Suzy Gershman's

BORN TO SHOP

NEW YORK

The Ultimate Guide for
People Who Love to Shop

11th Edition

WILEY

Wiley Publishing, Inc.

*To Paul, with thanks for breakfast at Tiffany's, dinner at
De Beers, and a million nights of Law & Order.*

Published by:

Wiley Publishing, Inc.
111 River St.
Hoboken, NJ 07030-5774

ISBN-13: 978-0-471-78743-3
ISBN-10: 0-471-78743-4

Editor: Leslie A. Shen
Production Editor: Suzanna R. Thompson
Photo Editor: Richard Fox
Cartographer: Guy Ruggiero
Production by Wiley Indianapolis Composition Services

For information on our other products and services or to obtain technical support, please contact our Customer Care Department within the
U.S. at 800/762-2974, outside the U.S. at 317/572-3993 or fax 317/
572-4002.

Wiley also publishes its books in a variety of electronic formats. Some
content that appears in print may not be available in electronic formats.

Manufactured in the United States of America

5   4   3   2   1

CONTENTS

MAP LIST

ABOUT THE AUTHORS

Suzy Gershman is a journalist, author, and self-professed shopping goddess who has worked in the fashion and fiber industry for more than 25 years. The Born to Shop series, which is over 20 years old, is translated into eight languages, making Gershman an international expert on retail and trade. Her essays on retailing have been used by the Harvard School of Business; her reportage on travel and retail has appeared in *Travel & Leisure, Travel Holiday, Travel Weekly,* and most of the major women's magazines. She writes in French and English for *Air France Madame,* published by Condé Nast France. When not in an airport, Gershman can be found in Paris, Provence, or San Antonio, Texas.

Aaron James is a singer-songwriter who lives and sings in L.A., where he has a day job at Warner Brothers Music. He is also a contributing editor for Born to Shop.

Jenny McCormick has just won her graduate degree in criminal justice. She can recite your Miranda rights or steer you to the best in fashion and trends for young women.

TO START WITH

I suffer from what I have to call New York Syndrome. I see a new store and I cannot remember what was there before. New York these days is giving me amnesia—many new faces, many new places. I guess they wouldn't call it New York if there weren't a lot that was new. In this edition, I not only try to keep up with it all, but I also incorporate a little bit of reporting from the Younger Generation—a couple of 20-somethings who have a few thoughts of their own.

Now that I am back living in the U.S. part-time, it's more fun than ever to visit New York—I can't imagine why anyone wouldn't schedule an annual trip, just to soak up the energy. Prices are high these days, but bargains are hidden and ready to be claimed. There's more and more luxury every day (wait till you see the De Beers diamond store), while at the same time there are more and more chances to buy cut rate.

This is deal city, and the deals are thriving. As always, I look for what can't be found elsewhere in the world—and, of course, I look for great prices. Since the laws on sales tax and the regulations on luggage allowance have both gotten stricter in the past years, I made a lot of trips to the post office to mail home many boxes. The shoes will be here any day now. Can't wait!

Note that all Born to Shop books have a slightly new format: Phone numbers and websites are included in the listings. If you don't see a website, the store did not have one as we went to press.

Special thanks go to New York correspondent Paul Baumrind, who does a lot of cutting, clipping, calling, and schlepping on my behalf.

Note: If you are shopping from Europe and euros are your currency, lucky you. At press time, the euro is 25% stronger than the dollar, making most of America one big bargain for you. By the time you read this, who knows what the rate of exchange will be. My advice to you? Go get it, guys.

Manhattan Neighborhoods

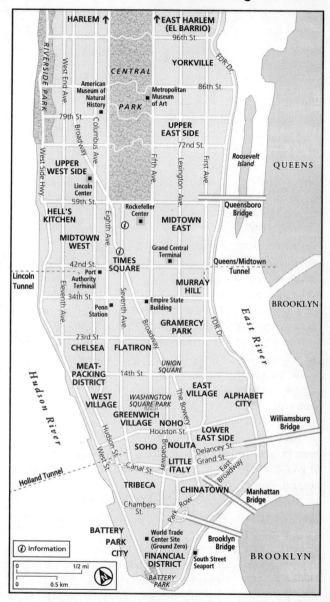

HARLEM ↑

↑EAST HARLEM (EL BARRIO)

96th St.

RIVERSIDE PARK

CENTRAL

YORKVILLE

FDR Dr.

West End Ave.

American Museum of Natural History ■

Metropolitan Museum of Art ■

86th St.

PARK

79th St.

Broadway

Columbus Ave.

UPPER EAST SIDE

72nd St.

West Side Hwy.

Fifth Ave.

Lexington Ave.

First Ave.

Roosevelt Island

QUEENS

UPPER WEST SIDE ■

Lincoln Center ■

59th St.

Rockefeller Center ■

Queensboro Bridge

HELL'S KITCHEN

Eighth Ave.

ⓘ

MIDTOWN EAST

MIDTOWN WEST

ⓘ

Grand Central Terminal ■

Queens/Midtown Tunnel

42nd St.

TIMES SQUARE

Lincoln Tunnel

Port Authority Terminal ■

MURRAY HILL

Eleventh Ave.

Seventh Ave.

34th St.

Penn Station ■

Empire State Building ■

BROOKLYN

GRAMERCY PARK

FDR Dr.

23rd St.

Broadway

CHELSEA

FLATIRON

East River

MEAT-PACKING DISTRICT

14th St.

UNION SQUARE

Hudson River

WEST VILLAGE

WASHINGTON SQUARE PARK

EAST VILLAGE

ALPHABET CITY

GREENWICH VILLAGE

NOHO

The Bowery

Williamsburg Bridge

Hudson St.

Houston St.

LOWER EAST SIDE

SOHO

Broadway

NOLITA

Delancey St.

West St.

LITTLE ITALY

Grand St.

Holland Tunnel

Canal St.

East Broadway

TRIBECA

CHINATOWN

Manhattan Bridge

Chambers St.

Park Row

BATTERY PARK CITY

World Trade Center Site (Ground Zero) ■

Brooklyn Bridge

FINANCIAL DISTRICT

South Street Seaport ■

BROOKLYN

ⓘ Information

BATTERY PARK

0   1/2 mi
0   0.5 km

Manhattan: 14th Street & Below

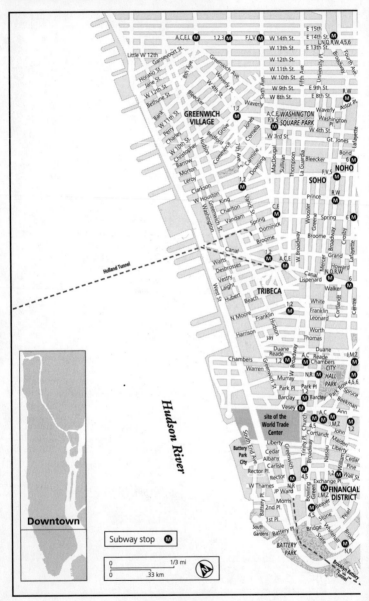

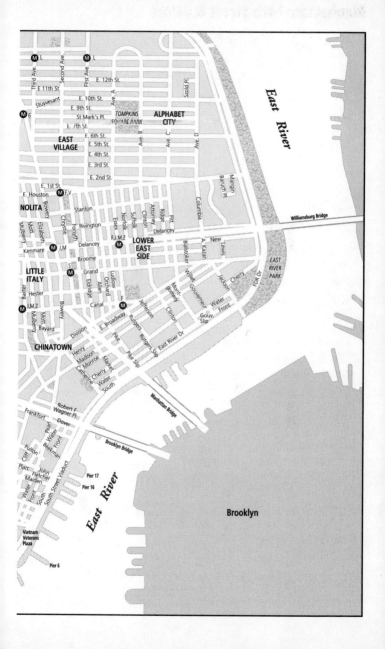

Manhattan: 14th Street & Above

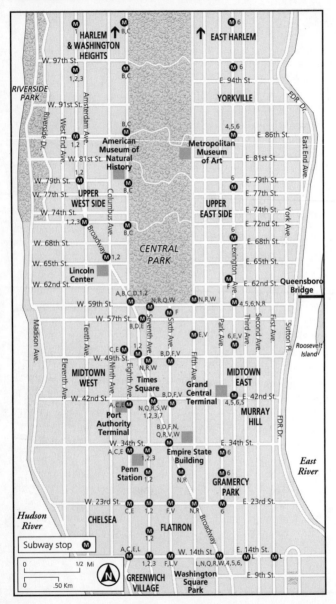

Manhattan Subways

SUBWAY LINES

- 1, 2, 3
- A, C, E
- B, D, F, V
- N, R, Q, W
- S
- 7
- L
- 4, 5, 6
- J, M, Z

○ Local stop

⊙ All trains stop

∽ Free transfer

Herald Square, Garment District, Times Square, Rockefeller Center & More

SHOPS

Aaron Faber **45**
Abercrombie & Fitch **32**
Alfred Dunhill **43**
American Girl Place **65**
Anne Fontaine **3**
Ann Taylor **5**
Anya Hindmarch **7**
Ascot Chang **28**
Asprey **33**
Aveda **45**
Avon Salon & Spa **32**
A/X Armani Exchange **43**
Baccarat **11**
Bally **6**
Banana Republic **55**
Barneys New York **5**
B&B Italia **16**
Belgian Loafers **36**
Bergdorf Goodman **27**
Bergdorf Goodman Men **27**
Bernardaud/Limoges **8**
Best of Scotland **69**
B&J Fabrics **82**
Blanc de Chine **49**
Bliss **25**
Bloomingdale's **14**
The Body Shop **56**
Borders **21**
Bottega Veneta **6**
Boyd's **17**
Bridge Kitchenware Corporation **47**
Brooks Brothers **43, 74**
Brookstone **66**
BuffSpa **27**
Bulgari **26**
Burberry **26**
Calvin Klein **2**
Caron **5**
Cartier **43**
Caswell-Massey **44, 60**
Celine **3**
Chanel **25**
Christian Dior **25**
Christie's **65**
Club Monaco **26, 43**
Coach **72**
Coliseum Books **84**
Colony Music **53**
CompUSA **93**
Concord Chemists **61**
Conway **96, 97**
Crabtree & Evelyn **45, 55**
Crate & Barrel **6**
Crouch & Fitzgerald **71**
Daffy's **20, 71, 97**
Dana Buchman **22**
Dean & DeLuca **65**
Diesel **11**
Disney Store **38**

DKNY **5**
Dooney & Bourke **4**
Drama Book Shop **82**
Dylan's Candy Bar **12**
Eileen Fisher **45**
Emporio Armani **24**
Ermenegildo Zegna **26**
Escada **38**
Ethan Allen **101**
Fauchon **34**
Felissimo **31**
Fendi **49**
Forman's **70, 88**
Fortunoff **38**
Frédéric Fekkai **26**
Gale Grant **48**
Galo **46**
Ghurka **22**
Gianni Versace **50**
Gucci **43**
Hammacher Schlemmer **18**
Harry Winston **32**
Henri Bendel **32**
H&M **50**
H. Stern **50**
H2O Plus **5**
Hyman Hendler & Sons **91**
Janet Sartin Institute **15**
J. Crew **75**
Jean-Claude Biguine **78**
Jos. A. Banks **72**
J. S. Suarez **21**
Kate's Paperie **29**
Kavanagh's **60**
Kmart **100**
Laila Rowe **10**
Lana Marks **5**
Laura Biagiotti **28**
L'Occitane **48**
Lord & Taylor **92**
Louis Vuitton **26**
Lush **96**
Mackenzie-Childs **28**
Macy's **98**
Manolo Blahnik **40**
Mary Quant **45**
Maternity Works **28**
Michael C. Fina **77**
Mimi Maternity **12**
M&J Trimming **95**
Mokuba New York **94**
NBA Store **50**
Nicole Farhi **5**
Niketown **23**
Nine West **19**
N. Peal **5**
Old Navy **98, 99**
Oliviers & Co. **76**
OMO Norma Kamali **31**
Original Levi's Store **11**
Origins **76**

Orvis **77**
OshKosh B'Gosh **64**
Paul Stuart **72**
Pierre Deux **24**
Pottery Barn **13**
Prada **22**
Qiora **44**
Rochester Big & Tall **51**
Saks Fifth Avenue **55**
Salvatore Ferragamo **49**
Sermoneta **24**
Sharper Image **28**
Sherpa Shop **71**
Smythson of Bond Street **26**
Sony Style **33**
St. John **49**
Strawberry **87**
Stuart Weitzman **6**
Takashimaya **43**
Talbots **44**
Talbots Mens **37**
T. Anthony **35**
Thomas Pink **44**
Tiffany & Co. **26**
Tod's **3**
Tourneau **6**
Toys "R" Us **80**
Trump Tower Atrium **32**
Van Cleef & Arpels **26**
Virgin Megastore **79**
Williams-Sonoma **13**

WHERE TO STAY

The Barclay InterContinental **60**
The Benjamin **58**
Doubletree Guest Suites **67**
Drake Swissôtel **34**
Four Seasons Hotel **22**
The Peninsula **39**
The Pierre **1**
Rihga Royal **42**
Sheraton New York Hotel & Towers **52**
The Waldorf-Astoria **57**
The Warwick **41**
W New York **59**
W New York-The Court **89**
W New York-The Tuscany **90**
W New York-Times Square **68**

WHERE TO DINE

Burger Heaven **37, 49, 62, 86**
Burke & Burke **30, 48**
DB Bistro Moderne **83**
ESPN Zone **81**
Gino **9**
Ollie's Noodle Shop **79**
Rainbow Room **54**
Vong **46**

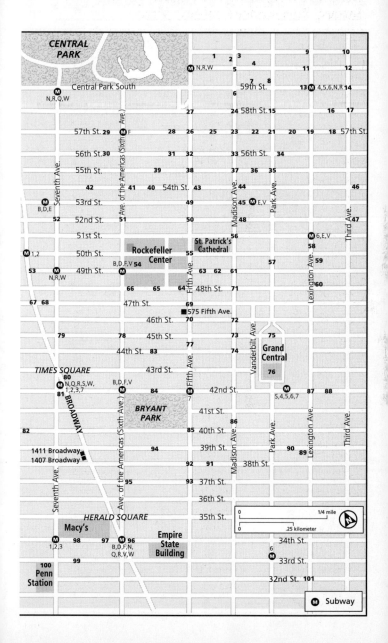

CENTRAL PARK

Central Park South
Ⓜ N,R,Q,W

Ⓜ N,R,W

59th St.

58th St.

57th St. **29** Ⓜ F 57th St.

56th St. **30**

55th St.

Seventh Ave.

Ave. of the Americas (Sixth Ave.)

54th St.

Madison Ave.

Park Ave.

Third Ave.

53rd St. Ⓜ B,D,E

52nd St.

51st St.

50th St. Ⓜ 1,2

Rockefeller Center

St. Patrick's Cathedral

Ⓜ 6,E,V

Lexington Ave.

53 Ⓜ N,R,W 49th St. Ⓜ B,D,F,V

48th St.

47th St.

575 Fifth Ave.

46th St.

45th St.

79 78

44th St.

Fifth Ave.

Vanderbilt Ave.

Grand Central

TIMES SQUARE

Ⓜ N,Q,R,S,W, 1,2,3,7

Ⓜ B,D,F,V

43rd St.

42nd St. Ⓜ 7

Ⓜ S,4,5,6,7

BRYANT PARK

41st St.

BROADWAY

82

40th St.

Madison Ave.

Park Ave.

Lexington Ave.

Third Ave.

1411 Broadway
1407 Broadway

39th St.

38th St.

37th St.

36th St.

HERALD SQUARE

35th St.

Macy's

Empire State Building

34th St.

Ⓜ 1,2,3 Ⓜ B,D,F,N, Q,R,V,W

Ⓜ 6

33rd St.

Penn Station

32nd St. **101**

0   1/4 mile
0   .25 kilometer

Ⓜ Subway

SoHo, NoHo, Nolita & the Lower East Side

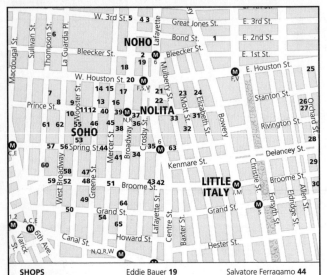

Flatiron, Union Square, Chelsea, Ladies' Mile & the Village

Ⓜ Subway stop

SHOPS

ABC Carpet & Home **30**
Alcone Company **13**
Alexander McQueen **39**
Anthropologie **29**
A/X Armani Exchange **25**
Banana Republic **29**
Barnes & Noble **20, 32**
Barneys Co-Op **12**
Bed, Bath & Beyond **22**
Best Buy **9**
Burlington Coat Factory **8**
Canine Styles **42**
Chelsea Market **38**
Club Monaco **24**
Condomania **56**
The Container Store **21**
Corniche Furs & Luxury
  Outerwear **2**
DSW **36**
Eileen Fisher **48**
Filene's Basement **22, 36**
Fishs Eddy **30**
Flight 001 **41**
Forbidden Planet **46**
Forever 21 **36**
Fresh **57**
Greenmarket **31**
H&M **27**

Home Depot **10**
Housing Works
  Thrift Shop **18**
Intermix **26**
Jam Paper **22**
J. Crew **28**
Jean-Claude Biguine **4**
Jensen-Lewis **15**
Jo Malone **23**
Keni Valenti
  Retro-Couture **1**
Kiehl's **47**
Kleinfeld **19**
Kmart **51**
L'Occitane **55**
Loehmann's **14**
Lucky Brand Jeans **23**
Lulu Guinness **58**
M.A.C. **23**
Marc Jacobs **58**
Old Navy **22**
Origins **23**
Paragon **30**
Paul Smith **29**
Petco **32**
Restoration Hardware **23**
Ricky's **11, 52, 43**
Rothman's **33**

Rugby **44**
Sephora **26**
Simon's Hardware **6**
Stella Dallas **53**
St. Mark's Comics **50**
Strand Book Store **46**
Swann Galleries **7**
T.J. Maxx **22**
Trader Joe's **34**
Trash and Vaudeville **50**
Urban Outfitters **37, 49, 54**
Virgin Megastore **35**
West Elm **17**
Whole Foods/
  Whole Body **3, 36**
Williams-Sonoma **14**
Zara **28**

WHERE TO STAY

Ramada Inn Eastside **5**
W New York-Union
  Square **33**

WHERE TO DINE

Cafeteria **16**
Coffee Shop **31**
Cornelia St. Café **55**
Pastis **40**
Terra **47 45**

Chapter One

....

THE BEST OF NEW YORK

If you are dashing about in a New York Minute, or thinking that all the possibilities in these pages are overwhelming, this at-a-glance chapter might help you get started quickly and easily. This chapter features some easy-to-locate shops where you can find what you need if you're short on time, as well as some easy-to-make choices when in a hurry. Each store mentioned here is explained in greater depth in later chapters, and, of course, there are plenty more shops discussed inside.

Addresses in all listings are given with cross streets so that you can find your destination more easily. When taking a taxi, tell the driver the cross streets as soon as you get in the car so there is no confusion.

If you're in a hurry, the subway may be your best bet—especially for long hauls, which can get tedious (and expensive) in traffic. Never take the uptown or downtown bus when you are in a hurry unless it's an express bus; cross-town buses, however, are worth the effort.

Note: I use 34th Street as the dividing line between uptown and downtown. This is not a traditional dividing line (many people use 14th St. or 23rd St. as the official dividing point and consider 34th St. as Midtown), but I find it very handy and use it throughout this text.

YOU HAVE ONLY 1 HOUR TO SHOP

If you have only an hour to shop, your choices really depend on what part of town you're in, what your goals are, and how frequently you get to New York. Sometimes I'm willing to blow my single hour in town on something totally nontraditional, and sometimes I'm forced to look for something as specific as a matching button. But let's concentrate on location in this chapter, since time is so tight here.

Upper East Side

I can walk from 57th Street to 79th Street along Madison Avenue in about 2 hours, poking into whatever stores interest me (but not doing serious shopping). You can do this same stroll in an hour if you stick to window-shopping. Few districts of the city give you a better overview of why New York is so special.

Midtown Fifth Avenue

Do you want an hour's worth of visual stimulation and excitement or do you want to do some serious shopping? If it's inspiration you seek (and maybe not that much in terms of durable goods), poke in quickly at **Takashimaya** (693 Fifth Ave., at 54th St.) and **Henri Bendel** (712 Fifth Ave., at 56th St.). Then stop by **Felissimo** (10 W. 56th St.), a shop filled with whimsy and wonder.

If you really need something and need it fast, do what I do and spend an hour at **Saks Fifth Avenue** (611 Fifth Ave., at 50th St.). Saks in New York is a festival unlike any other Saks in the world, but it's also a bit of a cop-out since it's very tame. I want you to have your hour at Saks, but I do hope you've got another hour to do some shopping that's more wild and crazy.

Herald Square

One hour divided between **Macy's** (Broadway, at 34th St.), **Forever 21** (50 W. 34th St.), and **Old Navy** (150 W. 34th St.) should get your shopping juices flowing. If you can do all this in an hour, you should possibly run the Kentucky Derby.

Meatpacking District & Chelsea

Take a taxi to **Jeffrey** (449 W. 14th St., near Tenth Ave.) and step on it. Walk over to **Barneys Co-Op** (236 W. 18th St., near Seventh Ave.) if you have time.

SoHo & Nolita

Sure, you can spend an hour breezily and easily in SoHo, but take time out and head for nearby Nolita! You'll only have time to window-shop, but you'll get a whirlwind tour of what's new and what's happening in New York retail. Head directly to **Calypso** (280 Mott St., near Prince St.).

YOU WANT TO SEE SOMETHING *VERY* NEW YORK

If you're visiting from Europe, much of American retail will seem new and fresh to you. If you're visiting from another American city, you'll find that many Manhattan versions of your favorite chain stores are bigger and better but fundamentally the same. Therefore, visiting those stores that are the epitome of New York style (even if they have stores in other cities as well) will give you supreme pleasure, whether you buy anything or not. For those reasons, check out:

ABC CARPET & HOME
888 Broadway, at 19th St. (Subway: R or W to 23rd St.).

EILEEN FISHER
521 Madison Ave., near 53rd St. (Subway: E or V to 5th Ave./53rd St.).

TAKASHIMAYA
693 Fifth Ave., at 54th St. (Subway: E or V to 5th Ave./ 53rd St.).

YOU WANT ONE-DESTINATION SHOPPING

SoHo. No doubt about it, SoHo is bursting with new stores— some original shops and some branches of big names. The big money (**Chanel, Louis Vuitton, Armani Casa**) continues to move here, so if you're looking for funky, hunt for it on the fringes. If you have the energy, there are plenty of great shopping areas (let's call them SoHo Adjacent) nearby. Stores open late, so make a day of it by adding on dinner at one of the hot restaurants in the vicinity.

YOU WANT SOME PLACE NEW TO DISCOVER

Way Downtown

It's Nolita for me, which is conveniently near SoHo, so if you have the time, you can shop 'em both.

Union Square

Union Square is hardly new, but now offers tons of new stores, lots of energy, and the chance to hit the **Greenmarket** as well. Check out **Whole Foods, Trader Joe's, Filene's Basement, DSW,** and **Forever 21.** There's also some fun and funky nearby shopping, and the L train will take you directly to trendy Williamsburg, Brooklyn. Can yu get more hip, dawg?

Midtown

Head for Columbus Circle and the **Time Warner Center,** which houses a hotel, a large mall, and a huge **Whole Foods.** The mall is sort of over-glitzy, but many of the stores are one-of-a-kinds or flagships, such as the only **Joseph Abboud** home store.

YOU WANT ONE ADDRESS TO TELL FRIENDS ABOUT

Get your fix at **Dylan's Candy Bar** (1011 Third Ave., near 60th St.), operated by none other than Ralph Lauren's daughter. This place has two floors of goodies and items not found anywhere else, including 24 colors of M&Ms. I would have preferred a more old-timey Polo kind of decor instead of this moderne take on a penny-candy store, but the sweets are moving like, uh, hot cakes. There's a basement floor as well as an old-fashioned soda fountain. You'll see plenty of gift ideas, including beautiful ready-made and custom-made gift baskets.

ONE ADDRESS YOU CAN'T BELIEVE YOU DON'T KNOW

Speaking of Ralph Lauren, you probably think you know it all and there's not much more to say. So, have you been to **Rugby** (99 University Place, at 12th St.) yet? This new store near the NYU campus is very Ralph, but has been tweaked just so for the college set. There's clothing and gear for all of life's needs, from active sportswear to dress-up.

SOMETHING FOR THE YOUNG ONES

Toys "R" Us is all over the U.S., but the best one is at Times Square—you ain't seen nuthin' like it, I promise you. I'll give you a hint: indoor Ferris wheel. Also in Midtown are the **Disney Store** (711 Fifth Ave., at 55th St.) and the **Metropolitan Museum of Art Store** at Rockefeller Center, which has a wonderful kids' department.

BEST ARRIVAL FROM OUT OF TOWN

Manhattan is constantly invaded by foreigners, but the arrival of **Sur La Table** (75 Spring St., at Crosby St.)—a tabletop-and-cookware store based in Seattle—takes the, uh, cake. This one isn't as large as many other branches, but it has an intimacy not often found in Manhattan and provides a nice change of pace for those looking for perfect table settings, gifts, or items for their own homes.

BEST DOWN & DIRTY BARGAINS

It's got to be **Ladies' Mile** (Sixth Ave., around 18th St.). And no, it's not just for ladies anymore. When the mayor of New York rezoned this part of downtown, discounters and off-pricers quickly moved in. The district now has off-pricers like **T.J. Maxx** and **Filene's Basement** (in the same building at 620 Sixth Ave., at 18th St.).

Although **Loehmann's** (101 Seventh Ave., at 16th St.) is not in this stretch, it's only a block away and should definitely be included in this neighborhood.

BEST STUFF FOR YOUR APARTMENT OR HOME

You won't believe you read this here, and I can't believe I'm writing it, but here goes: the East Side, mostly around the East 50s and 60s! We'll forego the James Robinson silver on Park Avenue and the original artworks in tony stores on East 67th Street and still have a good time.

Move over to Madison for **Crate & Barrel** (650 Madison Ave., at 59th St.). Or head straight for the **Terence Conran Shop** (407 E. 59th St.) and **Bed Bath & Beyond** (410 E. 61st St.), both under the 59th Street Bridge.

Not too far away, there's also a big department store at 59th Street and Lexington Avenue called **Bloomingdale's** (yep, you've heard of it before!), which has a terrific bed-linen selection that, when it goes on sale, equals discount prices. And for the final flourishes, head to **Gracious Home** (1217 Third Ave. and 1220 Third Ave., both at 70th St.).

You should also check out Lower Broadway and Ladies' Mile. Start at **ABC Carpet & Home** (888 Broadway, at 19th St.) and **Fishs Eddy** (889 Broadway, at 19th St.); then wander the side streets east of Broadway and look for the upholsterers and quiet fabric and furniture sources nestled in and around 20th Street. Or just head straight over to Ladies' Mile for **Bed Bath & Beyond** (620 Sixth Ave., at 18th St.). And while you're there, check out home style at **T.J. Maxx,** in the same building.

BEST GIFTS

Need to pick up a few quick gifts for friends? Here are a few ideas:

- A bag of gourmet coffee from **Bloomingdale's** ($15).
- Bath bombs from **Lush** ($5).
- Soap or a Dead Sea beauty treatment from **Sabon.**
- Something from **Tiffany & Co.** Small leather goods, scarves, and items in sterling silver are reasonably priced. I like the leather case that holds Post-it Notes ($30).
- Health, beauty, or well-being products from a brand with limited distribution—possibly unknown in your hometown,

---

Jenny's Five Best Buys in Brooklyn

1. Parcel "Boombox" purse: $22 at the Mini Mini Market (MMM) in the Williamsburg Mini Mall.
2. Astrological-sign drinking glasses: $7 each at Pilgrim (Home).
3. "McCormick Farm Equipment" Trucker Hats: $10 at Brooklyn Industries.
4. Burt's Bees facial kit: $10 at the Mini Mini Market.
5. An everything bagel with butter: $1.20 at the Bagel Store, at 247 Bedford Ave. (best bagel in the 'burg).

Aaron's Five Best Buys in New York

1. Vintage "Masters of the Universe" T-Shirt: $8 at Beacon's Closet.
2. *Vice Magazine:* Free at the Vice Store.
3. New York Soul hoodie: $45 at Triple Five Soul.
4. Hurley jeans: $40 at Brooklyn Industries.
5. Studded belt: $7 from street merchant.

like maybe the Slatkin Body Therapy line, sold only at **Bergdorf Goodman.**

- Art or folk art from any of the museum stores—or even the street. The **Metropolitan Museum of Art** has a shop in Macy's and one at Rockefeller Center; look for the tin plates patterned after French china ($7.50 each). Notebooks and stationery items are in the $6.95-to-$11 price range and make useful, stylish gifts.
- A gift for their pet—pet boutiques are the rage in New York. Try **Canine Styles** (43 Greenwich Ave., near Charles St.); the Statue of Liberty holding a dog bone is a winner at $9. The **Sherpa Shop** (400 Madison Ave., near 48th St.), inside Crouch & Fitzgerald, is where you'll find high-quality totes for cats and dogs.

BEST QUICKIE SHOPPER'S LUNCH

Burger Heaven. Yummy burgers. See p. 64 for locations.

BEST HOTEL LUNCH

Fancy hotels can offer very competitively priced luncheons, served in restaurants that are true hidden gems. **The Mark** (25 E. 77th St., near Madison Ave.) has a great menu and a fixed-price lunch, plus it's in the heart of the Madison Avenue shopping district.

The Surrey is home to **Café Boulud** (20 E. 76th St., near Madison Ave.), which also has a fixed-price lunch. **The Pierre** (2 E. 61st St., near Fifth Ave.) also has a sensational full lunch at Café Pierre.

BEST AFTERNOON TEA

The Rotunda at **The Pierre** (2 E. 61st St., near Fifth Ave.)—a gorgeous location.

BEST OVERALL DEPARTMENT STORE

Saks Fifth Avenue (611 Fifth Ave., at 50th St.) has it all.

BEST SALE

Nothing beats **Saks Fifth Avenue** (611 Fifth Ave., at 50th St.) when the sale merchandise gets marked down an additional 30% to 40%.

BEST OFF-PRICER

New York is suddenly teeming with off-pricers and discounters, so a new and better resource could pop up at any time. I left my heart at **Century 21,** which has locations in Manhattan (22 Cortlandt St., near Church St.) and Brooklyn (472 86th St., between Fourth and Fifth aves.).

BEST RESALE SHOPS

Try **Encore** (1132 Madison Ave., near 84th St., second floor) and **Michael's** (1041 Madison Ave., near 80th St., second floor).

BEST PLACE FOR A WEDDING GOWN

Filene's Basement now holds its famous bridal sale twice a year in New York, too! See p. 287 for details.

If you time it right, you can get to the **Vera Wang** sample sale, usually held at the Hotel Pennsylvania. Call © **212/628-3400** for the dates and details.

If you miss the sales and want to try wholesale, the best thing to do is to shop in the **Garment District.** Try 1375 and 1385 Broadway (near 38th St.). Many makers have moved out recently, but those remaining usually sell to the public.

Should you be willing to wear a used gown (of course you are), **Michael's** (1041 Madison Ave., near 80th St., second floor) has one of the best selections in town.

If nothing but the full regalia will do, and your mom wants to sip tea while you try on your train, **Saks Fifth Avenue** (611 Fifth Ave., at 50th St.) has been doing this for years and remains the last of the full-service wedding belles.

And finally, I have to remind you that **Kleinfeld** of Brooklyn has just come to Manhattan (110 W. 20th St., near Sixth Ave.)—by appointment only, dear. It has over 1,000 gowns on hand and all sorts of insider information, tips, and services for the bride and her entourage.

BEST HANDBAGS

I'd head straight for **J. S. Suarez** (450 Park Ave., at 57th St.) which sells a variety of designer-style handbags made in the same Italian factories as the big names (Gucci, Prada). We're not talking cheap here—there's probably little for under $100—but we are talking quality and less money than at big-name stores.

BEST "REGULAR" DRUGSTORE

Manhattan is dotted with drugstores. **CVS, Duane Reade,** and **Rite Aid** are fighting it out for the hearts and minds and teeth of New Yorkers, even in the best business districts in Midtown. Just about everywhere you wander, you can find a branch of one or all. They carry all the basics, from bottled water to beauty aids to condoms. Please note that prices on sundries in Manhattan are more expensive than anyplace else in the U.S., so you'll almost always pay less at home. Unless home is overseas.

Best for beauty supplies is **Ricky's,** which also sells wigs, jewelry, and funky gifts. See p. 226 for details and locations.

BEST FANCY DRUGSTORE

Go straight to **Clyde's** (926 Madison Ave., near 74th St.). Wait here please, James.

BEST MUSEUM STORE

METROPOLITAN MUSEUM OF ART STORE
Fifth Ave., at 82nd St. (Subway: 4, 5, or 6 to 86th St.).

The flagship inside the museum itself is the best, but there are multiple branches around town, including one inside Macy's and one at Rockefeller Center. ✆ **212/570-3894.** www.met museum.org/store.

BEST TRENDY SHOP

JEFFREY NEW YORK
449 W. 14th St., between Ninth and Tenth aves. (Subway: A, C, E, or L to 14th St./8th Ave.).

This place has trendsetting clothes and the attitude to go with them. There's an excellent service policy as well as a DJ. Time to rock 'n' roll. ✆ **212/206-1272.**

TRENDY WITH ARCHITECTURE

ADIDAS
610 Broadway, at Houston St. (Subway: B, D, F, or V to Broadway/Lafayette St.).

Not as large as Niketown, but the store is sleek and black and minimalist and functional all at once. ✆ **212/529-0081.** www. adidas.com.

JEAN-PAUL GAULTIER
759 Madison Ave., near 65th St. (Subway: 6 to 68th St./Hunter College).

Check out the Philippe Starck decor here. ✆ **212/249-0235.** www.jeanpaulgaultier.com.

PRADA
575 Broadway, near Prince St.

There are other Prada stores in Manhattan, but this is the one for style freaks and architecture buffs to check out. You don't have to buy anything; just bring a tissue in case you start to drool. In keeping with Miuccia's devotion to outstanding architecture statements, this store could be a museum. ✆ **212/ 334-8888.** www.prada.com.

BEST STORES IN NEW YORK

In alphabetical order:

ABC CARPET & HOME
888 Broadway, at 18th St. (Subway: R or W to 23rd St.).

Even if you buy nothing, step into this beautifully dressed showcase for tabletop, linens, fabrics, and, oh yeah, carpets. ✆ 212/473-3000. www.abchome.com.

APRIL CORNELL
487 Columbus Ave., at 83rd St. (Subway: B or C to 81st St.).

This place has home furnishings and clothes for women and little girls in swirly printed Indian fabrics that feel like the south of France. ✆ 212/799-4342. www.aprilcornell.com.

BOYD'S
968 Third Ave., at 58th St. (Subway: 4, 5, 6, N, R, or W to 59th St./Lexington Ave.).

"Drugstore" doesn't do it justice. Boyd's is a veritable department store of European beauty lines, health aids, accessories, and more. ✆ 212/838-6558. www.boydsnyc.com.

CENTURY 21
22 Cortlandt St., between Church St. and Broadway (Subway: R or W to City Hall or Rector St., until Cortlandt St. reopens in 2007); 472 86th St., between Fourth and Fifth aves., Brooklyn (Subway: R to 86th St. in Brooklyn).

If you crave the biggest designer names at discount prices, it's worth the subway ride to downtown Manhattan, the schlep to Brooklyn, and maybe even the trip to New York! Note that the Brooklyn branch is better than ever (with a new home store), but whatever you do, don't drive there—especially on a weekend. Instead, take the subway. ✆ 212/227-9092 for Manhattan; ✆ 718/748-3266 for Brooklyn. www.c21stores.com.

EILEEN FISHER
521 Madison Ave., near 53rd St. (Subway: E or V to 5th Ave./53rd St.).

Several branches around town offer droopy chic for women. Love those elastic waists! Silks and linens, bouclé wools, and a soft color palette a la Armani—but affordable. ✆ **212/759-9888.** www.eileenfisher.com.

KATE'S PAPERIE
561 Broadway, near Prince St. (Subway: R or W to Prince St.); 140 W. 57th St., between Sixth and Seventh aves. (Subway: F to 57th St.).

You'll find an eye-popping choice of papers, wraps, and ribbons here. ✆ **212/941-9816** for Broadway; ✆ **212/459-0700** for West 57th Street. www.katespaperie.com.

TAKASHIMAYA
693 Fifth Ave., near 54th St. (Subway: E or V to 5th Ave./53rd St.).

This place has gorgeous flowers and drop-dead lifestyle designs to gawk at. ✆ **212/350-0100.**

Chapter Two

....

NEW YORK DETAILS

BIG APPLE CIRCUS

....

Diamonds on the soles of your shoes? Diamonds and dust? Well, sparkle plenty and get ready to be blinded—New York is bigger and better and, yep, has more diamonds by the mile than ever before. Bring sunglasses, and save up for bling.

Whether you come from Europe with a fistful of strong euros, from another large U.S. city, or from the boonies, you're in for a head-spinning trip full of opportunities. No place has more shopping ops than New York City—and no single group of people is more likely to make your day as you go shopping and looking for bargains. Subway strike? Just keep walking and shopping. Disgruntled taxi drivers? Ask 'em how they like your smile. No matter what the work conditions, New York has so much to offer that you won't be able to stop grinning.

There are lots of new stores and many, many arrivals from international shores. Luxury keeps outdoing itself here, but big-box stores and suburban retailing styles have been blossoming as well—wait till you get down to Union Square. East 57th Street, east of Fifth Avenue, has practically reinvented itself; street vendors sell fake Bottega Veneta bags from Midtown corners; and secret sales and showrooms are popping up everywhere, even in people's homes.

Read on for more on what's new.

WHAT'S NEW, PUSSYCAT

- Middle America has invaded Manhattan. Get this: **Build-A-Bear Workshop** has opened, at 565 Fifth Ave. (at 46th St.). Obviously it is the end of civilization as I knew it.
- Suburbia has invaded Manhattan. **Red Lobster** (the cheese biscuits are to die for) opened right near Times Square, and **The Container Store** came to Ladies' Mile. **Target** is rumored to be arriving soon, and **Home Depot** is in a landmark building, at 40 W. 23rd St. (between Fifth and Sixth aves.).
- Suburban style has conquered Manhattan—or, at least, **Union Square.** Enormous chain stores are dotted all around Union Square, which—when teamed with the Greenmarket—is the hottest destination in town. There's everything from **Filene's Basement** to **DSW.** And **Sephora, Virgin Megastore,** and **Barnes & Noble** have been here for several years.
- Even Brooklyn has invaded Manhattan. The famous bridal shop **Kleinfeld** has opened up in Chelsea, at 110 W. 20th St. (near Sixth Ave.).
- Mass-market has gotten bigger and bolder—especially since this category of goods is selling so well. Check out the arrival of a chain called **Forever 21,** the poor gal's H&M. There are several branches around town.
- Being a Broadway baby no longer means you're bound for the Theater District. Retail on Broadway from the West 60s on up to the mid-70s is hot. There's a new underground **Bed Bath & Beyond** near **Gracious Home.** And many more stores are coming to the Upper West Side, including—get this—a **Barneys Co-Op!**
- This is not to imply that the only thing that's new in town is low-end or mass-market—oh no, sirree. For one, **De Beers** is here. Also note that New York is seeing a rise in cult shops that are pushing to become niche luxury icons, such as **Searle.** Searle has long been known to insiders, but now there are half a dozen locations, many with different looks and styles. They are eating up Manhattan with a bite stronger—and more chic—than Godzilla's.

- Museum stores have always been a great place to shop—
  no secret there. But with the reopening of MoMA comes
  the U.S. launch of Japanese lifestyle store **Muji.** This no-
  name minimalist label has stores all over London and various European cities. Turn to Muji for excellent plain designs
  at fair prices—including housewares, gift items, and some
  clothing.
- **SoHo** (short for "South of Houston") has turned out to be
  uptown in a downtown location. The area is now fancy and
  mainstream and has something for everyone. **Ralph Lauren** occupies an enormous space; **Bloomingdale's** has a
  small specialty store on Broadway; Armani opened **Armani
  Casa;** and **Chanel** came to SoHo and brought **Eres,** a brand
  that makes very, very chic underwear and bathing suits. **Sur
  La Table,** from Seattle, has just arrived in the 'hood, too,
  with cooking gear and tabletop.
- **Nolita** (short for "North of Little Italy") has become the new
  SoHo, sort of, but it's real and small and intimate and fabulous. I'm ready to move here and open up shop. Shhhh, don't
  tell anyone. This is where small stores are an art form and
  the retailer is the curator—and maybe the designer as well.
- The **Meatpacking District** (very far west on 14th St. and into
  Chelsea), though still working on the smells, is fast becoming a restaurant scene, while hip department store **Jeffrey**
  tries to hang on in the 'hood. The area has everything from
  art galleries to warehouse spaces to the **Comme des Garçons**
  boutique, which marries retail with a gallery feel and rede-
  fines the borders of Chelsea. While the area is a big sprawl
  best shopped with car and driver, it certainly is hot.
- **TriBeCa** (short for "Triangle below Canal Street") has its
  first big-name retailers, **Issey Miyake** and **Baker Furniture.**
  In fact, over 100 new faces opened in TriBeCa just last season. Watch this neighborhood.
- **Fifth Avenue** at its midpoint has become one giant mall, with
  a wider range of retail than ever before. You'll find this brave
  new shopping world right around Rockefeller Center, with

flagships representing everyone from **Banana Republic** to **Kenneth Cole.** And **Façonnable** recently moved in, too.

- But Fifth Avenue is not all down-market or mass-market. **De Beers,** the diamond dealers, just opened an eye-poppin' shop. **Fendi** has moved. **Bottega Veneta** gave up Madison Avenue and a splendid store there to open an even more incredible space right next to Takashimaya on Fifth.

- **Columbus Circle,** considered dead for the last decade, is now the address to boast about—it's become home to a chic hotel, apartments, and a luxury mall, all contained in the **Time Warner Center,** New York's latest architectural wonder. The building anchors a hot eating and shopping district. The mall is rather ho-hum, but the **Whole Foods** in the basement is a big hit.

- **Middle Madison Avenue** (in the 40s) is getting classier—first the rebirth of Grand Central Terminal (with great new stores, including **Oliviers & Co.** for imported olive oil) and now an enormous branch of **J. Crew.**

- **Ladies' Mile,** the section of Sixth Avenue where the first department stores in New York opened more than 100 years ago, has turned into superstore, discounter, and off-pricer heaven. Try the blocks from 17th to 20th streets for some rather amazing sights and discounts for all members of the family—yep, even the kids.

- **West 34th Street** claims that it's been revitalized. I'm iffy on this claim, but admit that I'm knocked out by the **Old Navy** store, which is across the street from **Macy's,** between Broadway and Seventh Avenue.

- The city is also becoming attractive for mainstream stores' experimental efforts. Word has it that **Crate & Barrel** is looking for a space in the Meatpacking District to open its spin-off line, **CB2.**

- Chain stores have discovered that Manhattan is so neighborhood-oriented, they need two or more addresses to succeed—often one uptown and one downtown, or one on the East Side and one on the West Side, and sometimes even a branch in a specialty retailing district like Carnegie Hill or the World Financial Center.

- Need to look, feel, or shop like a New Yorker? Log on to **www.dailycandy.com** to find out what's hot with the *Sex and the City* crowd.

THE NEW YORK RULE OF NATURAL SELECTION

New York offers more selection than any other marketplace in the United States, and probably in the world—and that includes Tokyo. (Okay, Tokyo may have more merchandise, but it won't all fit you.)

One of the things that make New York great is the fact that you can find things here that aren't available elsewhere or haven't yet been introduced in other parts of the country. Shopping in this city offers the biggest mental challenges of all time—can you bear to see this much stuff and not buy it all? Can you possibly choose the best thing for you at the best price? Shopping in New York is like living a game show.

Even though Midtown is now populated by stores that you may have back home (even if home is Paris), the New York Rule of Natural Selection is simple: If it's new, it comes to New York first.

True, consumer products are usually test-marketed in more average American cities, but once a firm has decided to go with a product, it rolls it out in New York first. It builds a flagship in New York. It decides to go for impact—in New York. That's why you'll be able to find things in New York that you can't find at home, even if you have the same stores back there.

WINDOW-SHOPPING 101

To me, the biggest bargains in New York are the education that you get from wandering around and the high that comes from absorbing so much energy and so many creative ideas.

Look at the men and women who rush past on their way to work—study what they're wearing and learn from them. Look at the store windows and displays; stare at mannequins and even at ads in the *New York Times*. If you want to buy a piece of the action (and of course you do), you'll have choices, depending upon how much you want to spend and what style of retail best fits your mood or your pocketbook . . . and depending on just how much effort you are willing to make and how much digging you are willing to do.

The windows are easy. The bargains take work. (See chapter 11 for more on bargains.)

GETTING THERE

Because it is the international hub city of the United States, just about every domestic and international carrier—and then some—serves New York. The trick is to realize that there are several airports and to know that you can avoid a traffic jam or even get a bargain by using an alternative airport.

John F. Kennedy International Airport (JFK) is the best-known airport, especially for international flights, but it's not the only game in town. **LaGuardia Airport (LGA)** takes mostly domestic flights, but it does serve cities in Canada, Bermuda, and a few other destinations outside the continental U.S. **Newark Liberty International Airport (EWR)**, in New Jersey, has grown dramatically as an international hub; new AirTrain service can get you from Newark to Manhattan in less than a half-hour.

Westchester County Airport (HPN), in White Plains, serves the suburbs directly north of New York. **Long Island Macarthur Airport (ISP)** is in Islip, on the south shore of Long Island. Upstate in the Hudson Valley, **Stewart International Airport (SWF)** hopes to become an international hub to take some of the pressure off JFK. The outer-fringe airports might not be convenient, but frequent promotions are available to encourage traffic through them. Maybe you wanted to see Westchester after all?

ARRIVAL & DEPARTURE

A few tricks of the trade:

- For international arrivals, luggage carts are free; for domestic, they are not. Use the machine, which takes credit cards and dispenses carts.
- There are porters at the airport, and you should pay them as you see fit—there is no fixed charge for baggage service in New York, as there is in many other cities. A dollar per bag is the going rate.
- Illegal taxi drivers will hustle you; ignore them and get in line for a real, legit New York City yellow cab.
- There are flat-rate fees for taxis to the city from JFK, but no outbound set fees. At press time, the fare is $45, plus tolls and tip.
- There is express bus service every 20 minutes to and from LaGuardia and JFK. Buses stop at a variety of hotels and major transportation centers such as Penn Station, the Port Authority, and Grand Central. For more info, go to www.nyairportservice.com or stop by the Transportation Desk in the terminal after you arrive. From Newark, there is bus service every 30 minutes; call © 877/894-9155 for details.

GETTING AROUND

There's no need to rent a car for your visit to New York. Driving is a nightmare, and parking is ridiculously expensive (and nearly impossible in some neighborhoods). It's much easier to get around using public transportation, taxis, and your own two feet. If you're going to visit Aunt Erma on Long Island or you have some other need to travel beyond the five boroughs, call one of the major car-rental companies, such as **National** (© 800/227-7368; www.nationalcar.com), **Hertz** (© 800/654-3131; www.hertz.com), or **Avis** (© 800/230-4898;

For More Bus & Subway Info

For transit information, visit **www.mta.info** or call the Metropolitan Transportation Authority's **New York City Transit Travel Information Center** (© 718/330-1234). Extensive automated information is available 24 hours a day, and live agents are on hand to answer questions and provide directions daily from 6am to 10pm.

You can get bus and subway maps at most information centers. A particularly helpful MTA desk is located at the Times Square Information Center, at 1560 Broadway, between 46th and 47th streets, where you can also buy MetroCards. Maps are usually available in subway stations (ask at the token booth), but rarely on buses.

www.avis.com), all of which have airport and Manhattan locations.

By Subway

You can ask for a free subway map at the token booth of any subway station, or use the black-and-white map on p. 5. To use the subway (and bus), buy a **MetroCard,** a magnetic card that is swiped at the turnstile as you enter a station. A ride costs $2. If you buy a card for $10 or more, you receive a 20% bonus, so a $20 card actually gives you 12 trips. Even better, there's a $24 card that provides 7 days' worth of unlimited travel. There is also a 1-day unlimited-ride Fun Pass for $7. Go to www.mta.info for details. *One of the best bargains in town:* Note that when you swipe your MetroCard at the subway, you get a free bus transfer if needed.

By Bus

Buses are easy to use and may feel safer to you than the subway; unfortunately, they are much slower. Buses cost the same as the subway ($2 per ride) and can be paid for with coins (exact change) or your MetroCard. *Note:* Word on the street is that buses will no longer accept cash at some point in the near future, so you'll have to use a MetroCard.

When you take the bus, you can get a free transfer that's good for travel within 2 hours. Bus routes are clearly marked on signposts, but ask the driver to confirm that you're headed the right way.

On Foot

If you want to get someplace in a hurry, do what all locals do: Walk.

By Taxi

If you just can't do the walk, flag a taxi. If the middle light on the top of the cab is lit, the car is available; if the outer lights on the top of the cab are lit, it is off-duty. Get into the taxi and shut the door before you give your destination. This avoids the hassle of the driver telling you he doesn't want to go where you want to go.

A fare hike may be in the works, but at press time, the flag drops at $2.50 once you get into the cab, and then the meter starts up from there; taxi drivers expect a 15% tip. Note that the city has implemented flat-rate fees for taxi service from JFK into the city ($45), but does not have a flat fee out to the airport. These rates do not include tips or tolls.

By Car Service

While limos are standard fare in New York, you can also get a sedan to drive you around for less than a limousine. And frankly, who really needs a limo? Just be sure you book through a legit car service.

Car services can be booked by the hour, by the job, or for a standard run—such as going to the airport. Rates do not include tolls (this is most applicable to airport runs) or tips. A 15% tip may be automatically added onto your bill.

You may want to try **Dial 7 Car Service,** my regular. From Manhattan, it charges a flat $46 to JFK or Newark and $31 to LaGuardia, not including tips and tolls. Its phone number is easy to memorize (© 212/777-7777), or go to www.dial7.com. If you're traveling with a dog, say so when you book.

DIRECTIONS

You're hot to trot, but please, study up on your New York neighborhoods before you pounce (see the map on p. 1).

Most of Manhattan is laid out on a grid system. Avenues run north and south, while streets run east and west. Fifth Avenue divides the East and West sides, so building numbers start at 1 heading east or west from Fifth.

In many places in the world, "downtown" is a specific place. Not in Manhattan, however. Here, all directions are given in reference to where you are standing and where you are going: Uptown is north and downtown is south.

If you're looking for a specific address on a numbered street (not an avenue), the even numbers are usually on the south side of the street and the odd numbers are on the north side of the street.

If you are at all concerned about where a shop or address may be, call ahead for directions. Ask for the nearest cross streets to know exactly where in the grid of Manhattan you will be going. There are a few parts of Manhattan that do not work on a grid, but you can spot these on a map.

INFORMATION SOURCES

I love this one: It's called **It's Easy** (© 866/ITS-EASY or 212/286-8500; www.itseasypassport.com). It arranges travel needs, including passports, visas, passport photos, and more. You pay; they do the hard work. It's Easy is located on the second floor of the Satellite Airline Terminal building, at 125 Park Ave., between 41st and 42nd streets.

Other quite helpful sources include the visitor centers in some department stores. The welcome desk at **Saks Fifth Avenue** is almost like a concierge service—it has free copies of local guide magazines like *Where* and *In New York,* which are advertisement-driven but still useful. The visitor center at **Bloomingdale's** changes currency and sells MetroCards and phone cards. These centers frequently offer a promotional gift (like a store-logo tote bag) if you bring your receipts in after a day's shopping. The minimum for the gift is usually $50, but this can vary from store to store.

SAFETY

According to current crime statistics, New York is safer than any other big American city. While that's quite encouraging for all of us, it's still important to take precautions. Visitors in particular should be vigilant, as swindlers and criminals are expert at spotting newcomers who appear vulnerable.

Panhandlers are seldom dangerous and can simply be ignored (more aggressive pleas can be answered with a firm "Sorry"). If a stranger walks up to you on the street with a long sob story ("I live in the suburbs and was just attacked and don't have the money to get home"), it's likely to be a scam, so don't feel any moral compulsion to help.

Be wary of an individual who "accidentally" falls in front of you or causes some other commotion, as he or she may be working with someone else who will take your wallet when you try to help. *And remember:* You *will* lose if you place a bet on a sidewalk card game or shell game.

ONLINE & PRINT GUIDES TO NEW YORK

If you're tempted to buy a lot of guidebooks about New York—don't. *Frommer's New York City* is a great tool to help you navigate the city. It includes hotel and restaurant reviews,

Site-Seeing: The Big Apple on the Web

The official site of **NYC & Company** (formerly known as the New York Convention & Visitors Bureau), **www.nycvisit.com**, is an excellent resource offering tons of information on the city.

New York Today (**www.nytoday.com**) is the online arts, leisure, and entertainment arm of the venerable *New York Times*. You'll find comprehensive listings, including museum schedules and sports events, plus the newspaper's definitive restaurant reviews.

Citysearch (**www.newyork.citysearch.com**) and **AOL CityGuide New York** (**http://cityguide.aol.com/newyork**) are hipper general-information sites, with reviews and listings for restaurants, shops, hotels, attractions, and nightlife.

About.com maintains a useful New York page at **www.gonyc.about.com**, hosted by an insightful and opinionated local expert.

Each of the city's high-profile weekly magazines also maintains a useful site, including *New York* (**www.newyorkmetro.com**), *Time Out New York* (**www.timeoutny.com**), the *Village Voice* (**www.villagevoice.com**), and the *New Yorker* (**www.newyorker.com**).

details on attractions, walking tours, and nightlife listings. The free package from **NYC & Company** (www.nycvisit.com) is a good starting point as well. Then you might want to think about purchasing a *Zagat* dining map or guide.

In your search for basic and up-to-date information, check out the monthly magazine *Where,* which is distributed free at hotels and at the welcome desk at Saks. Besides listing the expected tourist information, *Where* announces the big fashion shows, designer house shows, antiques sales, public sales, and auctions. Don't panic if a favorite store or restaurant isn't included in *Where*—it features only paying clients. Nonetheless, it's a valuable source.

Want a guide to area sample sales? Try the *S&B Report* (www.lazarshopping.com), described on p. 302. There's also a weekly column of sales and bargains in *New York* (www. newyorkmetro.com) and *Time Out New York* (www.time outny.com).

SHOPPING HOURS

As the town that never sleeps, New York prides itself on having some retail services available on a 24-hour basis. Not at Bloomingdale's, mind you, but there are some stores open whenever you may need them.

Regular retail hours are roughly 10am to 5:30 or 6pm, Monday through Saturday. Thursday is the late night, with stores usually open until 9pm. But irregular is often the rule, so you should call ahead to make sure. Here are some guidelines:

- Stores in business areas, such as Wall Street, tend to open rather early in the morning to serve locals on their way to work. Stores often open at 7:30 or 8am on weekdays and are frequently closed on Saturday and Sunday.
- Power chains with enough money and staff often keep their stores open more nights of the week or later every night of the week. **Barneys** is open until 9pm 6 nights a week.
- Midtown stores that sell business apparel usually open at 9am. But stores that open at 9am may close at 5 or 5:30pm.
- Monday and Thursday are traditional late nights for department stores, which stay open until 9pm. But if a store has only one late night per week, then it's Thursday night.
- Bookstores seem to have their own rules about hours, especially now that certain ones have become the substitute for the village green. Some are even open until midnight.
- During Christmas season, anything goes.
- In summer, fancy stores—such as Madison Avenue boutiques—close at noon on Saturday or don't even open at all.
- Most stores close earlier on Saturday evening than during the work week, be it at 5 or 5:30pm, maybe 6pm. Few stay

open until 9pm on Saturday. There are exceptions; this is a general rule for traditional retail.

Sunday Shopping

I can't go so far as to say everything is open, but Sunday is a huge day for retail in Manhattan. Certain neighborhoods have a big social-retail-dining scene, like SoHo and the Upper West Side. Locals go out for brunch and then go shopping.

Not only are all major department stores and chains open on Sunday, but the hours they keep also seem to be extending. While regular Sunday hours seem to be from noon to 5pm, the opening times are creeping earlier and earlier. Many stores open at 11am now, and a few even open at 10am.

Religious Hours

Please note that stores owned and operated by observant Jewish people may have special hours; they will close at 2pm on Friday and remain closed throughout Saturday. They then reopen first thing on Sunday morning. This is true of many businesses on the Lower East Side as well as individual stores here and there.

Holiday Hours

If it's a shopping holiday (like Christmas), look for extended hours. If it's summer, look for retracted hours. Do note that more and more stores need cash and will do whatever it takes to keep the electricity on, so store hours are becoming more flexible (and extended).

Funky Hours

Now that so many funky neighborhoods have become "in," a whole new set of operating hours is coming into style. Most stores in downtown areas (SoHo, Nolita) open at 11am and stay open until 8pm. They may open at 10am on Saturday, but then again, they may not.

BEHIND CLOSED DOORS: PRIVATE SALES

There is enormous business being done privately in Manhattan. People with taste, a little money, and a few friends are pursuing their personal interests and selling from their collections on a private basis. They usually sell out of their homes, which is why their numbers and addresses are kept quiet.

While there are a few clothing and accessories people who operate this way, the bulk of the business is in antiques and collectibles—especially items picked up at markets around the world and brought in on an individual basis. If you have an area of interest, ask dealers if they can recommend any private resources who might help out. You'll need an appointment and usually the name of your connection before you can get the address.

BAD BUYS OF NEW YORK

There are people who will tell you that anything you buy in New York that costs full retail is a bad buy, but I'm not one of them. I think the things to avoid are the things you can buy at home at much cheaper rates, such as dry-cleaning services, some makeup, vitamins, and pantyhose.

Computers, electronics, and cameras may be available for less in your hometown if you live in a major U.S. city. I've done some rather extensive electronics research for this edition and have discovered the basic operating ploy for the Midtown Fifth Avenue and even Sixth Avenue electronics stores that claim to offer such incredible deals: Typically, they base their prices on what those goods sell for in Europe and Japan and in the world's most expensive duty-free stores. That way, the prices seem like bargains to international visitors. These Midtown stores survive because the people who frequent them often live out of town and may never come back to New York again to complain—or because people don't know that they can do much better. Don't get taken.

PERSONAL/SPECIAL SHOPPERS

Large New York stores offer many free services to help busy people with their shopping. If you've ever been on one of those whirlwind business trips where you mean to get out for a few minutes to your favorite store but you never make it, a personal shopper may work wonders for you. Every department store has a service that will run errands for you and mail out your purchases (from that store only) or will pull together everything you want to look at and then have it ready for you to peruse on an appointment basis at your convenience.

A special shopper will work the entire store with you, helping to coordinate your outfits or put together table settings for a dinner party. Or a special shopper will pick clothes *for* you and then invite you into the store to try them on. They can even bring them to your home if you don't like to go to stores or if you have time constraints.

Store translators are generally available if you would prefer to work in a language other than English. Make an appointment and specify what language you will be speaking.

You should not pay extra for the services of a shopper, since they are employees of the department store. Special shoppers will not use outside resources for your buying, and they won't tell you where to get bargains or discounts. They may give you fashion tips and point you toward a good buy, but their job is to sell the store's merchandise. Note that this service is not just for women—many men also use special shoppers.

CHARGE & SEND

If you are on a mad shopping spree, your concierge can call a messenger to pick up your packages at the stores and deliver them to the hotel on the same day (for a fee, of course).

Most department stores have shopping services that will deliver to your hotel for you. Department stores will also usually mail-order any item you see advertised in the newspaper.

Many of the fancy boutiques offer shop-by-phone and online options as well.

Stores will happily send a package to any address for you—but they'll probably bill you a flat fee for the packing, wrapping, and mailing. Insurance is probably not included. Technically, mail costs should be charged by weight and distance—but many stores guess at the weight and charge you a flat fee for the whole works.

Businesses traditionally ship their merchandise via **UPS,** which takes several days depending on your delivery zone, or **FedEx,** which offers next- or second-day delivery. Every now and then, a store will throw in free shipping for you.

Tip: The old send-it-to-avoid-New-York-sales-tax doesn't always work anymore. New York now has a rule that requires shoppers to pay sales tax for anything purchased here—whether you ship it or not. However, shipping your merchandise home does mean that at least you won't have to worry about airline overweight fees, or about thieves who may break into luggage that must stay unlocked.

If you want to go with the U.S. Postal Service, it offers **Express Mail,** which promises next- or second-day delivery. There's also **Priority Mail,** which is good for small packages. You can use these services yourself through any post office.

NEW YORK SALES TAX

This one is tricky, as it has changed several times in the last few years. Forget everything you knew or thought; here's the skinny as we go to press.

Most items are taxed at a relatively high 8.375%. Ever since 2005, however, the city sales tax of 4% is waived on clothing or footwear purchases under $110, meaning you pay only the state's 4.375% sales tax.

New York has two tax-free weeks a year—usually one in January and one in June—when the sales tax is waived.

Note that some people shop in New Jersey or Pennsylvania specifically to avoid New York sales taxes, as taxes there can be lower or nonexistent. Sometimes you can also avoid sales tax through postal tricks (see above), but New York has recently cracked down on shipping purchases out of state in order to get a tax break—you're supposed to pay the tax at the point of purchase.

There are no refunds on tax (VAT) for international visitors.

Chapter Three

....

SHOPPING TIPS FOR INTERNATIONAL VISITORS

THROUGH MY EYES

There are wonderful things to buy in Europe, and I do indeed write an entire series of books about those items, but no one makes or merchandises low-cost merchandise like the United States. The cost of living—and living well—in Europe is not as high as in New York, but with the euro as strong as it is right now, shopping with dollars becomes a real treat.

There may be financial problems all over the world, but there's always a bargain in New York. Step this way, *venez par ici.*

American Retail

American retailers sell at every point along the price spectrum in order to get their products to people of all socioeconomic backgrounds. Sometimes the exact same merchandise is sold in different packaging or with different labels at different prices. The U.S. retail scene also offers a wide number of sales, promotional events, and outlet stores (see chapter 11).

Come Sale with Me

National governments usually control European sales, and although European sales are very nice, they do not compare with American ones, where the intent is to clear out all the merchandise before the store has to give it away. Visitors from abroad will be amazed by the promotional events that bring super-low prices in the U.S. You should seriously consider flying to New York for the summer or after-Christmas sales.

Welcome to Deal City

Yes *(sí, oui, ja, da)*, if you are visiting from another country, there are plenty of tips throughout this guide; believe me, this isn't the only chapter to read. Of course, I want you to read the whole book, but be sure to see the chapter on bargains (chapter 11) and the information on factory outlets (such as **Woodbury Common;** see p. 297) to learn some tricks of the retail trade so that you go home with a smile on your face and an extra piece of luggage!

Remember, excess baggage from the U.S. to your home destination is in most cases charged by the unit, not the size or the weight. One extra piece of luggage outward bound is usually charged about $100; this can be one of the best investments of your trip.

So if the shopping is going well and you can pack more than $100 worth of savings into an extra suitcase, it may be worth expanding your horizons. The bad news: You may have to pay duty on your purchases when you return to the E.U.—a situation made worse if you have extra luggage crammed with evidence of your shopping spree.

Cash on Demand

If you don't have any U.S. dollars in your wallet, don't fret. They are expensive if you buy them at a *cambio* in Europe or Canada, so wait until you get to the airport at your U.S. port of entry and use your bank card there. Then go to a shop and buy a newspaper or a candy bar and get change in $1 bills. *Remember:* The $1 bill is your key to tipping in the U.S.

If you plan to ride the bus or the subway, you will need a MetroCard or exact change in coins. Get coins ahead of time if you suspect you will need them for fares.

ARRIVING IN NEW YORK

Most international travelers come to the Big Apple via **John F. Kennedy International Airport (JFK)**, in Queens; or **Newark Liberty International Airport (EWR)**, in New Jersey. **LaGuardia Airport (LGA)** frequently gets arrivals from Canada.

Of these three airports, JFK has the most international traffic and therefore is the most congested and most likely to be confusing; Newark is a lot newer and, I think, easier to use. JFK has also become infamous for its scams on travelers who do not know enough about New York to know they are being cheated. While police have cracked down on these scams in order to protect international visitors, you sometimes don't know you're in trouble until it's too late. Therefore, a few tips:

Luggage Carts

In international terminals, they're free. Otherwise, pay for them with a credit card.

Skycaps

If you page a skycap to help you with your luggage, there is no predetermined fee, as there is in many European airports or train stations. You tip at your own discretion. The norm is $1 per bag.

Getting a Taxi at the Airport

Ignore all drivers who approach you and offer you a ride; this includes well-dressed limo drivers or people with "honest" faces.

Use only a yellow licensed cab. When you get into your taxi, take out a pen and paper and copy down your taxi driver's name, shield number, and the name of the cab company. Make sure he or she sees you doing this little ritual. The New York City Taxi and Limousine Commission states that a driver's license will be revoked if he or she is caught overcharging a passenger by more than $10.

There is now a fixed price for taxis into the city from JFK: $47.50. This fee does not include the tip or bridge and tunnel tolls. The fixed-price situation does not work in reverse; you pay the meter price in a taxi from the city to any of the airports. There is also a fixed price for trips from Newark.

Other Ground Transportation

There is public transportation from each airport into Manhattan and to the suburbs. Go to the Ground Transportation desk, located across from the baggage carousels or in the lobby outside of U.S. Customs after arrival. You have your choice of bus, subway, or private transport to take you into the city and suburbs of the Tri-State area (New York, New Jersey, and Connecticut).

SIZING UP AMERICAN SIZES
....

For a conversion chart of U.S., Continental, and British clothing and shoe sizes, see the inside front cover of this book.

Also note that towels and bed linens in the U.S. rarely match their Continental or British counterparts, but may work with some successful juggling or recalculating.

It helps to bring a tape measure with you that has metric measurements on one side and the U.S. measuring system on the other. My friend Ruth, who lives in London, says an American queen-size sheet fits two British twin beds pushed together.

Meanwhile, when it comes to clothing styles, you should know that a European cut is different from an American one;

that Far Eastern sizes are often scaled to the petite; and that size charts are a beginning, but nothing to bet on—always try clothes on and go by fit, not by label.

There are various names for sizes and types of cuts in the U.S. For example, size charts usually refer to women's sizes in even numbers—sizes 4, 6, 8, 10, and so on. They don't tell you that in America we also have junior sizes, sometimes called misses sizes, which are sizes 3, 5, 7, 9, 11, and so on. Misses sizes are usually a tad shorter, rounder, and roomier in the bust, and should not be confused with petite sizes, which usually have a P next to the size number and are proportionately smaller all over.

Large sizes for women come with a variety of names, from "queen size" to "women's size" to "plus size" to simply 1X, 2X, 3X. In addition to sizes that are written as S (small), M (medium), and L (large), there are usually also XL for extra-large and sometimes XXL for extra-extra-large. See p. 207 for special-size resources.

Men's sizes are found up to about size 44, or maybe 46, in regular stores; after that you need a store for "big and tall" men (p. 206).

FRAGRANCE DIFFERENCES

Fragrances in the United States, even when labeled MADE IN FRANCE, are made with denatured alcohol rather than with potato alcohol, which is the base for European perfumes. This type of alcohol may wear differently on your skin, even if the scent in the bottle smells the same. Huh?

It all has to do with the U.S. Food & Drug Administration (FDA) and what it will allow onto American shores. For this same reason, many shades of cosmetics are different in the United States and other parts of the world. They may or may not bear the same color name, number, or designation.

ELECTRONIC DIFFERENCES

Despite the number of stores that sell low-cost DVDs and videos—to say nothing of street vendors who offer up illegal copies of the same—there are several things to watch out for: the difference in voltage and in current, as well as in DVD zones and even TV types. Most newer-model European TVs play NICAM and NTSC. Do not buy videos unless you know for sure that your TV plays NTSC or you are willing to invest in a new set. See "Gadget Lowdown" (p. 54) for more information.

CLOTHING COLOR DIFFERENCES

Global marketing has brought brand names from their countries of origin to stores all over the world, and colorations are geared for specific markets—European colors for Gap are often darker than U.S. colors. Don't be surprised if you find styles or color groups in the States that are not available in Europe.

Colors in fashion will usually match if they're from same-season collections, but colors may not match if the goods were made, or dyed, in different parts of the world.

As I mentioned before, shades of makeup can have the same code numbers throughout the world and yet still be different colors in different parts of the world. In fact, many cosmetics colors don't match up at all!

If you're not flexible, don't buy in the U.S.

PRICES IN NEW YORK

Most international visitors to New York are so dazzled by the price tags at regular retail that they fail to understand the concept of bargain shopping—to realize that there are places where you can get the same, or similar, merchandise for less money.

The first step toward getting a bargain is to create a list of target acquisitions and their prices and availability at home. List the regular retail prices and then check out convenient bargain resources, alternative retail (such as resale shops), and factory outlets.

Value-Added Tax (VAT) & Sales Tax

European shoppers may at first be shocked that the ticketed price on an item in the United States is not the final price, so an advance warning: Once you go to the cash register, *taxes are added on.*

Unfortunately, the U.S. does not presently have a value-added tax (VAT) or an export-tax program. We may get one, but we haven't got it now. International visitors are required to pay the state sales tax and cannot get a refund on this money when they leave the country. Sorry, I know that doesn't sound very fair, but that's the way it works.

Sales tax varies from state to state. Some states have no tax on clothes, no tax on clothing items up to a certain amount, or no tax at all. New York happens to have one of the highest sales taxes anywhere in the United States, currently at 8.375%. However, the city sales tax of 4% is waived on clothing or footwear purchases under $110, meaning you pay only the state's 4.375% sales tax on those items. New York also has two tax-free weeks a year—usually one in January and one in June—when all sales tax is waived.

Some stores are very conscious of the fact that the United States has no VAT refund, and thus go out of their way to give a discount to international visitors. **Conway** (p. 285) does this—just show your passport at the time of purchase. Ask at other stores about such policies.

MONEY CHANGING

One of the best bets is to buy traveler's checks in U.S. dollars before you leave home. Although there is usually a fee for doing this, it allows you to freeze your rate of exchange at the time of purchase.

Some stores and businesses will accept Canadian currency at an automatic (and possibly unfair) discount rate; few stores will accept other foreign currency. **Bloomingdale's** has a foreign exchange office within its store; it's right next door to its American Express Travel Services office, open Monday through Saturday from 10am to 6pm; Thursday until 8pm; closed Sunday.

While you can change funds at airports and most banks, several services in Midtown specialize in money exchange and international traveler's checks. Most are open 7 days a week. These include **American Express,** with multiple locations, including branches at 374 Park Ave. (at 53rd St.) and 1185 Sixth Ave. (at 47th St.); **Chequepoint,** at 22 Central Park S. (between Fifth and Sixth aves.), 1568 Broadway (at 47th St.), 551 Madison Ave. (at 55th St.) and 820 Second Ave. (at 44th St.); and **Thomas Cook,** at locations including 1590 Broadway (at 48th St.), 317 Madison Ave. (at 42nd St.), and 1271 Broadway (at 32nd St.).

Global use of international banking systems is not yet here; a British friend who uses NatWest in London had no luck in a branch of NatWest on Fifth Avenue when trying to transfer dollars to his account.

If you travel to the United States frequently and stockpile cash, you may want to keep track of what you paid for your money. With currency fluctuations, you may find it smarter to sit on your cash and convert new funds, or to rely mostly on credit cards for a better rate of exchange.

INTERNATIONAL MAILING & SHIPPING

If you've bought more than you can carry home, you may want to send some packages overseas. The small-package airmail rate is the least expensive and has minimal paperwork. Once you get into big or heavy packages, however, it does get more expensive, especially if you send by airmail. Even surface mail (which is by sea) gets pricey if the item is large or heavy.

For surface mail to Europe or Asia, figure 6 to 8 weeks before your package will arrive; for airmail, about 1 week. Various courier services carry overnight mail around the world, although with time changes and the international date line, the service is rarely overnight. It will take 2 to 4 days, depending on the destination. (Too bad you can't fax yourself a sweater!) The U.S. Postal Service does have 3-day international airmail that is similar to courier service but is less expensive.

The biggest problems with shipping are not American prices or laws, but laws on the receiving end—many people cannot afford the duty on the gifts that you send them. You could always ship your old, dirty, travel-worn belongings home and pack your new purchases in your luggage.

Note: It is usually less expensive to pay for an additional piece of luggage as excess baggage when you fly home than to ship a package home.

POSTCARDS

Postcards are sold just about everywhere; the best prices are on those sold in minibulk from touristy electronics shops in Midtown. These stores sell cards at three for $1 on Fifth Avenue in the 50s; six for $1 on Madison Avenue in the 40s; and 10 for $1 on Broadway in the 40s, on West 34th Street, and on Fifth Avenue below the New York Public Library at 42nd Street.

Your hotel should have free postcards, featuring the hotel, of course. Postage for an international postcard is 75¢; a letter (up to ½ oz.) is 85¢. A two-page letter may cost more.

E-MAIL

Most hotels have dataports in each room, or they have separate business centers where you can send and retrieve e-mail. You'll have to bring your own cables or rent them from your hotel, so call in advance to find out what the options are.

Internet cafes are dotted around the city. Try **easyInternet-café**, 234 W. 42nd St., between Seventh and Eighth avenues, which is open daily from 7am to 1am.

SALE SEASONS

Sales are held much more frequently in the United States than in Europe. Because Americans think that a good sale is part of the American way, retailers look for any occasion to host a blowout or a promotion that will make shoppers think they are saving money. The events can be seasonal, pegged to holidays, or once-a-year events.

Yes, there are big January and July sales in New York as in every other city in the world, but there are also sales you may have never heard of, such as:

Thanksgiving: The Christmas season officially begins with this American holiday, which is celebrated on the fourth Thursday in November. The following day, Friday, is usually the single biggest day in retail for the year. Sometimes stores begin their pre-Christmas sales on this date.

Pre-Christmas: Recently created to goose Christmas shoppers with the warning that the store has less merchandise than usual, these sales prod you to buy before it sells out.

Post-Christmas: Various stores have their own patterns for post-holiday sales—some stores begin their sales at 8:30am the day after Christmas, while some stores wait until after January 1. It's rare for a store to wait until Epiphany, because it's rare to find an American who knows when (or what) Epiphany is.

Whites: Usually in January, this is a sale of bed linens, rarely white these days since colors and patterns replaced traditional whites in the 1960s.

January Clearance: While most department stores have their end-of-season sales right after Christmas or New Year's, most of the European boutiques in New York have their clearance sales toward the end of January, starting around the 20th. These events, even at stores as exclusive as Hermès, are often advertised in the *New York Times*.

Valentine's Day: February 14 is Valentine's Day, a big day for lovers to express their feelings with traditional gifts such as flowers, chocolates, or fancy undies. These types of items, along with fragrances, jewelry, and anything with a heart-shaped motif, are heavily promoted.

Presidents' Day: Promotional sales are usually on for this entire holiday weekend in late February. This is a good time to pick up winter clothes and ski equipment.

Memorial Day: Stores hold promotional events for summer merchandise during the long weekend at the end of May.

Fourth of July: Bathing suits and some summer apparel go on sale before the Fourth of July weekend. Fourth of July weekend sees blowout sales events, summer clearance sales, various specials offered for a day or two, and special-event sales. Outlet stores in the New York area often do big sales at this time.

Midsummer Clearance: From late July throughout August, there are major summer sales on European brands. Sales on American brands usually begin right before Fourth of July weekend.

Back-to-School: During the last 2 weeks in August, there are promotional sales for school supplies, furnishings, and clothing.

Columbus Day: Coats and early fall clothing are sold at these sales in early October.

Election Day: These sales in November are a good time to buy coats and fall merchandise that you can still wear this season.

HOTEL PROMOTIONS

American hotels are far bigger on promotional deals than European hotels, so there may be freebies and extras that you are not used to asking for or getting. Most frequently, these promotions are for weekends, but there are hotels that offer upgrades at check-in, discounted parking, breakfast, or even a free T-shirt. It never hurts to ask.

PRIX-FIXE MEALS & RESTAURANT PROMOTIONS

Almost every famous restaurant in New York has a fixed-price lunch or dinner. The fixed price usually does not include wine and rarely includes tip. Pre-theater fixed-price meals offer perhaps the best deals you can find. However, you must eat dinner before 7pm, which many visitors consider uncivilized. Even the most famous restaurants in Manhattan offer these promotions, including the Four Seasons and 21.

During New York's Restaurant Week, held twice a year, in late June/early July and late January/early February (see www. nycvisit.com for details), all kinds of swanky restaurants offer three-course lunches at a special price—in 2006, it was $24.07. Some restaurants also offer dinner deals for an additional $10 or so.

TIPPING

When in doubt, give a dollar. The basic tip in America for **small services** (luggage porters and so on) is the $1 bill, although $1 coins are in greater circulation these days, and these will also do the trick. Just learn the size and weight differences between a quarter and a dollar coin so that no one (on either end of the transaction) gets slighted.

It is rare for an American restaurant to automatically add in a service charge or tip unless you are part of a party of eight or more diners. At **restaurants,** tip between 15% and 20% of the total bill *before* the tax was added. In **taxis,** give the driver a percentage of the total meter cost, usually 15%. At **beauty salons** and **spas,** tip 15% to 20%.

Please pay attention to the fine print regarding tipping, especially in hotels. It is very common for a hotel to add the tip for room service and to then leave a second blank space labeled "gratuity" so that those people who are not paying attention will add in another 10% to 15%. Be careful!

BOOZE NEWS

This is a tricky category, so you may want to stay sober enough to take notes. Liquor in Manhattan, especially when sold from fancy liquor stores near the city's finest hotels, is outrageously expensive. Outrageously. I mean, liquor can cost 50% more than it should. Compared to these inflated prices, duty-free liquor is a bargain. But wait! If you can get to a part of America or even Manhattan where real people live (instead of superstars), liquor prices in regular stores are lower than in the duty-free shops.

Now then, should you have the choice of buying a miniature bottle of liquor from your hotel minibar or a small bottle of liquor from an overpriced store, you have to figure out just how much you are going to drink. Miniatures in expensive Midtown liquor stores are at least $4 each; a small bottle of Chivas costs about $20.

GADGET LOWDOWN

Many a European visitor has come to the United States and planned his or her free time around electronics shopping, since electronics and small business machines cost about 30% less in the U.S. than in Europe.

Since there are many pitfalls awaiting you, I have lots of guidance. Electronics are not as easy to buy as you think they will be. Proceed with care. I personally went through hell in order to fulfill an order for a personal computer for my friend Richard. It took approximately 20 hours of my time to research the buy, several transatlantic phone calls back and forth to make sure Richard understood the findings, and then a week of bated breath while we waited for a computer guru in Nice to figure out if the parts would work. Throughout the research and the agony, I kept screaming at Richard: "No amount of savings is worth going through this!" Think about it.

When I first moved to France, I bought French electronics, but they break down frequently and I have begun to bring over some small American electronic products. Results are 50/50 in terms of satisfaction and success. The most nerve-racking buy was the digital camera, which, even with an adapter, does not charge in France. I brought it back to the U.S., planning to take it to J&R, but the camera charged perfectly in an American electrical socket. Go figure.

AMERICAN BRANDS

As a general rule, international brands cost less in the country of origin than they do when exported. Therefore, a trip to the U.S. is the time to stock up on brands like Levi's, Gap, Coach, OshKosh, Estée Lauder, Donna Karan, Calvin Klein, and so on.

European shoppers should only consider buying European brands if the items are on sale or are being sold at a factory outlet or discount source.

DUTY CALLS

All airlines have duty-free shopping onboard, and frequently publish a beautiful color brochure in the seatback in front of you with the other magazines. In many cases, the airline duty-free price is lower than the airport duty-free price. The best way to be sure is to look at the brochure (take it along with you) and price what you want on outbound travel. When you leave the United States, price the item in the airport duty-free shop. Then look it up in your brochure to decide if you want to buy on the plane or not.

Speaking of airport duty-free stores, various terminals at JFK have different shops—some are downright sorry-looking while others are more gorgeous than in any U.S. mall. Many of them publish a price guide. If you have a lot of time before a flight, you might want to wander.

Note: "Duty-free" stores in Manhattan offer no serious bargains. You'll do better at discount sources.

Chapter Four

....

EATING & SLEEPING IN NEW YORK

MORE TO EAT THAN APPLES

I've based the restaurant selections in this chapter on my personal needs as a shopper and visitor, with the assumption that good meals and never-to-be-forgotten dining experiences are among the things you are shopping for while you're in New York. The restaurant information below will also help you get a great meal at a great price.

Chapters 5, 6, and 7 contain additional dining suggestions, which are related to specific New York neighborhoods.

Hotel Dining Deals

One of the most important lessons I've learned as a traveler is that hotels are always looking for lunch business in their dining rooms, even when their dining rooms are famous. As a result, you can often get some of the best lunch deals around at the top hotels in town. Several of the city's snazziest places, and I'm talking **The Pierre** and **The Mark** here, have fixed-price luncheon menus that allow you to enjoy three courses for a flat price that varies from about $20 to $25 per person. At many other places in town, you'd have to pay that same amount and get less food, less service, less atmosphere, and less quality.

Pre-Theater Deals

Broadway curtains usually rise at 8pm, and most restaurants in Midtown offer pre-theater dinner specials that allow you to get a fabulous meal at a fabulous price—if you eat early enough. You don't have to show your theater tickets at the door to prove that you're going to the theater; you just have to come to terms with eating dinner at 6pm. A three-course pre-theater meal at a good restaurant usually comes in at around $32 to $35 per person, which is considerably less than it would cost if eaten a la carte after 8pm.

Big Chefs

I was recently taken to Café Boulud, one of Daniel Boulud's restaurants, and was shocked to see a three-course lunch menu for $24.07, a special due to New York's **Restaurant Week,** held twice each year (see www.nycvisit.com for details). Granted, after iced tea, wine, and tip, the total comes to more than $24.07 per person, but this is still an extraordinary value.

There are all sorts of dining deals like this; some are offered in slow seasons, others are offered year-round, and still others are available only during promotional periods. Ask around and check the website above to find out what dining deals are on during your stay in New York.

Also, following a trend that started in Europe, many big-name, big-time, big-price chefs have opened smaller cafes or bistros that offer great food at affordable prices—a real New York experience.

The listings below are arranged by chef.

DANIEL BOULUD

A French chef more famous in the U.S. than in France, Boulud has some of the best tables in the city. Check it all out at www. danielnyc.com.

Cafe Boulud
20 E. 76th St., between Fifth and Madison aves. (Subway: 6 to 77th St.).

This is not the most low-key of Boulud's eateries, but it's still less expensive than the star chef's fanciest restaurant. Café Boulud is located in a fabulous shopping neighborhood and is right around the corner from my beloved Mark Hotel. © 212/772-2600.

DB Bistro Moderne
55 W. 44th St., between Fifth and Sixth aves. (Subway: B, D, F, or V to 42nd St./Bryant Park).

A casual spot near the Theater District, DB Bistro is the home of the famous DB burger—stuffed with foie gras or truffles and sold for the whopping price of about $35. To be honest, my burger sort of crumbled in my hands and was more of a concept than a heavenly meal. Takeout lunches are available. © 212/391-2400.

THOMAS KELLER

Keller came to fame with the French Laundry, in Napa Valley, and is often considered the reigning American chef in the galaxy of big names that dot the U.S.

Per Se
Time Warner Center, 10 Columbus Circle (Subway: A, B, C, D, or 1 to 59th St./Columbus Circle).

Per Se is per expensive and not as elaborate as the French Laundry. © 212/823-9335. www.frenchlaundry.com.

GRAY KUNZ

The chef from the very tony Lespinasse has now opened a restaurant in the Time Warner Center.

CAFE GRAY

Time Warner Center, 10 Columbus Circle (Subway: A, B, C, D, or 1 to 59th St./Columbus Circle).

The lighting is terrifyingly bright, the decor is overbearing, the service is not great, but the food is terrific. Prices aren't bad considering the location and the pedigree of the chef; dinner for two with a glass of wine for each, plus tip, ran $225. Open for dinner daily, lunch Monday through Saturday. **212/823-6338.** www.cafegray.com.

JEAN-GEORGES VONGERICHTEN

This is the French chef with the Alsatian name so difficult for Americans to pronounce that he is most often called Jean-Georges, which is also the name of his fanciest restaurant. Go to www.jean-georges.com for all the details.

NOUGATINE

1 Central Park West, between 60th and 61st sts. (Subway: A, B, C, D, or 1 to 59th St./Columbus Circle).

The cafe portion of Jean-Georges's most famous eatery serves breakfast, lunch, and dinner, and is not as expensive as the main dining room. © **212/299-3900.**

PERRY STREET

176 Perry St., near West St. (Subway: 1 to Christopher St./Sheridan Sq.).

If you're a Jean-Georges groupie like I am, then you're ready to move on to his latest, which is near the Meatpacking District but not in the midst of the shopping world. You have to go out of your way not only to get here, but also to grab a table, as the place is small. If you're looking for a better location while out on a spree—and if you can stand the crush and the hipsters—then Spice Market is still the best bet. © **212/352-1900.**

SPICE MARKET
403 W. 13th St., at Ninth Ave. (Subway: A, C, E, or L to 14th St./8th Ave.).

This restaurant, which Vongerichten created with chef Gray Kunz (see above), is similar to Market, Vongerichten's restaurant in Paris. The food is great—an even broader version of the cuisine at Vong. The crowd is trendy beyond belief. ✆ 212/675-2322.

VONG
200 E. 54th St., between Third and Second aves. (Subway: 6 to 51st St.; or E or V to Lexington Ave./53rd St.).

This is one of Jean-Georges's first restaurants, serving French-influenced Thai cuisine. It's a great choice for a somewhat spicy meal in an exotic atmosphere. Come here for the food rather than the people-watching. ✆ 212/486-9592.

Legends & Landmarks

Some cities offer dining experiences so sublime that I consider them "legends and landmarks." Just once in your life, you'll probably want to try the following restaurants—you don't go for the food alone, but for the whole gestalt.

IL VAGABONDO
351 E. 62nd St., between First and Second aves. (Subway: F to Lexington Ave./63rd St.).

Perhaps this is a legend and a landmark only to those of us who came of age in Manhattan in the '60s. Il Vagabondo is the funky, dumpy, Italian home-style restaurant of your dreams, with more atmosphere than you can imagine: There's even a bocce court right in the center of the dining space. ✆ 212/832-9221. www.ilvagabondo.com.

RAINBOW ROOM
*30 Rockefeller Plaza, between 49th and 50th sts., 65th floor
(Subway: B, D, F, or V to Rockefeller Center).*

Here's the answer to your burning question: Yes, the Rainbow
Room is open to civilians, with a few restrictions. You can eat
in the Rainbow Grill—dinner and cocktails—every day of the
week. The Rainbow Room ballroom is open for dinner and
dancing on select Friday and Saturday nights. There is also a
grand brunch buffet in the ballroom on Sunday. © 212/632-
5100. www.rainbowroom.com.

TAVERN ON THE GREEN
*Central Park West, at 67th St. (Subway: 1 to 66th St./
Lincoln Center; or B or C to 72nd St.).*

Despite the fact that tourists flock here, the beauty of Tavern
on the Green (first built in 1870 for sheep, believe it or not)
is that it's still frequented by celebs and beautiful people. The
food is surprisingly good and the prices offer real value. Plus,
there's often free dancing in the garden, where little golden lights
twinkle in the trees. A pre-theater three-course meal costs
$25. It also does lunch all week and brunch on Sunday. © 212/
873-3200. www.tavernonthegreen.com.

In-Store Dining

All of the major department stores have a place for you to eat,
and some of them actually have several places to eat, offering
a variety of dining experiences. Such is modern retail.

Cafes have become really important to smaller shops; you'll
find one or two in the basement or on the mezzanine of just
about every name brand in New York, from **Old Navy** to **DKNY**
to **Armani** to **Frédéric Fekkai** to the **NBA Store.** Most of these
cafes have a gimmick: There are bagels and health-food snacks
at DKNY, a 1950s-style diner at Old Navy, and so on. **ABC
Carpet & Home** now has a branch of **Le Pain Quotidien,** a
Belgian chain known for the quality of its bread (say "kwoh-
tee-*dyen*"); **Burberry** has—of course—a tearoom. Some stores

have gone the extra step and now offer fine dining: The **Nicole Farhi** store on East 60th Street has a noisy and fun restaurant that serves really nice Continental food (including great breads). Her downtown outpost, **202,** doubles as an eatery as well.

BARNEYS NEW YORK
660 Madison Ave., at 61st St. (Subway: 4, 5, 6, N, R, or W to 59th St./Lexington Ave.).

Fred's, the stylish cafe in the uptown Barneys store, has a sort of moderne Milan feel. This is very much the place to be seen having a nosh. In fact, I'm not a big fan because it's simply too too, my dear. But you should do it at least once in your life. Without the kids, please. © **212/833-2200.** www.barneys.com.

BERGDORF GOODMAN
754 Fifth Ave., between 57th and 58th sts. (Subway: F to 57th St.).

The Café on 5 is on, duh, the fifth floor; there's also a cafe in the basement in the new beauty portion of the store. I sometimes go across the street to Bergdorf Men to eat at Café 745, a tiny cafe with great salads and no tourists. © **212/753-7300.** www.bergdorfgoodman.com.

BLOOMINGDALE'S
1000 Third Ave., at 59th St. (Subway: 4, 5, 6, N, R, or W to 59th St./Lexington Ave.).

Several choices for several different eating styles: Le Train Bleu (a sit-down restaurant that resembles the inside of the famous French train from the Belle Epoque), 40 Carrots (health food), Showtime Cafe (a cafeteria), and the new David Burke at Bloomingdale's. © **212/705-2000.** www.bloomingdales.com.

HENRI BENDEL
712 Fifth Ave., near 56th St. (Subway: F to 57th St.).

The tearoom on the first floor serves light lunches and teas. The view is of Fifth Avenue through Lalique windows. Teapots line the walls, and each table has a shelf above your lap for your handbag. The food is adequate and midpriced (entrees are around $15), and the salads are especially nice. © 212/247-1100. www.henribendel.com.

MACY'S
151 W. 34th St., at Broadway (Subway: B, D, F, N, R, Q, V, or W to 34th St./Herald Sq.).

There are dining choices on every floor, offering a variety of ethnic eats, old faves, and even a Starbucks. The Cellar in the basement is like the Harrods food halls in London, while the Cucina marketplace is a relatively classy and healthy fast-food option. © 212/695-4400. www.macys.com.

SAKS FIFTH AVENUE
611 Fifth Ave., at 50th St. (Subway: E or V to 5th Ave./ 53rd St.).

Cafe SFA is one of my favorite places for lunch in New York. It's elegant without being stuffy, serves a great raisin-and-walnut bread, offers a good choice of light fare for those who want only a salad or such, and boasts moderate prices. © 212/753-4000. www.saksfifthavenue.com.

Snack & Shop

When I am having an intense shopping day, I do not want a 2-hour lunch, nor do I want to spend what is the equivalent of a pair of shoes for my lunch. I want quick, I want cheap, I want convenient, and I want good (though charming and chic are nice bonuses).

BURGER HEAVEN
9 E. 53rd St., near Fifth Ave. (Subway: E or V to 5th Ave./ 53rd St.); 291 Madison Ave., between 40th and 41st sts. (Subway: 4, 5, 6, 7, or S to Grand Central/42nd St.); 20 E. 49th St., between Fifth and Madison aves. (Subway: B, D, F,

*or V to Rockefeller Center); 536 Madison Ave., between
54th and 55th sts. (Subway: E or V to 5th Ave./53rd St.);
804 Lexington Ave., at 62nd St. (Subway: 4, 5, 6, N, R, or
W to 59th St./Lexington Ave.).*

There's an entire menu with a variety of choices, but I dream
of the Roquefort burger. There are a handful of locations; my
regular is right off Fifth Avenue on East 53rd Street, a great
shopping location. © **212/752-0340.** www.burgerheaven.com.

BURKE & BURKE
*2 E. 23rd St., at Broadway (Subway: R or W to 23rd St.);
485 Madison Ave., at 52nd St. (Subway: E or V to 5th
Ave./53rd St.); 156 W. 56th St., between Sixth and Seventh
aves. (Subway: A, B, C, D, or 1 to 59th St./Columbus Circle); multiple other locations.*

Another chain dotted all over Manhattan, Burke & Burke is a
gourmet sandwich shop. It delivers, so you can actually order
in to your hotel (few of the shops have table service). I fall for
the same old sandwich time after time: Make mine the turkey
and Brie with honey mustard on a baguette. When you pass a
Burke & Burke during your wanderings, pick up a menu—it
lists all of the addresses so you'll be prepared wherever you may
be. © **212/505-2020** for East 23rd Street location.

OLLIE'S NOODLE SHOP
*200 W. 44th St., near Seventh Ave. (Subway: 1, 2, 3, 7, N,
Q, R, or W to Times Sq./42nd St.); 1991 Broadway, between
67th and 68th sts. (Subway: 1 to 66th St./Lincoln Center);
2315 Broadway, at 84th St. (Subway: 1 to 86th St.).*

This is a low-priced noodle shop that actually has a full Chinese menu as well as dim sum and then some. I like the one
on Broadway and 84th Street for a break while shopping in
that area, but the business has grown and opened up all over
town, even in the Theater District, where Ollie's makes an attractive pre- or post-theater possibility. © **212/921-5988** for West
44th Street location.

Teatime

Although tea is a British tradition, it's especially welcome in New York, where you can easily get exhausted by a hard day on your feet. Tea is also a great option when you are going out to the theater and not having dinner until 11pm—it will curb your appetite before the play without making you full. There are only a few specialty teahouses in New York, but all of the major hotels do a big business in tea.

For this section, I tested some of the big Fifth Avenue hotel names that are generally associated with afternoon tea, and was quite disappointed with some of the most famous ones. So if I don't mention your favorite, it might be that I wasn't wild about it.

THE BARCLAY INTER-CONTINENTAL
111 E. 48th St., at Lexington Ave. (Subway: 4, 5, 6, 7, or S to Grand Central/42nd St.).

This is one of my regular spots for tea. It's in a very convenient location, especially if you're meeting someone who is coming in through Grand Central. The style is traditional English. © 212/906-3130. www.new-york-barclay.intercontinental.com.

BURBERRY
9 E. 57th St., between Fifth and Madison aves. (Subway: N, R, or W to 5th Ave./59th St.).

Since everything else about Burberry is new and cutting edge, why shouldn't they also serve tea? © 212/407-7100. www.burberry.com.

THE PIERRE
2 E. 61st St., between Fifth and Madison aves. (Subway: N, R, or W to 5th Ave./59th St.).

Rotunda Tea is what they call it. I've never seen anything like this in my life—I came for tea and wanted to stay for retirement. And I don't mean bedtime. The Rotunda is a small and intimate space, with beautiful painted murals and drop-dead decor, located in the middle of the Pierre Hotel. A pot of tea is a mere $5! You can also get snacks or a light bite. © 212/838-8000. www.tajhotels.com/pierre.

SoHo So Great

You'll have no problem getting something to eat in SoHo: There are grocers, kiosks, fast-food joints, takeout places, and cutting-edge chic restaurants. I visit one of two regulars, depending on my ability to get a reservation.

BALTHAZAR
80 Spring St., between Broadway and Crosby St. (Subway: R or W to Prince St., or 6 to Spring St.).

Right near the most commercial area of SoHo shopping, Balthazar is a Paris-style bistro with a great crowd and affordable prices. Naturally, you can get a good steak and fries here. It also has a takeout department and a bread shop. Reservations can be hard to get, although lunch is much easier to do than dinner. You can also go for morning café au lait. © 212/965-1785. www.balthazarny.com.

BAROLO
398 West Broadway, between Spring and Broome sts. (Subway: C or E to Spring St.).

Before Balthazar, this was my regular place. Barolo is great for pasta, and there's a garden for alfresco dining. I do it for a late lunch—I get to beat the crowds and can usually escape calling ahead if I come at 1:30pm or later. © 212/226-1102. www.nybarolo.com.

SLEEPING IN NEW YORK

There seem to be two completely different schools of thought when it comes to booking hotels. Some people say, "Hey, I'm only sleeping there," and want the least expensive room they can get in a safe neighborhood. Not me. I usually want my hotel to be part of my whole travel experience. I travel to make my life something it isn't when I'm at home, so I want service and location and pretty flowers and sheets made of very crisp, real linen.

Since the kinds of hotels I like are generally very expensive, I am constantly looking for deals—or at least little extras that make luxury a smart choice. I've devoted less space to the totally glam hotels and more to the specialty hotels below, as I have been very freaked out by the high cost of accommodations. I recently called the New York Hilton and was quoted a price of $550 per night—without tax—as the least expensive room in the house.

The kind of hotels I now seek out tend to be renovated old places that were once considered not ready for prime time; they cost about $200 to $250 per night with promotional rates and $250 to $300 in high season—pretty good deals for big cities these days. Rack rates (the published rates) tend to run higher, of course, but there's no reason for anyone to pay those prices.

Various websites, such as www.hotels.com, offer hotel deals. If you do use a website, check to see what kind of flexibility you have and whether there is a cancellation fee.

The hotels that I have chosen for this chapter are all in locations that are convenient for shoppers.

Parking Concepts

If you have a car with you, pick your hotel with parking needs in mind. I don't want to sound discouraging, but some hotels charge up to $50 a day for parking! This is unusually high, but the norm is about $25 per day. One of the reasons I have been devoted to **The Warwick** (see below) is that when you stay at the hotel, the lot next door charges only $18 for overnight parking.

New York Hotel Deals

You may want to keep in mind a few standing promotions for which you might qualify:

CONVENTION RATES   Professionals visiting New York for a convention should be aware of special rates offered by certain hotels that cater to conventions or to visitors coming for market weeks. Even Garment District buyers coming to work the market qualify.

CORPORATE RATES   Most hotels offer corporate discounts, often a 20% discount off rack rates. Since the rack rate can be outrageously high, though, this still may not be the best rate the hotel has available; ask and compare. At some chains, you can fill out a form to become a corporate member. Leading Hotels of the World (www.lhw.com) has such a policy and offers a fine corporate price break for all of its properties.

NEW HOTEL RATES   When a new luxury hotel opens, there are often get-acquainted deals.

THEATER PACKAGES   Many hotels, especially the ones in the Theater District, offer packages that include theater tickets. This can mean either that the hotel's concierge will get theater tickets for you, which you will then pay for, or that the price of the tickets is included in the package. Make sure this is all clear when you book.

WEEKEND RATES   Because there are so many business travelers visiting the Big Apple during the week, hotel prices are steep—and climbing every year. However, when those guys go home, weekend rates make a city stay attractively affordable. The rates vary with the time of year and with availability, but so do the choices.

Weekend visitors should check the Sunday Travel section of the *New York Times* for various weekend rates and promotions—note that some are per room and some are per person. Ask which days are considered weekend days, since some

Hotel Tax Alert

While New York's occupancy tax has been lowered, it's still high—13.375%—and can add a shocking amount to your total bill. If price is a consideration, you might want to ask a few questions before you book, such as what the total rate will be including city tax, hotel tax, and any other extras that might not be included. Don't be shocked when you check out; be prepared before you check in.

hotels include Sunday as part of the weekend while others do not. Usually a weekend is only Friday and Saturday nights.

The **Waldorf-Astoria** (301 Park Ave., between 49th and 50th sts.; ✆ **212/355-3000**) sometimes offers weekend rates at under $200 per night. The **Rihga Royal** (151 W. 54th St., between Sixth and Seventh aves.; ✆ **212/307-5000**), a terrific all-suite hotel, has weekend rates starting at $229. These two hotels are very different, as are their locations—you really need to do some thinking before you pounce on a deal. But you should know that there are some truly splendid rooms out there for a decent price, if you get lucky. Otherwise, you can end up at the Hilton for $550 a night.

Seasonal Discounts

Room rates can vary dramatically—by hundreds of dollars in some cases—depending on the time of year. Winter, January through March, is best for bargains, with summer (especially July–Aug) second best. Fall is the busiest and most expensive season after Christmas, but November tends to be quiet and rather affordable, as long as you're not booking a parade-route hotel on Thanksgiving weekend. All bets are off at Christmastime—expect to pay top dollar for everything.

Consolidators & Discounters

If you crave the deluxe hotels but aren't quite ready to pay top dollar, give a call to a few consolidators and see if they have bought a block of rooms in a hotel to be sold at a discounted price. This strategy usually doesn't work during heavily booked convention times, but it's always worth a try. Try **Hotel Discounts** (© 800/964-6835; www.180096hotel.com) or **Cheap Trips Online** (© 800/444-7666; www.accommodationsxpress.com). *Please note:* Check the hotel's prices first—sometimes a consolidator will get you a room . . . but at no discount!

Online Savings

Every traveler has a few favorite websites for bargains. My suggestions: **www.hotels.com** and **www.priceline.com**. Know that the price of the same room can vary depending on the site. You may also want to play against the middle; after you obtain a few quotes from online services, call the hotel directly and see what it can offer after hearing the online rates and offers. Admit to being confused, and then ask for the best deal, with extra amenities thrown in, please (upgrades, breakfasts, and so on).

Luxury Shopping Hotels

Luxury hotels are New York's middle name; if you're coming to New York to be part of the scene, then you'll want to stay in one, if only for a night or two. Between the **St. Regis** (2 E. 55th St., near Fifth Ave.; © 212/753-4500), the **Peninsula New York** (700 Fifth Ave., at 55th St.; © 212/956-2888), the **Sherry-Netherland** (781 Fifth Ave., near 59th St.; © 212/355-2800), and the hotels listed below, you can have all the luxury you crave and still be a few feet from a fine shopping district. Many luxury hotels are members of Leading Hotels of the World and can be booked by calling © 800/223-6800.

FOUR SEASONS HOTEL
57 E. 57th St., between Madison and Park aves. (Subway: 4, 5, 6, N, R, or W to 59th St./Lexington Ave.).

This is perhaps my favorite location when money is no object. The Four Seasons is more expensive than most other luxury properties, but it also has a cachet that money can't buy . . . and a fabulous restaurant. This place is modern, luxe, and boasts every latest technology. The rooms are big, the bathrooms huge.

A room here will cost at least $600 per night. The business center charges $1 per minute for e-mail, and I was hit with a fee of an additional $40 to print out 20 pages—so if you're on a budget, the Four Seasons might not be for you. On the other hand, it's half a block from a great discount store (Daffy's), so you need not look in the Chanel–Dior direction. © 800/223-6800 or 212/758-5700. www.fourseasons.com.

THE MARK
25 E. 77th St., between Fifth and Madison aves. (Subway: 6 to 77th St.).

I'm loyal to the Mark for several reasons: The area is great for shopping, the location is good for getting to area airports without having to drive through Midtown traffic, the hotel is pet-friendly, and you can get a room with a kitchen—which works for me because I often load up on groceries when I'm in Manhattan.

Of course, this place is also luxury personified—rooms are decorated in grand style, like they jumped off the pages of *Architectural Digest*. There's a well-being center in the hotel, and the Mark is affiliated with a spa across the street, plus there's a direct phone line to Zitomer. The cost? A room can be yours for under $400 a night during a promotion. © 800/526-6566 or 212/744-4300. www.mandarinoriental.com.

THE PIERRE
2 E. 61st St., between Fifth and Madison aves. (Subway: N, R, or W to 5th Ave./59th St.).

If you think all luxury hotels are created equal and it doesn't matter which one you pick, meet the Pierre. While it's a pricey choice (about $550 per night), it happens to be the least expensive of the drop-dead fancy hotels in Manhattan. It's also the only one with elevator operators. They wear white gloves, of course.

The decor is old-fashioned and elegant, and the rooms vary enormously. The bathrooms are usually good, but aren't in the same league as the ones at some of the newfangled hotels (although the toiletries are by Bulgari). The Pierre has a residential feel to it (you can even buy an apartment here), so it's more like a private club than a hotel . . . and that's what you're paying for. The bad news: The business center charged me $2 per minute for e-mail. The good news: I bought so many things that I couldn't cram them all into my luggage, so I shipped a box home to Texas (where I used to live) through the concierge by way of UPS. Total charge: a mere $15. © 800/ 223-6800 or 212/838-8000. www.tajhotels.com/pierre.

Four-Star Shopping Hotels

I've never found a four-star hotel in New York that compares with the city's luxury five-star hotels. And I'm not just talking about fancy rooms or better bars of soap: A five-star luxury hotel functions in a seamless manner that a four-star hotel simply can't quite get down pat. It may not seriously offend you and the price difference may be worth the inconvenience, but never make the mistake of considering a four-star property as close cousin to a five-star property. Four-star properties are for those who don't mind the difference and like saving the cash.

THE BENJAMIN
125 E. 50th St., near Lexington Ave. (Subway: 6 to 51st St., or E or V to Lexington Ave./53rd St.).

This used to be the Beverly Hotel, which was one of my secret finds in New York. Now it's been redone, renamed, and repositioned. Rates are around $300 a night, but you can often get a promotional deal. © **212/715-2500**. www.the benjamin.com.

THE DRAKE SWISSÔTEL
440 Park Ave., at 56th St. (Subway: 6 to 51st St.; or E or V to Lexington Ave./53rd St.).

The Drake's fine reputation has been based on its reasonable prices and great location. This place is considered a secret find by many Ladies Who Lunch, as well as by businesspeople who stay here during the week. Both sets know that this was once a residential hotel, so it has an intimate feeling and boasts rooms that aren't cubicles. The newly renovated rooms and suites are decorated in faux Biedermeier, which is a novel idea.

The hotel has a new spa and a branch of French pastry-maker Fauchon. There's a bed-and-breakfast package with rates of $295 in a deluxe room. Note that standard and deluxe rooms are more or less the same size. © **800/DRAKE-NY** or 212/421-0900. www.swissotel.com.

HOTEL WALES
1295 Madison Ave., near 92nd St. (Subway: 6 to 96th St.).

For those interested in proximity to Museum Mile, the enclave of Upper Madison Avenue shopping in Carnegie Hill, or the idea of a secret hotel at a good price, this is a find. It was once a residential hotel, but renovations have made it chic. The hotel's restaurant is none other than Sarabeth's, a cult favorite for home-style cooking. Room rates are around $229 with online promotions. © **866/WALES-HOTEL** or 212/876-6000. www.wales hotel.com.

SURREY HOTEL
20 E. 76th St., between Madison and Fifth aves. (Subway: 6 to 77th St.).

I found this hotel by accident while I was shopping on Madison Avenue; you certainly can't beat the location or the fact that Café Boulud is in the lobby.

This was once an apartment building and is now part of the Affinia group. The lobby is simple, but moderately swank. The rooms may remind you of furnished apartments—the basics are there and they're fine, but the decor is nothing special. But then again, you're here for the location, the price, and the wow of it all. Daily, monthly, promotional, and weekend rates are all available. A studio begins at $290 double. © **866/246-2203** or 212/288-3700. www.affinia.com.

THE WARWICK
65 W. 54th St., between Fifth and Sixth aves. (Subway: E or V to 5th Ave./53rd St.).

This is the kind of find that every smart shopper wants to know about, mostly because the rates are about half that of a five-star hotel and the rooms are large. If price and location are of paramount importance, you'll be thrilled with this choice.

The Warwick is an old, very famous New York hotel that went downhill for a while and therefore may have fallen off your list. However, the place has been completely refurbished. Know that it has a tiny lobby, but *grrrreat* rooms with rates around $300 per night. © **800/203-3232** or 212/247-2700. www.warwickhotels.com.

Unusual Locations (Great for Shopping)

60 THOMPSON
60 Thompson St., between Broome and Spring sts. (Subway: C or E to Spring St.).

This is a small luxury hotel in such an incredibly fabulous Village/SoHo shopping area that you may never leave downtown. © **877/431-0400** or 212/431-0400. www.60thompson.com.

SOHO GRAND HOTEL
310 West Broadway, between Grand and Canal sts. (Subway: A, C, or E to Canal St.).

Located conveniently on the edge of SoHo, the Soho Grand is swank and moderne—in keeping with the cutting-edge nature of this neighborhood. Rooms are stark, small, and very chic; rates begin at $150 per night. © **212/965-3000.** www.soho grand.com.

Chains for Deals

APPLE CORE HOTELS
This is a group of five hotels, in about the three-star category, that are in great Manhattan locations and that keep prices below $200 per night—some are even $150 a night.

They include **Comfort Inn Midtown,** 129 W. 46th St., near Sixth Avenue (© **800/517-8364); La Quinta Manhattan,** 17 W. 32nd St., off Fifth Avenue (© **800/551-2303); and Ramada Inn Eastside,** 161 Lexington Ave., at 30th Street (© **800/625-5980).** Rooms have the usual luxuries (including free Wi-Fi) and are nicely but not extravagantly decorated. © **800/567-7720.** www.applecorehotels.com.

DOUBLETREE GUEST SUITES
1568 Broadway, at 47th St. (Subway: N, R, or W to 49th St.).

All of the rooms here are suites, the location is right in the thick of Times Square and the Theater District, and the prices begin at $250. That was the good news. When I called the hotel for a room, I was offered a rate of $450 for 1 night! There are packages for theater visits, for weekends, and so on, but your timing has to be just right. © **800/222-TREE** or 212/719-1600. www.doubletreehotels.com.

SHERATON NEW YORK HOTEL & TOWERS
811 Seventh Ave., at 53rd St. (Subway: B, D, or E to 7th Ave./53rd St.).

It might not be romantic, but the Sheraton offers various shopping promotions. You may get coupons for discounts in stores or a gift upon check-in; rates on weekend deals begin at $79, which is per room, not per person! To get the promotional rates, you have to request them and sometimes need a promotional code. Ask. ✆ 877/782-0018 or 212/581-1000. www.sheraton. com.

W HOTELS

W New York, 541 Lexington Ave., at 49th St. (Subway: 6 to 51st St.; or E or V to Lexington Ave./53rd St.); W New York–The Court, 130 E. 39th St., at Lexington Ave. (Subway: 4, 5, 6, 7, or S to Grand Central/42nd St.); W New York–The Tuscany: 120 E. 39th St., between Park and Lexington aves. (Subway: 4, 5, 6, 7, or S to Grand Central/ 42nd St.); W New York–Times Square: 1567 Broadway, at 47th St. (Subway: N, R, or W to 49th St.); W New York– Union Square: 201 Park Ave. S., at 17th St. (Subway: 4, 5, 6, L, N, Q, R, or W to 14th St./Union Sq.).

The W is a concept hotel chain—modern, minimal, and high chic at low prices. It has taken over several older Manhattan properties, redone them, and created a whole new hotel picture with very realistic prices, often under $250 a night if you get a promotional deal.

When I booked, it was $269 per night, but that was a weeknight. Since the company keeps taking on more and more properties, you need to call and get the lowdown on which is the best location for you and offers the best deal. I admit to not being wildly impressed by the Lexington Avenue hotel, but I'm extremely impressed by the W Tuscany. ✆ 877/W-HOTELS. www.whotels.com.

Chapter Five

....

UPTOWN SHOPPING NEIGHBORHOODS: WEST

DIRECTIONALLY SPEAKING

There is no other city in the world that I know of where what you call the various parts of town depends on where you're standing. There is no precise center of New York called "downtown." Although it generally refers to anything below 14th Street, "downtown" also means down from where you are standing—unless you are in the river below the bottom of the island, and then it's all uptown.

Since this is all so arbitrary, I've created a few random map boundaries in these pages: I decree 34th Street the divider between uptown and downtown. Fifth Avenue has always been the divider between east and west. In this book, uptown neighborhoods for the East Side and West Side are in two different chapters, followed by a chapter on downtown.

Sometimes the best way to shop is to head for a general destination and then let your feet do the wandering. I have included some lunch possibilities here as well, although there is another section on restaurants in chapter 4.

WEST 34TH STREET

The West 34th Street neighborhood stretches from Penn Station (between Seventh and Eighth aves.) to Fifth Avenue. The addition of **Kmart,** right near Penn Station, has extended the shopping district and given everyone a place for one-stop shopping. But the real energy comes from **Old Navy** and **H&M,** both across the street from Macy's. There is also a branch of **Daffy's** (one of New York's most famous off-pricers—although this is not my favorite location), a **Gap,** and a big **Banana Republic.** Right on the corner of 34th Street and Broadway is **Victoria's Secret.** Another off-pricer, **Conway,** has several stores dotted around here. Conway is down-market, but I have fun there. You may not.

Remember that just because a lot of this strip has been revitalized, it's still not Fifth Avenue. In fact, shopping here is far from chic—it's practical. To get the most out of this area, you really have to consider it an extension of the greater shopping neighborhood that includes the **Garment District, Lord & Taylor** (424 Fifth Ave., at 38th St.), and the row of stores on Fifth Avenue south of Lord & Taylor until about 34th Street.

Postcards in this part of town go 10 for $1—a good buy. There are a few street vendors around here; many sell fake designer perfumes or big-name perfumes bought in the Caribbean. Let the buyer beware.

You can take the A, C, E, 1, 2, or 3 train to 34th Street/Penn Station; or the B, D, F, N, Q, R, V, or W to 34th Street/Herald Square.

KMART
1 Penn Plaza (W. 34th St., at Seventh Ave.).

Maybe Kmart isn't your idea of a find, but if you live in New York, this discount drugstore-and-more is a godsend. ✆ **212/760-1188.** www.kmart.com.

OLD NAVY
150 W. 34th St., between Broadway and Seventh Ave.

This is the Old Navy flagship in Manhattan, and all I can say is wow—it's retail entertainment at its finest. See p. 171 for more on the Old Navy brand. ✆ **212/594-0049.** www.oldnavy.com.

Eats

The department stores have several choices for lunch—if you decide to dine in one of them, go before or after the usual lunch hour to avoid crowds. There's a 1950s-style diner downstairs in the **Old Navy** store.

GARMENT DISTRICT

....

The Garment District is the name of a neighborhood on the west side of Manhattan where most, but not all, of the needle trades have their showrooms, offices and, sometimes, cutting rooms. The main area, where you'll see the racks whizzing by with their dozens of brand-new fashions, is on Seventh Avenue around 40th Street.

Broadway bisects Sixth Avenue at 34th Street, so this part of Broadway, which is very close to Seventh Avenue, also houses much of the trade. Many buildings have two different entrances (and sometimes two different addresses): one on Broadway and one on Seventh Avenue.

The Garment District is different things to different people: Some salivate, others shudder. For the person who has fabric in the blood, it's one of the most exciting places on earth. For others, the hustle and bustle of the pipe racks, the screaming and swearing of the workers, and the unglamorous workrooms can cause severe headaches.

Some people like to wander around the Garment District buildings on a Saturday to see what vibes (and bargains) they can pick up. The big Broadway buildings (1407 and 1411) are totally locked up, but the smaller buildings have an elevator operator on duty who will take you to a specific floor for an appointment. *A note to the crafty:* These elevator operators are savvy professionals; they can spot a tourist a mile away. Don't try to fool them. Simply ask if any of the showrooms do business on Saturday. Many sample sales are posted on the elevator or building doors in the lobby; the doormen know everything.

Sample-Sale Venue

Parsons School of Design (as seen on *Project Runway*) is in this neighborhood, at 560 Seventh Ave. (at 40th St.). Frequent sample sales and shopping events are held in the school's auditorium. Call © **212/229-8959** for further information.

If you're not keen on wandering around this area blindly, get a copy of the *S&B Report,* which lists sample sales in the area. See p. 302 for more information.

Note: The **Fur District** is adjacent to the Garment District, farther downtown. The streets around 30th Street and Seventh Avenue house small mom-and-pop furriers and suppliers as well as a few skyscrapers packed with showrooms.

DUTY FREE APPAREL
204 W. 35th St., between Seventh and Eighth aves.

This place is sometimes called "Sample Sale." It's not a real sample sale, but rather a store that concentrates on Italian brands for the Italian-visitors market. The hours are a bit unusual: Tuesday through Friday from 10am to 6pm. © **212/967-6548.** www.dutyfreeapparel.com.

WEST 42ND STREET

The block of 42nd Street just west of Fifth Avenue is not glam, but because one of Manhattan's best bookstores has moved here—and because fashion shows are held in Bryant Park, across the street—it's an area to consider passing through. During Fashion Week (usually held in Sept and Feb), hostesses on the street often hand out free magazines or even products and samples.

COLISEUM BOOKS
11 W. 42nd St., between Fifth and Sixth aves.

This is my favorite bookstore in Manhattan, so I am thrilled that it has resurfaced after closing on West 57th Street. This is one of the few independent bookstores left, and it offers many specialized customer services and an enormous selection of books. You are more likely to find unusual titles or small publishers represented here than at the big chains. © 212/803-5890. www.coliseumbooks.com.

TIMES SQUARE

I wish I could tell you that the new Times Square is a must-do neighborhood and a shopper's heaven. However, though the area has undergone an enormous cleanup and has been vastly improved, this is still not a retail paradise. You'll find chains such as the **Disney Store, Sephora,** and **Virgin Megastore,** as well as snazzy hotels and even the new Condé Nast building—but mostly this is an area that is far from classy.

The **Times Square Information Center,** 1560 Broadway, near 47th Street (© 212/768-1560; www.timessquarenyc.org), is a good one-stop source for information, MetroCards, maps, and so on.

You can take the 1, 2, 3, N, Q, R, S, W, or 7 train to Times Square/42nd Street.

TKTS
Duffy Sq., Broadway, at 47th St.

I tell you about this with a heavy heart, as I hate to see you spend precious New York time standing in line. On the other hand, bargains are bargains, so here goes: This discount booth sells same-day, half-price theater tickets. Cash and traveler's checks only. © 212/221-0013. www.tdf.org/tkts.

Toys "R" Us
1514 Broadway, at 45th St.

If you're interested in retail as theater, check out this amazing branch of the toy retailer. They ain't got one like this back home. © **646/366-8800**. www.toysrus.com.

Eats

I am amused by the McDonald's on West 42nd with the Broadway-style marquee; I also think it's funny that Red Lobster came here from suburbia. Those going to the theater often prefer the side streets around Sixth Avenue, especially on West 44th and West 45th streets, where there are plenty of really nice restaurants, many of them in hotels. For you guys out there, the **ESPN Zone** (1472 Broadway, near 42nd St.) is incredible, with food, games, retail, and large screens for watching sports.

THEATER DISTRICT

The Theater District is a subset of Times Square, located in the area from West 42nd to West 52nd streets, mostly west of Seventh Avenue. I mention it because there is a small amount of specialty retail here. Most Broadway productions have their own merchandise, sold in the lobby of the theater: This is "You've seen the play, now wear the T-shirt" kind of stuff. There are also the usual TTs (tourist traps) with souvenirs.

Take the 1, 2, 3, N, Q, R, S, W, or 7 train to Times Square/42nd Street; or the 1, N, R, or W to 49th Street.

Colony Music
1619 Broadway, at 49th St.

Musical scores, sheet music, CDs, posters, and other print materials—be still, my heart. You can go nuts here. Open late for after-theater browsing. © **212/265-2050**. www.colony music.com.

DRAMA BOOK SHOP
250 W. 40th St., between Seventh and Eighth aves.

This place has a complete selection of plays and theater-related publications. ✆ **212/944-0595.** www.dramabookshop.com.

MANNY'S MUSIC
156 W. 48th St., between Sixth and Seventh aves.

This is a musician's source for instruments and supplies such as strings. Not to be confused with shoe-guru Manolo Blahnik. ✆ **212/819-0576.** www.mannysmusic.com.

ROCKEFELLER CENTER
....

On the west side of Fifth Avenue, you have everything from the new **Façonnable** to the somewhat new **Anne Fontaine.** The promenade leading to the skating rink has specialty bookstores, chocolate shops, and a branch of **Brookstone.**

Take the B, D, F, or V train to Rockefeller Center.

WEST 57TH STREET
....

No visit to New York is complete without worshipping at the corners of Fifth Avenue and 57th Street—all four of them. Even if you don't buy anything, between the window-shopping and the crowd-staring, this is what you came for.

The block of 57th Street between Fifth and Sixth avenues has all sorts of retail. Italian hotshots such as **Bulgari** and **Laura Biagiotti** show no sign of being disappointed with the location, and there's also **Club Monaco** and the British stationery retailer **Smythson of Bond Street**—quite a creative mix of stores. For cheapie teen outfits, don't miss the chain **Strawberry,** at the Sixth Avenue end. The feel of the street changes as you head west, but there is some very interesting retail around Seventh Avenue, so do explore.

Take the F to 57th Street/6th Avenue, or the N, R, or W to 5th Avenue/59th Street.

ASCOT CHANG
7 W. 57th St., between Fifth and Sixth aves.

This Hong Kong shirtmaker to the rich and famous creates custom-made shirts here for about $75 each. See p. 199 for more. © 212/759-3333. www.ascotchang.com.

KATE'S PAPERIE
140 W. 57th St., between Sixth and Seventh aves.

See p. 118 for details on this fabulous paper store. © 212/459-0700. www.katespaperie.com.

OMO NORMA KAMALI
11 W. 56th St., between Fifth and Sixth aves.

Even though this store is not officially on West 57th Street, it fits in with the whole vibe of that street. This is cutting-edge chic for those who like unique clothes, from Indian saris to reflective Lycra sportswear. © 212/957-9797. www.norma kamalicollection.com.

Eats

Bergdorf's, of course (p. 63).

COLUMBUS CIRCLE

Oh me! Oh my! What a difference a decade makes. This neighborhood has been born again and is now the hottest place in town, home to many big-time chefs and a new high-rise.

Welcome to the new **Time Warner Center,** with a Mandarin Oriental hotel and a large "retail complex," which is basically business-speak for "mall." Not charming, but filled with fashion's big names. If you have limited time in New York, it's a one-stop shopping zone for luxury goods.

A shocking contrast to all that glitz is my regular branch of beauty-supply chain **Ricky's** (332 W. 57th St., near Eighth Ave.). See p. 226 for more info and locations.

Take the A, B, C, D, 1, or 9 train to 59th Street/Columbus Circle.

Eats

Pop into the Time Warner Center and explore either the hotel (**Mandarin Oriental**), the new **Whole Foods** (with a sushi bar and sit-down area!), or the mall for eats.

UPPER WEST SIDE

Broadway has become home to numerous superstores, discounters, and lifestyle resources, while Columbus Avenue has lost its energy and seems to function more as a mall, with branches of chain stores. Amsterdam Avenue has been slower to develop, but it has a few funky stores, antiques dealers, and resale shops. I've come to like the area best for the food stores on Broadway.

Take the 1, 2, 3, B, or C train to 72nd Street; or the 1 to 79th Street; or the B or C to 81st Street/Museum of Natural History.

Broadway

Many of the old staples are clustered from the high 60s to the mid-80s. There's **Talbots** (2289 Broadway, at 82nd St.) and an **Ann Taylor** (2017 Broadway, near 69th St.). Choose from two **Gap** stores (2109 Broadway, near 69th St.; and 2373

Broadway, near 86th St.), plus **Gap Kids** (2373 Broadway, near 86th St.). Check out the **Body Shop** (2159 Broadway, near 76th St.), and don't forget **Urban Outfitters** (2081 Broadway, at 72nd St.) for teens and tweens. For off-price retail, pop into **Filene's Basement** (2222 Broadway, at 79th St.), though its other Manhattan locations are better. You'll see street vendors selling used books around West 72nd Street, or stop in **Barnes & Noble** (1972 Broadway, at 66th St.) for new ones.

This area has become very residential, so there are stores for real people who live here. The grocery store **Fairway** (2127 Broadway, at 74th St.) has redone itself and competes more than ever with **Zabar's** (2245 Broadway, near 80th St.). For home decor, choose from **Pottery Barn** (1965 Broadway, at 67th St.) and **Gracious Home** (1992 Broadway, at 67th St.).

Amsterdam Avenue

If you stroll along the whole avenue, you may think I've sent you to the wrong neighborhood. So aim high—head straight to the blocks in the 70s and 80s.

ALLAN & SUZI
416 Amsterdam Ave., at 80th St.

If you're looking for an eye-popping ensemble at a bargain price, look no further. Don't even stop to stare at the funky 8-inch platform shoes in the window; just dash right in and start trying on "gently worn" designer items. With prices that run from $10 to $8,000, there's something here for everyone's taste and budget. ✆ **212/724-7445.** www.allanandsuzi.net.

Columbus Avenue

Welcome to the mall. There's no other area in all of Manhattan with a greater concentration of stores that you'd find in any suburban shopping mall. Some unique retailing gems are still here, but you have to look past all the big chains to find them. But since all the shopping giants are so handy, why not check out the whole scene? Please note that many of the stores in this neighborhood do not open until 11am, and be warned that this area is super-crowded on weekends.

APRIL CORNELL
487 Columbus Ave., at 83rd St.

This is one of the most likely places to find items you don't see very often—but that you'll love for yourself, your home, or a special little girl. The look is unique, colorful, and, I think, sensational. Remember those paisley and madras bedspreads from the 1960s? Now the prints (which look surprisingly like some from Pierre Deux; see p. 98) have been pieced together and sewn into bedspreads and quilts. Tablecloths and napkins are a sea of color. Refreshing and unpretentious, colorful and quaint, charming and delicious. There's an excellent sale rack in the back, and twice a year, in January and July, sales are worth flying in for. © **212/799-4342.** www.aprilcornell.com.

BETSEY JOHNSON
248 Columbus Ave., near 72nd St.

Teen angel, are you with me? I've never met a teenage girl who didn't crave to be dressed by Betsey. So here you go, moms and daughters alike—have a look. The clothes are slightly on the cutting edge without being too crazy. © **212/362-3364.** www.betseyjohnson.com.

DANSKIN
159 Columbus Ave., at 67th St.

This place has a wide selection of gym and dance attire for women and girls. It also carries plus sizes. © **212/724-2992.** www.danskin.com.

Eileen Fisher
341 Columbus Ave., at 77th St.

One of the branch stores of my heroine; see p. 94 for more about her. © **212/362-3000.** www.eileenfisher.com.

Eats

Try the cafe upstairs at **Fairway** (2127 Broadway, at 74th St.).

Chapter Six

·················

UPTOWN SHOPPING NEIGHBORHOODS: EAST

DIRECTIONS

Since this is the eastern portion of the uptown neighborhoods chapters of this guide, I have again used 34th Street as the dividing line between uptown and downtown.

EAST 42ND STREET

East 42nd Street is not much of a neighborhood, per se. But wait—there's action on two fronts here, maybe more. **Grand Central Terminal** (42nd St., between Vanderbilt and Lexington aves.) is gorgeous and filled with great stores (and an excellent market). And farther east, at Lexington Avenue and 42nd Street, is the first official **Ann Taylor LOFT** (LOFT is Ann Taylor's discount brand, which used to be reserved for outlet malls). The eastern portion of shopping on East 42nd Street, and the subsequent opportunities on Third Avenue up toward 50th Street, will mostly make you feel like you're in a mall. It's convenient for those using Grand Central; it has nothing that you need to go out of your way to find.

Take the 4, 5, 6, 7, or S train to Grand Central/42nd Street.

SEAN JOHN
475 Fifth Ave., at 41st St.

Although I don't really think you need or want this address,
I don't want you to think that I am out of it and don't know
cool when I see it. This is the first store in Sean "P. Diddy"
Combs's retail empire. The clothes are urban casual and great
for young men with high style and fashion attitude. © **212/220-
2633.** www.seanjohn.com.

MIDTOWN FIFTH AVENUE

What locals refer to as Midtown is what visitors consider the
main shopping guts of the city. It's also one of the main business areas—between 57th Street and 34th Street. Main Street
USA in this case is Fifth Avenue, which is a legend in its own
time.

To get in the spirit, begin your tour at Fifth Avenue and 58th
Street. Walk down Fifth all the way to 34th Street, noting the
changes in the crowds, the types of stores, and the very feel of
the air. It's fancy uptown and gets less so as you walk downtown. The specialty department stores are **Bergdorf Goodman**
(two stores on Fifth Ave., near 58th St.) and **Takashimaya** (693
Fifth Ave., at 54th St.), a drop-dead elegant place that despite
its Japanese name is not particularly Japanese in style.

I'm not certain which is more a tribute to human spirit and
imagination, the **Disney Store** (711 Fifth Ave.) or **Gianni Versace** (647 Fifth Ave.). The **NBA Store** (666 Fifth Ave.) is in a
class by itself. Even if you don't buy anything, go in and
stare—this is what sizzle is all about. There are plenty of
affordable places now: Get a look at the new **Mexx** (650 Fifth
Ave., at 52nd St.), a Dutch brand that's slightly more upmarket than H&M.

My favorite subway line is the F train, which will get you
to Rockefeller Center, or you can take the E train to 5th
Avenue/53rd Street, exactly where you want to be.

FORMAN'S
560 Fifth Ave., near 46th St.

Forman's is part of the family of off-price stores dotting downtown and Midtown. I like other branches better, but this is a good start if you're in the area. Major American brands are discounted about 25%; I load up on Jones New York. ✆ 212/719-1000.

H&M
640 Fifth Ave., at 51st St.

H&M is the signal to the world that Fifth Avenue has changed. This Swedish chain sells clothes for men, women, and kids; it can knock off the latest trends from the catwalks faster than you can say, "What's new, pussycat?" ✆ 212/489-0390. www.hm.com.

NBA STORE
666 Fifth Ave., at 52nd St.

From the sublime to the ridiculous, perhaps, but this store is unlike anything in the world—a new generation of retail entertainment that owes its inspiration to Niketown (but has more bells and whistles). To say nothing of WNBA Barbie! ✆ 212/515-6221. http://store.nba.com.

TAKASHIMAYA
693 Fifth Ave., near 54th St.

If you have time to see only one store in Manhattan and you may not even have time to buy, let me make life easy for you—speed through Takashimaya. The store is a museum of good taste; every little detail is breathtaking to behold. It all looks incredibly expensive, but some of it is actually affordable. The point, however, is not to buy. Feasting your eyes and your soul is the most important thing. Takashimaya artfully blends Asian inspiration with country French and sophisticated Continental looks to provide one smooth international arena of finesse and magic. The florist is Christian Tortu, the toast of Paris. © 212/350-0100.

Eats

I'm always at **Burger Heaven** (p. 64), but you can also pop into the cafe at **Saks Fifth Avenue** or choose from any number of eats at **Rockefeller Center.** (There's a **Dean & DeLuca** gourmet grocery at Rock Center with tables upstairs.) If you're with the kids, try the cafe at the **NBA Store.**

MIDDLE MADISON AVENUE

I call Midtown Madison Avenue (from 57th St. to 42nd St.) "Middle Mad." The lower end of the stretch, in the 40s, is geared toward haberdashery. If you're looking for the older version of **Brooks Brothers** (346 Madison Ave., at 44th St.), you'll still find it, along with **Jos. A. Bank** (366 Madison Ave., at 46th St.), **Paul Stuart** (350 Madison Ave., at 45th St.), and **Thomas Pink** (520 Madison Ave., at 53rd St.).

The stretch beginning around 54th Street is filled with big chains. A new flagship **J. Crew** (347 Madison Ave., near 44th St.) recently opened, and there's an okay branch of the off-pricer **Daffy's** (335 Madison Ave., at 44th St.) as well. Don't forget **Talbots** (525 Madison Ave.), **Talbots Mens** (527 Madison Ave.), and **H2O Plus** (511 Madison Ave.). This is very real shopping without being overly glam—it's just all here.

You can use the E or V stop at 5th Avenue/53rd Street. If you're beginning lower on Madison and then plan to walk uptown (a good idea), take the 4, 5, 6, 7, or S train to Grand Central/42nd Street.

AMERICAN GIRL PLACE
609 Fifth Ave., at 49th St.

If you have a young daughter, you know about this amazing series of dolls and the marketing concept that goes behind them.

This new store has dolls, a tearoom, and a theater for events. © 877/247-5223. www.americangirlplace.com.

BELGIAN SHOES
110 E. 55th St., between Park and Lexington aves.

There is no place more "in" and "New York" than this shoe store, which has its own look and is, therefore, an icon of style—flat shoes in zillions of colors and styles, with a distinctive cut and shape. © 212/755-7372. www.belgianshoes.com.

CROUCH & FITZGERALD/THE SHERPA SHOP
400 Madison Ave., near 48th St.

A staple for fine leather goods for as long as I can recall, this store has been sold and downsized but still has plenty of great merchandise, including briefcases and carry-alls for business-women and travelers. The house-brand luggage is crafted from canvas and belting leather—handsome, practical, and well made. Better yet is the in-store **Sherpa Shop,** which sells doggy totes and travel gear. © 212/755-5888. www.crouchand fitzgerald.com.

DAFFY'S
335 Madison Ave., at 44th St.

This branch isn't the largest Daffy's, but you'll make do here, just as I do. Sometimes you find the big names; sometimes you don't. The discount is hard to measure because you rarely find current merchandise here. Don't worry about it. © 212/557-4422. www.daffys.com.

EILEEN FISHER
521 Madison Ave., near 53rd St.

Positioned as a way-of-life dress style, Fisher's clothes are moderately priced yet high in fashion, chic, and comfort. Colors are the selling point: They are always new, with an almost European palette. The mainly pull-on styles are mostly in solids—all you do is mix and match—but because of the quality of the fabric and the fabulous colors, they make a great fashion statement. There are other stores around town; shop them all. The outlets in Secaucus (p. 295) and Woodbury Common (p. 297) are worth the schlep. © **212/759-9888.** www.eileen fisher.com.

Eats

Try **Burger Heaven,** on Madison Avenue between 54th and 55th streets (p. 64).

PARK AVENUE

For the most part, Park Avenue is not a street with too much retail. Instead, it has tulips. However, there are some nuggets right in the heart of town, in the mid-50s. **J. S. Suarez** (450 Park Ave., at 57th St.) is a leading resource for designer-style handbags without the designer label or price tag (p. 185). **T. Anthony** (445 Park Ave., at 56th St.) sells distinctive and chic canvas and leather luggage. And **Syms** (400 Park Ave., at 54th St.) is an off-pricer with men's, women's, and kids' clothing—lotsa Italian designer stuff.

Take the N, R, or W train to 5th Avenue/59th Street; or the 4, 5, or 6 train to 59th Street/Lexington Avenue.

EAST 57TH STREET

This is what you've come for: 57th Street is both a state of mind and a neighborhood. It's a high-ticket address for residential and retail, especially where it bisects Fifth Avenue. It's also the new home of casual chic designers, like those represented by the **LVMH** group. Everyone from **Dior** to **Chanel** is here.

The luxe shopping area begins at Park Avenue and ends between Fifth and Sixth avenues. In these blocks, you'll find a few galleries and antiques shops (many are upstairs), elite European boutiques, and America's own retail landmark, **Tiffany & Co.**

You'll also find a few surprises: **Daffy's** (on E. 57th St., between Lexington and Park aves.) brings stylish discounting right to the upper crust; and **Louis Vuitton** just took over the Warner Brothers Studio Store space at 1 E. 57th St., at Fifth Avenue, for its new flagship.

I've always considered Fifth Avenue at 57th Street to be the center of Manhattan shopping and a destination you will come upon as if drawn by a supernatural force. If the mystic forces don't work, then hop an F train to 57th Street/6th Avenue, or an N, R, or W train to 5th Avenue/59th Street.

DANA BUCHMAN
65 E. 57th St., near Park Ave.

Owned by the Liz Claiborne people, the more upscale Dana Buchman line is now available in its first free-standing store. This is a good standard resource for the career woman. Some looks are boring; others are classics. © **212/319-3257.** www.danabuchman.com.

FREDERIC FEKKAI
15 E. 57th St., between Fifth and Madison aves.

Talk about hidden! This salon-cum-spa doesn't even have frontage on the street. Fekkai was the star hairstylist of Bergdorf's before corporate France snapped him up and forced him to open an incredibly chic villalike series of spaces in the Chanel high-rise here. You can have your hair done, get a spa treatment, or simply sip a coffee. The salon sells beauty products as well as handbags and headbands. © **212/753-9500.** www.fredericfekkai.com.

SONY STYLE
550 Madison Ave., at 56th St.

The Sony Style flagship is home of the Sony Wonder Technology Lab, a virtual-reality amusement park/museum, kind of like a Nike store that doesn't have any shoes. You can explore all sorts of technology here. © **212/833-8800.** www.sonystyle.com.

Eats

My secret spot is the cafe in **Bergdorf Goodman Men,** 745 Fifth Ave., at 58th Street (p. 63). If there's something to celebrate, I head for **5757,** the restaurant inside the Four Seasons (p. 72). A secret spot for coffee: upstairs at **Frédéric Fekkai** (p. 96). There's also a **Burger Heaven** at 536 Madison Ave., at 55th Street (p. 64).

UPPER MADISON AVENUE (57TH STREET & BEYOND)

The average visitor to Manhattan perceives Madison Avenue as a dream shopping stretch that begins at 57th Street and works its way uptown. Although the street has changed its personality many times, it's still a great place to enjoy stores representing the big names in European style and international creativity. The stroll from 57th to 79th is a must-do, even if you're just window-shopping. The little whimsical stores are long gone, but the series of fancy "drugstores" here are enormous fun. The street offers all price points, so don't assume it's too expensive for you.

A lot of stores have moved around, including **Hermès** (691 Madison Ave., near 62nd St.), which moved here from East 57th Street. Many stores have bailed out of their expensive leases and moved to side streets right off Madison. For example, **Dooney & Bourke** is now at 20 E. 60th St. For a list of many of the big-name designers with shops in this area, see p. 184.

I walk from the F stop at 57th Street/6th Avenue, but you can also take a bus uptown and pop off at any point on Madison Avenue.

CLYDE'S
926 Madison Ave., near 74th St.

Clyde's is one of the fanciest drugstores you've ever seen. It's also neater and more sophisticated than the competition (namely, Boyd's and Zitomer). The store carries an enormous number of hard-to-find beauty lines from Europe, as well as many American brands that you may have never seen before. © 212/744-5050. www.clydesonmadison.com.

GHURKA
683 Madison Ave., between 61st and 62nd sts.

The new Ghurka flagship sells a fabulous line of canvas and leather items made in a very specific look, which I call "Ralph Lauren Fisherman Meets Isak Dinesen on Safari." They're outrageously expensive, very statusy, and quite chic. There's an outlet at Woodbury Common (p. 297). © **212/826-8300.** www.ghurka.com.

JEAN-PAUL GAULTIER
759 Madison Ave., near 65th St.

While numerous designer stores are listed on p. 137 in the "New York Resources A to Z" chapter, I have made particular note of this store because of its design properties—it is the first boutique in New York created by hot designer Philippe Starck. © 212/249-0235. www.jeanpaulgaultier.com.

PIERRE DEUX
625 Madison Ave., near 59th St.

This is a new location for a New York icon. The store has a revised look, but it still specializes in French country home and lifestyle items. See p. 266 for more. © **212/521-8012.** www. pierredeux.com.

RALPH LAUREN
867 Madison Ave., at 72nd St.; and 888 Madison Ave., at 72nd St.

I realize that you don't need me to tell you about Ralph Lauren, but here goes anyway: You absolutely must visit these stores, if only to get a look-see. The Rhinelander Mansion, at 867 Madison Ave., is one of the most beautiful stores you will ever see in your life. And then there's the new store across the street that specializes in active sporting gear. Both could be tourist sights—if they sold tickets for admission, I would certainly pay up. See p. 246 for more on Lauren's home style. ✆ 212/606-2100. www.polo.com.

ZITOMER
969 Madison Ave., near 76th St.

Zitomer began as a pharmacy but is really a tiny department store, with even a pet boutique selling fancy dog toys. Every nook and cranny is filled with beauty, health, and luxury items. It also carries a wide range of costume jewelry, hair accessories, and a cashmere shawl or two in season; I saw real (not fake) Judith Leiber handbags when I was here last. See p. 232 for more. ✆ 212/737-2016. www.zitomer.com.

Eats

I like both **Café Boulud** (p. 59) and the restaurant in **The Mark** (p. 72), but I also like a diner called **Three Guys** (960 Madison Ave., near 75th St.), which serves breakfast all day long. If you're walking all the way up Madison, shopping as you go, there are two other branches of this diner: 1232 Madison Ave., near 88th Street; and 1381 Madison Ave., near 96th Street.

BLOOMINGDALE'S COUNTRY

Bloomingdale's may be the promised land of retail, but there is plenty of nearby shopping as well. There are good stores on

Lexington Avenue leading up to Bloomingdale's from East 57th Street, and on Third Avenue heading uptown. To explore the neighborhood fully, start at Bloomingdale's and then branch out.

On the Lex side, you'll find mostly teen-oriented stores. **Diesel,** 770 Lexington Ave., at 60th Street, is the flagship for the Italian brand of jeans and other trendsetting clothing.

On Third Avenue, you get more upmarket chains, such as **Club Monaco** (1111 Third Ave., near 65th St.), along with **Dylan's Candy Bar** (1011 Third Ave., near 60th St.), a fancy penny-candy store with sweets and lovely gift baskets. At 70th Street, don't miss **Gracious Home,** which stocks everything you'd ever want for renovating your home (p. 251).

Farther away, but worth a hike if you're furnishing a home, are superstore **Bed Bath & Beyond** and the **Terence Conran Shop** (see below), both under the 59th Street Bridge.

There's a nice big subway station right under Bloomie's; you can reach it by taking the 4, 5, 6, N, R, or W train to 59th Street/Lexington Avenue. If you're going a bit farther uptown, take the 6 train to 68th Street/Hunter College. Stay away from this whole area on weekends if you can.

AVEDA
1122 Third Ave., near 65th St.

This is one of a handful of Aveda shops in the city; the hair and beauty products are sensational and are of such high quality that you won't mind the correspondingly high prices. Although the products are sold all over the world, it's a very New York kind of line and makes a great gift or souvenir. Hair products are the best items to buy. © **212/744-3113.** www.aveda.com.

KATE'S PAPERIE
1282 Third Ave., near 74th St.

Another branch of the fancy paper-and-crafts store. See p. 118 for details. © **212/396-3670.** www.katespaperie.com.

MARIMEKKO
1262 Third Ave., near 72nd St.

This Finnish line's splash-printed fabrics, clothes, and accessories have great colors and high style. Good gift items and kids' stuff, too. © 212/628-8400. www.kiitosmarimekko.com.

SCOOP
1275 Third Ave., near 73rd St.

A trendy chain-let of Manhattan boutiques filled with lines like James Jeans, Marc by Marc Jacobs, and Theory for Scoop (created just for these stores). © 212/535-5577. www.scoopnyc.com.

SEPHORA
1149 Third Ave., at 67th St.

Beauty supermarket Sephora is the purveyor of many brands you may have never heard of. It sells the Bourjois line, made in the same factories as Chanel cosmetics. © 212/452-3336. www.sephora.com.

TERENCE CONRAN SHOP
407 E. 59th St., at First Ave., under 59th St. Bridge.

For international travelers who know the Conran Shop, note the difference here—this one uses Sir Conran's full name because of legal technicalities in the U.S. It's the same chain, though, and it still specializes in Terence Conran's brand of home style and wit. See p. 252 for more. © 212/755-9079. www. conran.com.

Eats

Gino (780 Lexington Ave., at 61st St.; © 212/758-4466) is the locals' Italian restaurant of choice. (Cash only! No reservations!) If you want something quicker, there are eats right inside **Bloomie's** as well. If you're farther east by the 59th Street Bridge, you can eat at the **Terence Conran Shop.**

CARNEGIE HILL/UPPER MADISON

A residential area of grace and refinement, Carnegie Hill, in the low 90s, has a few select shops clustered on Madison Avenue (I call this area "Upper Mad"). Some are branches of European stores (**Jacadi**, 1296 Madison Ave., at 92nd St.; and **Bonpoint**, 1269 Madison Ave., at 91st St.), while others are original retailers, like the innovative kiddie store **Penny Whistle Toys** (1283 Madison Ave., near 91st St.).

The neighborhood gets less European and more Midtown-esque as you head downtown, so by the time you get to 86th Street, you'll have passed branches of big chains, like kitchen fave **Williams-Sonoma** (1175 Madison Ave.).

If you haven't yet caught up with **Eileen Fisher** (p. 94 for my rave), there's a branch at 1039 Madison Ave., at 79th Street. **Adrien Linford** (p. 255) is a great little gift shop at 1339 Madison Ave., at 94th Street.

Mixed in with the specialty stores and the chains are several resale shops (p. 304). Most of them have upstairs addresses, so don't be afraid to climb a flight of stairs.

To get to this neighborhood, take the 4, 5, or 6 train to 86th Street/Lexington Avenue; or the 6 train to 96th Street/Lexington Avenue.

Chapter Seven

....

DOWNTOWN SHOPPING NEIGHBORHOODS INCLUDING BROOKLYN

DOWNTOWN IS A STATE OF MIND

....

Downtown is more than a state of mind in Manhattan—it's a place and it's an attitude; it's a complete way of life. There are people who nowadays never leave downtown; there are businesses that have made it uptown and opened branches downtown; there are people already moving out because too many people (and stores) are moving in.

Downtown has become so uptown that limos pull into districts that once gave people the creepy-crawlies, and the Meatpacking District is the epitome of trendy. Union Square? It's never been so hip to be that square.

Meanwhile, a lot more than a tree is growing across the bridge in Brooklyn. Two areas, DUMBO and Williamsburg, are blooming in full force and attracting many young people who can't afford to live in Manhattan. And Carroll Gardens, which sounds like an address from Monopoly, is developing a hot retail strip on Smith Street.

Note that the expression "downtown" also refers to the Wall Street and Ground Zero areas. Several new hotels and businesses have opened at the water's edge, and the new PATH station—for trains to New Jersey—has opened as well. You'll feel a few somber moments when you pass The Site, but that's part of what New York is about—a phoenix rises from heartbreak and ashes.

LOWER FIFTH AVENUE

Hop off the Fifth Avenue bus at the Flatiron Building (23rd St.) and check out the scene on Lower Fifth Avenue, south of the Flatiron, which some call SoFi. You will be walking downtown on Fifth Avenue, headed toward 14th Street; this area is now so safe and clean it's almost a mall.

Lower Fifth was the start of something big years ago; now it doesn't have as much energy. However, it's still well situated and definitely worth a visit since the neighborhood puts you within walking distance of **Union Square,** one of the hottest parts of town these days. While you're here, you can hit the **Greenmarket,** the over-the-top emporium **ABC Carpet & Home,** all the discounters and big-box stores on Sixth Avenue, and the streets of SoHo and the Village. If you're really up for a walk, you can even make it to **Jeffrey** (449 W. 14th St., near Tenth Ave.).

If you take Broadway farther downtown from Union Square, you'll hit **Forbidden Planet** (840 Broadway, at 13th St.), for comics galore; and the **Strand Book Store** (828 Broadway, at 12th St.), for discounted new and well-priced used books. By the time you get to East 12th Street, you will be in an antiques neighborhood (p. 277). At East 9th Street, you'll hit an array of stores so hip and hot that they attract busloads of Japanese tourists. Head east on 9th to get to the heart of this area.

Fifth Avenue buses stop at the Flatiron Building before continuing downtown on Fifth. If you want to really see the whole area, pop off the subway at either 23rd Street/6th Avenue (take the F or V) or 23rd Street/Broadway (take the R or W). Or you can take any train to Union Square and work your way west and uptown.

Note: This part of Manhattan is also the kicking-off point for further tours to Brooklyn, SoHo, or the Village. If you're curious about exploring Williamsburg (p. 129), in the "new" Brooklyn, take the L to Bedford Avenue. To get to DUMBO ("I can fly!"), take the F to York Street.

ABC Carpet & Home
888 Broadway, at 19th St.

Be still, my heart. If I were making a movie of New York's best stores, this would be the star. Years ago, it was just a carpet store. But then it expanded into bed linens and now it has everything you could possibly need (or want) for your home—and with its focus on selection over price, you may find yourself wanting a lot more than you can reasonably buy.

Note: This store's look changes more frequently than I do—the zen period seems to be over, and some of the old boho swagger has been restored. The addition of the **Silk Trading Co.** doesn't change the whole gestalt, but it does add another reason to visit. See p. 266 for details. © **212/473-3000.** www. abchome.com.

Anthropologie
85 Fifth Ave., at 16th St.

Anthropologie, the brainchild of the man who created Urban Outfitters, sells clothes, home furnishings, gift items, and even some pet accessories. It's a very warehouse-cum-touch-this-and-that-store, with a look that's rich hippie chic; prices are not bad. You'll also find some ethnic style here, in the form of French, Indian, and other overseas merchandise and decor. I love this place—it's certainly one of my favorite stores in New York. There's another branch in SoHo, but this one is the cherry on the whipped cream of this shopping district. I find that teens and tweens adore it, too. © **212/627-5885.** www.anthropologie.com.

Club Monaco
160 Fifth Ave., at 21st St.

This is the flagship of a Canadian chain, now owned by Ralph Lauren. It's great for trendy fashion at affordable prices. © **212/ 352-0936**. www.clubmonaco.com.

FISHS EDDY
889 Broadway, at 19th St.

Stop sweating, palms! Please, take my credit cards away before I do it again! Did someone say dishes? I am bonkers for dishes. And thus for Fishs. Fishs Eddy's original concept was to resell restaurant supply and hotel has-beens, but the store has become so popular that it now casts old molds and sets its own trends. Prices vary from what-a-deal to stratospheric for almost-ready-for-the-big-time collectibles. Dinner plates from a fine London hotel go for about $50 a pop—not cheap. But you'll have a ball as you explore this small, crammed museum of old dishes and hotel services. Amen, and pass the gravy boat. © **212/420-9020**. www.fishseddy.com.

GREENMARKET
Broadway, between 14th and 17th sts.

I don't care if you're a visitor or a local—you do too need a greenmarket. This one has a very special New York feel about it, especially in fall, when the whole city celebrates the change from the dog days of summer to the crisp autumn. The best apples I've ever eaten in my life came from this market. Vendors sell all kinds of fruits and veggies, cheeses, wines and ciders, and even flowers. It is simply heaven . . . although I'm not sure if heaven is this crowded on a Saturday. While the market is held Monday, Wednesday, Friday, and Saturday year-round, it is a tad sparse in the winter months. Saturday is always the busiest day. There's not too much in the way of prepared foods, but Whole Foods is right across Union Square. © **212/ 788-7476**. www.cenyc.org.

JO MALONE
949 Broadway, near 23rd St.

Hip to Be Square

The era of Union Square being seedy is over—the glory days are on the way. The 14th Street side of the square is home to a whole slew of new stores that will make bargain and organic shoppers (that's the same thing, right?) quite pleased with themselves. **Whole Foods** and **Trader Joe's**, plus the **Greenmarket**, reinforce the area's status as a food festival.

Next to Whole Foods are **Forever 21** (the poor teen's H&M), **DSW**, and **Filene's Basement**. While the big-box action—**Petco, Barnes & Noble, Virgin Megastore**, and so on—is on the streets directly surrounding Union Square, there are some new arrivals on the side streets as well. To fight back, **H&M** has recently come to the area, on Fifth Avenue and 18th Street in the old Daffy's space.

The stores selling the products of Jo Malone, British cult heroine in the world of scent and beauty, are now owned by Lauder, hence the New York locations. The prices are outrageously high, but the product is unique. Note that while this shop is in the Flatiron Building, it faces east. See p. 234 for more. ☎ **212/673-2220**. www.jomalone.com.

PAUL SMITH
108 Fifth Ave., at 16th St.

Smith is a London designer known for his inventive touches. His traditional-looking clothes have a tiny twist, such as the use of unusual colors or fabrics. He makes both men's and women's wear, much of it very hip. Prices are high to match the quality, but the store does have regular sales. ☎ **212/627-9770**. www.paulsmith.co.uk.

Eats

Hit **Terra 47** (47 E. 12th St., near Broadway; ☎ **212/358-0103**) for an organic lunch, often with celebrity diners. There is also a cafe inside **ABC Carpet & Home.** Don't miss the **Greenmarket** at Union Square—and if you like it funky, go to the coffee shop called **Coffee Shop** (29 Union Sq. W., at 16th St.), a Brazilian spot that's a scene to be seen.

MEATPACKING DISTRICT

Don't look now, but the Meatpacking District is now known as MePa by some people. There goes the neighborhood.

I think this is one of my favorite parts of the new New York, not because everyone says it is *the* spot, but because it still feels, uh, raw. Yes, there are wholesale butchers and sights to unsettle you. It is very, very real down here, especially on 14th Street itself, right around Ninth and Tenth avenues. But like many other places, it's becoming more and more gentrified every day.

Blame it all on **Jeffrey New York** (449 W. 14th St., near Tenth Ave.), an alternate version of Barneys in what was once the middle of nowhere. Jeffrey made this part of New York important to know about. Unfortunately, the store is not doing too well, which just goes to show that you can build it and they will come, but they might not buy enough to pay the rent. For more on Jeffrey, see p. 162.

Even before Jeffrey arrived, there were signs of the times here: clubs, galleries, restaurants, and uptowners slumming it with a smugness that bordered on glee. Several name designers have moved into the area, such as **Stella McCartney** (429 W. 14th St.) and **Alexander McQueen** (417 W. 14th St.); now the hairdressers and day spas are coming along. Try to book into **Sally Hershberger Downtown** (425 W. 14th St.; © 212/ 206-8700) if you want to be as blond as Meg Ryan.

As for how to get here, I don't want to sound like a wimp, or someone who doesn't do public transportation, but I usually take a taxi to Jeffrey and then explore on foot from there. I do this because the area is extremely spread out and even the subway stations don't get you that close. Do note, however, that you *can* take the A, C, E, or L to 14th Street/8th Avenue, or the crosstown bus on 14th Street. Free transfers on buses, you know!

Eats

There's always a hot new restaurant to try in this district, but **Pastis** (9 Ninth Ave., at Little W. 12th St.; ☎ **212/929-4844**) is an icon where you can worship trendiness and take in the whole scene. This French bistro is more gorgeous than a movie set, and the crowd is more chic than any set of extras standing by the bar. The insecure should not try this.

CHELSEA

The dimensions of Chelsea, one of the city's hot neighborhoods, are changing enormously: Chelsea is now considered the area from the West 20s all the way down to West 14th Street, and from Seventh Avenue to Eleventh Avenue.

Formerly a mostly residential area, Chelsea began to make news when many art galleries from SoHo relocated to this district. Then **Comme des Garçons** became the first must-see clothing boutique—and you must see it: part gallery, part boutique, part museum of modern art.

Now almost all of the SoHo art galleries have moved to Chelsea. In fact, Chelsea has expanded so much that it endangered the best flea market in New York: The Annex was forced to move to Hell's Kitchen because the parking lot it called home was sold to developers.

Note that Chelsea is huge, and the distances between the avenues are so far that you cannot stroll and shop as easily as you can in SoHo and Nolita. By subway, take the 1 to 23rd Street/7th Avenue or the C or E to 23rd Street/8th Avenue; be prepared to walk.

ALCONE COMPANY
235 W. 19th St., between Seventh and Eighth aves.

Alcone is a beauty-supply store that sells theatrical and professional makeup. It has an enormous selection, including brands you may have never seen before. This place is a hangout for celebs and those in the know. See p. 224 for more info. © 212/633-0551. www.alconeco.com.

BARNEYS CO-OP
236 W. 18th St., between Seventh and Eighth aves.

Barneys' answer to Jeffrey on West 14th Street is this store, housed in part of the company's old warehouse, and meant to be young, hip, and attractive to the kids of the regular Barneys shoppers. © 212/593-7800. www.barneys.com.

BARNEYS WAREHOUSE SALE
255 W. 17th St., between Seventh and Eighth aves.

Twice a year, Barneys still hosts its famous warehouse sale at this facility near the Co-Op store. The sale is quite an event, and people really do line up. Prices change daily, so markdowns can be 50% to 80% off on clothing for men, women, and children, as well as gifts. The hours of the sale are announced in ads in publications like the *New York Times* and *Time Out New York;* note that they do differ as the sale progresses. © 212/450-8400. www.barneys.com.

CHELSEA MARKET
75 Ninth Ave., at 15th St.

This monster building, once a factory for the National Biscuit Company, serves as a cutie-pie-renovation-turned-retail space. It mostly sells food, though occasionally there are design sample sales here. (Honest.) Great for one-stop shopping or snacking, this place is truly visually exciting. www.chelseamarket.com.

COMME DES GARÇONS
520 W. 22nd St., near Tenth Ave.

It's worth cab fare to head directly to this address; don't miss it if you love avant-garde retail, architecture, creativity, and chutzpah. ✆ **212/604-9200.**

Eats

For lunch, try **Cafeteria** (119 Seventh Ave., at 18th St.; ✆ **212/ 414-1717**)—I love the crowd and the food, especially the lemon soufflé pancakes.

LADIES' MILE

Ladies' Mile is in the district some people call Chelsea. Around the time of the Civil War, when department stores were just beginning to catch on and ladies were allowed to go shopping without chaperones, the great names in New York retail stood in a row along Sixth Avenue and stretched from 14th Street to 23rd Street. Remember that the world of Manhattan was built from the bottom up, and 14th Street was sort of the edge of civilization at that time, so it would have been an exciting area to be in.

Although some of the retailers who had stores here have stayed in business, most of them moved uptown as trade moved uptown. As a result of this exodus, most of the buildings stood empty and abandoned. For almost 100 years, Ladies' Mile was a wasteland of gorgeous, empty, hulking cast-iron beauties. Then, voilà, they were rediscovered! Most have now been saved and are occupied by famous retailers and big-box stores.

Most of the tenants here are value-oriented, making this a serious shopping destination. The area is continuing to develop, not just on Ladies' Mile itself, but also on the side streets. And more big-box retailers from the suburbs are moving in—don't miss the new **Home Depot** (40 W. 23rd St., between Fifth and Sixth aves.), even if only to gawk at the building.

Stores right on Sixth Avenue include everything from **Old Navy** to **Filene's Basement,** plus **T.J. Maxx, Bed Bath &**

Beyond, Burlington Coat Factory, and The Container Store. West 17th Street is hoppin' (**West Elm** recently opened here), and off-pricer **Loehmann's** is a block over on Seventh Avenue near West 16th Street.

I usually arrive by subway (take the 1 to 18th St., or the F or V to 14th St.) and depart via the Sixth Avenue bus, which heads uptown. *Note:* Weekends are usually a zoo in these parts. However, most of the stores stay open until 9pm Monday through Saturday.

BARNES & NOBLE
675 Sixth Ave., at 21st St.

While there are several B&N superstores in Manhattan, this one is special because it helps round out the personality of the neighborhood and makes a great pit stop. If your feet are swollen from too much shopping, simply plop down here for a coffee and something to read. I bring Euro visitors here for the discounts and selection; they love it. ✆ **212/727-1227.** www.bn.com.

THE CONTAINER STORE
629 Sixth Ave., at 19th St.

This is the new kid on the block for locals, although it's been a suburban landmark for years. The Container Store is known for its chic storage devices and organizational goods. If you're furnishing a home, trying to better organize your life, or looking for household souvenirs to take back to Europe, this is the place to start. ✆ **212/366-4200.** www.containerstore.com.

HOUSING WORKS THRIFT SHOP
143 W. 17th St., between Sixth and Seventh aves.

Okay, this is my method: Arrive by subway, go to Loehmann's, eat at Cafeteria, walk east on West 17th Street, stop at the assorted thrift shops on the way to Sixth Avenue, then turn left onto Sixth Avenue, and walk uptown through the Ladies'

Mile area. Of the thrift shops, Housing Works is my favorite—partly because of the store's uptown clients. Most of the place is devoted to home style, but you'll also find some clothes. ✆ **212/366-0820. www.housingworks.org.**

JAM PAPER
611 Sixth Ave., near 17th St.

I confess to being a paper, stationery, and office-supply freak, so I love this warehouse-style shop of papers, envelopes, shopping bags, and sometimes gift wrap. Stock isn't regular, so you're bound to find anything and must visit often if you live in these parts. *Note for foreign visitors:* European paper sizes are different, so don't buy paper for computer printing projects. ✆ **212/255-4593. www.jampaper.com.**

Eats

For lunch, there's **Cafeteria** (p. 111), which always gets my vote and my stomach. Snacks can be found at the cafe inside **Bed Bath & Beyond.**

EAST VILLAGE

For my purposes, the area I refer to as the East Village extends east of Broadway from 14th Street down to Houston Street. This is where independent designers and artists take advantage of the relatively low rents to open wonderful storefront shops and galleries.

Shopping in the East Village is not for the faint of heart. You'll have to push past bikers in leather, a crush of NYU students, and panhandlers who compete for sidewalk space with street vendors. It's not overly cute, but it is funky. In order to enjoy this area, you must have a spirit of adventure and the desire to find the finds before Barneys or Bergdorf's do.

If you're out with teenagers, a trip down St. Marks Place (E. 8th St.) will immediately establish you as the coolest grown-up around and give you a taste of the East Village. If you like what you see, take off and explore the other streets and avenues between Third Avenue and Avenue A, and between 14th Street and Houston.

Begin your tour at St. Marks and Third Avenue, the corner of the busiest block in the East Village, and walk east. An eclectic mix of stores and restaurants is crammed into this short block. You'll find CD and record shops, bookstores, and boutiques advertising "Rock Star Clothing." Check out **St. Mark's Comics** (11 St. Marks Place) for a huge selection of comic books and T-shirts. If skin-tight leather pants are your teen's style—or yours—don't miss **Trash and Vaudeville** (4 St. Marks Place) for the best in punk gear.

As you cross Second Avenue and continue east, the crush of shops gives way to hipper-than-thou cafes and cutting-edge boutiques. Stroll East 9th Street between Third Avenue and Avenue A to see the newest trends in everything from home furnishings to lingerie.

And, yes, I have trolled the **Kmart** (770 Broadway, at 9th St.) here, waiting to be impressed. I like the branch at Penn Station, but this one doesn't seem as good. But you didn't come to this part of town for Kmart, now did you?

The easiest way to take in the whole area is to hop the 6 train to Astor Place, get out, and prowl. *Note:* Most of these stores open late in the morning (around 11am)—this is not an area for early birds.

EILEEN FISHER
314 E. 9th St., between First and Second aves.

You can't read much of this book without noticing that I am wild for Eileen Fisher, a designer of easy-to-wear chic with a handful of shops around town. Her outlet stores are out in the 'burbs—in Secaucus (p. 295) and Woodbury Common (p. 297)—but this strange little store in the East Village has samples, markdowns, and odd rejects along with the regular merchandise, so you can just enter and go straight to heaven.

I bought a silk blouse for $25 (originally $89) and a dress for $62 (originally $139). Even though my dress had a slight defect, the savings made it invisible to me. If you shop nowhere else on East 9th Street, a visit to this store is worth the trip. ✆ 212/529-5715. www.eileenfisher.com.

JOHN DERIAN
6 E. 2nd St., between Second Ave. and Bowery.

See p. 256 for details. ✆ 212/677-3917. www.johnderian.com.

KIEHL'S
109 Third Ave., at 13th St.

It's hard to call Kiehl's a find since it's been around for well over 100 years, its products are sold in many uptown department stores, and it has a cult following that includes just about everyone in New York. But if you're from out of town, you might not know that the original Kiehl's store—home to all sorts of beauty lotions and potions—is right here, and has been since 1851. See p. 232 for more. ✆ 212/677-3171. www.kiehls.com.

SOHO

SoHo stands for "South of Houston" (say "*house*-ton"). Today, it has become more of a destination than ever, partly because real-estate prices have risen and partly because European visitors and retailers are comfortable here. So the stakes have risen and the area is all but deluxe . . . and boring, oversaturated as it is with every big name and brand in the world and lacking in the true charm that turned us on in the old days. Plain-old funky doesn't cut it here anymore. Expensive funky is the trend, and mainstream funky is following quickly.

But wait! There are still a few people with a sense of humor. **Todd Oldham by La-Z-Boy** (73 Wooster St., near Spring St.), for one, brings a breath of fresh air to SoHo.

There are plenty of names that must be wincing at the arrival of La-Z-Boy to these refined blocks: **Chanel** (139 Spring St., at Wooster St.), **Louis Vuitton** (116 Greene St., between Prince and Spring sts.), and **Ralph Lauren** (379 West Broadway, near Broome St.), to name a few. You'll also find your chicer-than-thou types, such as **Helmut Lang** (80 Greene St., between Spring and Broome sts.) and **Marc Jacobs** (163 Mercer St., between Houston and Prince sts.).

Meanwhile, mass-market merchants keep opening stores. What's new changes constantly down here. Don't miss the **Apple Store** (103 Prince St., between Mercer and Greene sts.), with its Genius Bar set up in an old post office; **Taschen** (107 Greene St., between Prince and Spring sts.), the German bookstore with cool architecture and well-priced tomes on pop culture and the arts; **Sur La Table** (75 Spring St., at Crosby St.), the Seattle-based kitchen-and-tabletop store; and the new branch of **Daffy's** (462 Broadway, at Grand St.)—which proves that the neighborhood has room for everything, even a good off-pricer.

Before those of you in the know start thinking SoHo is going to the dogs, or isn't worth your time because you hate designer labels, shuffle over to Lafayette Street, where much of the new excitement in SoHo is coming from. Lots of little home-furnishings boutiques are opening up here in the cheaper real estate to the east, and SoHo excels in the home-decor market (see chapter 10).

Don't let the scant number of listings below throw you: I could do a whole book on SoHo alone, since just about every store of note has a branch in these environs, many of them flagships or showcases. But to simplify things, for example, I have not listed **Eileen Fisher** (395 West Broadway, between Spring and Broome sts.) below since there are many pages of this book devoted to her work . . . and yet the Eileen Fisher store in SoHo is three times bigger than any other location in Manhattan. (See p. 94 for more on Fisher.)

You should devote at least a whole day to SoHo, and you should consider your visit an event, a time to celebrate retail at its best. When referring to addresses in this or any guide, keep in mind that stores in SoHo open and close at such a rapid pace that you'll probably do better just wandering and enjoying.

Note: Stores tend to open at 11am or later in these parts. *Warning:* I recently came down here on a Sunday afternoon and left screaming—it was a zoo.

Take the C or E to Spring Street/6th Avenue, the 6 to Spring Street/Lafayette Street, or the R or W to Prince Street/Broadway. SoHo is also an easy walk from many other neighborhoods (Chelsea, the Village), so you have no excuse not to visit.

Suzy's Faves

AMORE PACIFIC
114 Spring St., between Mercer and Greene sts.

This looks like a spa, but it also sells beauty and skin-care products from Korea—sublime, expensive, and worth every penny. The cult brand is sold uptown at Bergdorf's. See p. 238 for more. © 212/966-0400. www.amorepacific.com.

ANTHROPOLOGIE
375 W. Broadway, between Broome and Spring sts.

See p. 105 for details on this store; I mention it here because I've rarely met an Anthropologie store I could resist. © 212/343-7070. www.anthropologie.com.

CATHERINE MALANDRINO
468 Broome St., between Greene and Mercer sts.

Catherine is the new best friend (of the moment) of every fashion editor in town. She was involved in the relaunch of Diane von Furstenberg, but this is her own store and her own vision. Clothing here is very Gallic, whimsical, and *charmant*. © 212/925-6765. www.catherinemalandrino.com.

HOTEL VENUS
382 West Broadway, between Spring and Broome sts.

Silly you, it's not a hotel at all! Patricia Field has long been one of the most famous names in downtown fashion (you know her as the woman who pulled all the clothes for *Sex and the City*). Her SoHo shop sells affordable funky styles—think color and disco. ✆ **212/966-4066.** www.patriciafield.com.

KATE'S PAPERIE
561 Broadway, between Prince and Spring sts.

This SoHo shop sums up all that SoHo was ever meant to be. Kate's sells assorted handmade and art papers by the sheet, notebooks, stationery, artsy-fartsy this and that, rubber stamps, and even papier-mâché. It's sheer heaven. Not cheap, but great fun and very sophisticated. You haven't seen the best of Broadway if you miss Kate's. ✆ **212/941-9816.** www.katespaperie.com.

KIRNA ZABÊTE
96 Greene St., between Prince and Spring sts.

This hot boutique space has fashionistas drooling over its Euro designer names, many of them difficult to find in the U.S. The downstairs features lotions, potions, and aromatherapy notions. The upstairs is full-service, with everything from clothes to shoes to accessories. Kirna Zabête is famous for cool pieces that have style but also whimsy, from either a famous designer such as Balenciaga or from a not-so-well-known member of the Antwerp group. ✆ **212/941-9656.** www.kirna zabete.com.

LAFCO/SANTA MARIA NOVELLA
285 Lafayette St., near Houston St.

If you can't get to the centuries-old *farmacia* in Firenze for Santa Maria Novella beauty products, then a trip to SoHo is in order. This store also offers Italian design for the home in a wow setting—ranging from furniture to tabletop objects. It's a good stop for gifts. © **212/925-0001.** www.lafcony.com.

MORGANE LE FAY
67 Wooster St., between Broome and Spring sts.

I saw the dreamiest chiffon dresses in the world here, including some in white that would make magnificent wedding gowns. Some things that I loved were $180 and others were $630. Ouch. Still, the shop is pure heaven—everything you want a stylish, secret, SoHo source to be. There's also a Madison Avenue location, for those of you who are too uptown to call my name. © **212/219-7672.** www.morganelefay.com.

PRADA
575 Broadway, near Prince St.

Yeah, yeah, I know, I said I wasn't gonna list the obvious. This flagship store is anything but normal, though, and a must-see by anyone interested in architecture, interior design, retail theory, or moments of thunderstruck wonder. It was designed by Rem Koolhaas. I'm not saying any more. © **212/334-8888.** www.prada.com.

PYLONES
69 Spring St., near Crosby St.

This French chain of novelty/gift shops is a recent arrival. It sells whimsical, offbeat, and odd pieces that will make you smile. © **212/431-3244.** www.pylones-usa.com.

YASO
62 Grand St., between W. Broadway and Wooster St.

Yaso specializes in one-size, flowing dresses and charming hats, and it also boasts a new line of home goods. The dresses cost close to $200 (half-price sale twice a year!) and are usually made of luxurious fabrics. © **212/941-8506.**

Eats

Mercer Kitchen (Mercer Hotel, 99 Prince St., at Mercer St.; © 212/966-5454) offers great fresh-made pizza and boasts a lively brunch scene on Sunday. See p. 67 for more ideas.

CANAL STREET

While you're in SoHo, you might want to wander south on Broadway until you reach Canal Street, at the edge of Chinatown, where all the fake designer goods in the world are sold.

I don't actually suggest that you buy any of this junk, unless you're looking for joke gifts, but friends from Europe love it here and teenagers seem to think that these items ("name brand" handbags, watches, sunglasses, and more) are musthaves. Trust me, very little down here will fool anyone. This is seedy fun for those who enjoy down-market atmosphere and want to buy fake merchandise. Not for bluebloods.

But wait, before I toss you out on your fake Chanel earrings, let's talk about the Chinese department store **Pearl River Mart** (477 Broadway, between Grand and Broome sts.). I've seen better in San Francisco and much better in Hong Kong. Nonetheless, it is so popular that it now has a spiffy brand-new store.

If you don't walk here from SoHo, take the A, C, E, J, M, N, R, Q, W, Z, 1, or 6 train to Canal Street.

Eats

Chow down on six dumplings that come with a free egg roll—pick any of the zillions of Chinese restaurants in the area.

NOLITA

Although the name of this area is derived from the term "North of Little Italy," the area is also adjacent to SoHo. My guess is that the two will soon merge.

The defining feature of the whole neighborhood, other than the fact that rents are lower than they are in SoHo, and that it's within walking distance of SoHo, is that store owners in this part of town make real personal statements with their spaces, much as if their boutiques were art galleries. Here, the owner is the star of the show—and often the sole employee. If you're thinking low prices, forget it. If you're thinking cutting-edge chic, you've come to the right place.

To get here, take the 6 to Spring Street/Lafayette Street. The best streets in the area are Elizabeth and Mott in the blocks from Houston to Prince. Around here, the storefronts are very tiny, you can feel the energy of all the creativity in the air, and it's absolutely charming to browse.

CALYPSO
280 Mott St., between Houston and Prince sts.

Christiane Celle has been so successful with her boho-hippie-chic fashions that she has also opened up stores uptown. In addition, she owns the nearby Calypso Bijoux (252 Mott St.) and several shops in SoHo, including Calypso Enfant (426 Broome St.) and Calypso Home (199 Lafayette St.; p. 245). © 212/965-0990. www.calypso-celle.com.

CATH KIDSTON
201 Mulberry St., between Kenmare and Spring sts.

Cath Kidston, the British textile designer with several shops in London, has finally come to the U.S. Her work is an update of 1930s kitsch. © 212/343-0223. www.cathkidston.co.uk.

SEIZE SUR VINGT
243 Elizabeth St., between Houston and Prince sts.

This is mainly a men's store; the name (16/20) refers to an excellent grade in the French school system, which marks up to 20. It does both off-the-rack and custom work; the vibe is sort of preppy-rich chic with an edge. © 212/343-0476. www.16sur20. com.

ZERO MARIA CORNEJO
225 Mott St., between Prince and Spring sts.

Maria Cornejo, icon to the stylish street fashion crowd, calls her work "conceptual fashion." (Conceptual fashion means that if you're over 30, you're too old.) Worship here and tell people you've been—you can't talk the talk without visiting this store. ✆ **212/925-3825.** www.mariacornejo.com.

NOHO

This is a hot area of town for savvy shoppers—more fun than SoHo and far more original. Nolita borders on Houston Street, so you have to cross over Houston to get to NoHo (shorthand for "North of Houston").

By train, take the 6 to Bleecker Street.

BOND 07
7 Bond St., between Broadway and Lafayette St.

This is one of the shrines to alternative retail, fashion, and tight pants. It helped make the street what it is today. ✆ **212/677-8487.** www.selimaoptique.com.

DARYL K
21 Bond St., between Lafayette St. and Bowery.

The grandma of downtown, and the first tenant to really make Bond Street worth the trip, Daryl K is known to dress celebs and rock stars. Daryl K also wholesales and is sold in a few hip SoHo boutiques. ✆ **212/529-8790.** www.darylk.com.

Announcement: Lafayette, We Are Here

Lafayette Street runs through both NoHo and SoHo, so don't get confused.

SoHo Style Near NoHo:
Aaron & Jenny Do Lafayette Street

Triple Five Soul (290 Lafayette St., between Houston and Prince sts.) is one of the coolest clothing lines in stores today. The T-shirts, jeans, sports coats, messenger bags, jackets, and hoodies always push the boundaries of design in a unique and interesting direction. The SoHo store has a huge selection and a few healthy discounts. Strongly recommended.

The creators of one of New York's finest underground magazines also own the **Vice Store** (252 Lafayette St., between Prince and Spring sts.). The free magazine, best known for its hilarious "Do's and Don'ts" section, is always on the cutting edge of new trends in the city, be they in fashion or music, and this SoHo store is just the same. Loud indie rock blares as you look through racks of ridiculously priced denim and sneakers. The sale rack at the front of the store can be pretty reasonable—it was home to the cheapest Evisu Genes I've ever seen (which were still ridiculously expensive).

TRIBECA

This one stands for the "Triangle below Canal Street." TriBeCa is a funkier version of SoHo, with less retail and a much less commercial feel. I used to think of TriBeCa as the end of civilization and the point of no return, but it's quickly becoming more and more gentrified. TriBeCa is just a stone's throw from the West Village, so you have no excuse not to visit this neighborhood!

To get here, take the 1 to Franklin Street/Varick Street. *Note:* This is an area of warehouses and interesting buildings from the cast-iron and brick decades; it's perfectly safe, but there are plenty of areas that are not gentrified yet . . . so you may find yourself walking around wondering where the cute is.

BAKER TRIBECA
129 Hudson St., at Beach St.

Baker Furniture is as mainstream and highbrow as it gets—so
this outpost really signals the arrival of a neighborhood that
will become a powerful force in the spending of downtown
dollars. Although the line is known for traditional looks, it
includes contemporary pieces and 1930s-inspired designs from
Barbara Barry. ✆ 212/343-2956. www.bakerfurniture.com.

ISSEY MIYAKE
119 Hudson St., near N. Moore St.

This you-gotta-see-it space was designed in conjunction with
Frank Gehry. Offerings include Miyake's APOC ("A Piece of
Cloth"), a very creative line that allows you to make the
clothes yourself. Sort of. You'll have to see for yourself. ✆ 212/
226-0100. www.isseymiyake.com.

Eats

Frankly, I don't usually find enough serious shopping in
TriBeCa to end up eating a meal here, but there are quite a
few well-known restaurants in the area, including Japanese hot
spot **Nobu** (105 Hudson St., at Franklin St.; ✆ 212/219-0500);
David Bouley's **Danube** (30 Hudson St., near Duane St.; ✆ 212/
791-3771); **Tribeca Grill** (375 W. Greenwich, at Franklin St.;
✆ 212/941-3900), owned by Robert DeNiro; and the bistro
Odeon (145 West Broadway, at Thomas St.; ✆ 212/233-0507),
which helped start the area on its rise to trendiness.

WEST VILLAGE

Also known as Greenwich Village, or even the Village, this is
the area west of Fifth Avenue, from 14th Street to Houston
Street, which actually comprises several neighborhoods woven
into a warren of little colonial streets.

There's teen heaven on West 8th Street (very touristy); there's a gay and lesbian area around Christopher and West 4th streets; and there's the funky antiques-store-heavy part of town, mostly on Bleecker Street (my main drag), which boasts a nice variety of design, antiques, clothing, gift, and aroma-therapy shops. You'll see a few name brands, such as bath-and-beauty people **Fresh** (388 Bleecker St., near Perry St.), along with the antiques shop that many knew as Pierre Deux—now called **Les Pierre Antiques** (369 Bleecker St., between Charles and Perry sts.) since both of the Pierres have passed on. Don't miss hip travel boutique **Flight 001** (96 Greenwich Ave., near Jane St.) or **Condomania** (351 Bleecker St., between Charles and W. 10th sts.) for condoms, party favors, and cheap laughs.

Anyone over the age of 15 who thinks that West 8th Street has good shopping is someone I don't particularly want to shop with. There are a number of shoe stores selling cheap junk, and shops where you can have body parts pierced or tattooed, but I mean, really.

Deeper into the West Village, it gets better. I could spend days wandering the maze of streets with names like Bank, Perry, Charles, Christopher, and West 10th. This is one of the most tranquil neighborhoods in all of New York City.

To get here, take the 1 train to Christopher Street/Sheridan Square. I suggest spending an afternoon wandering . . . but if you have only a limited amount of time, a short walk down Bleecker provides a microcosm of West Village shopping. Start where Sixth Avenue intersects Bleecker Street. You'll begin in a very commercial area, but once you cross Seventh Avenue, you'll be in heaven: Perfectly kept brownstones on tree-lined blocks are companions to charming restaurants and an eclectic assortment of well-appointed shops selling everything from antiques to clothing to crafts.

Eats

Cornelia Street Café (29 Cornelia St., between Bleecker and W. 4th sts.; © **212/989-9319**) is open all day and evening for meals, snacks, and people-watching, and offers a full schedule of music, theater, poetry readings, and other entertainment.

SOUTH STREET SEAPORT

I count this as a neighborhood, even though it consists of only a couple malls and a strip of stores. Built around the old Fulton Fish Market, South Street Seaport is wedged against the water on the east side of Lower Manhattan. Many of the shops are branches of chains, such as **J. Crew, Brookstone,** and **Abercrombie & Fitch.** The Wall Streeters are particularly dense during lunchtime; visitors take over on weekends. The maritime museum here is interesting, especially for kids.

To get here, take the 2, 3, 4, or 5 train to Fulton Street.

WALL STREET & WORLD TRADE CENTER

Century 21 (22 Cortlandt St., between Church St. and Broadway), the city's best off-pricer, is open, newly expanded, and waiting for you . . . reason enough to head downtown.

Take the R or W to City Hall or Rector Street (until the Cortlandt St. station reopens in early 2007), the E to World Trade Center, or the 1 to Rector Street.

LOWER EAST SIDE

There's no question that the Lower East Side has changed, that it's no longer the discount area it once was . . . but the next SoHo? Not yet. I'll let you know when this area is really ready for prime time.

Take the J, M, or Z train to Essex Street/Delancey Street, or the F or V to 2nd Avenue or Delancey Street.

A. W. KAUFMAN
73 Orchard St., between Broome and Grand sts.

If you are hooked on fancy-schmancy American, Japanese, or European underwear, you just might find it significantly discounted here. Harking back to the old-fashioned way: You don't touch the merchandise and you can't try it on. You know what you want, you ask for it, you pay for it. Cash is good. © 212/226-1629. www.awkaufman.com.

FINE & KLEIN
119 Orchard St., between Rivington and Delancey sts.

While Fine & Klein is one of the most famous stores in the area, and generations of women have been coming here for, well, generations, I find this place singularly boring, and the crowds of people make me crazy. However, there are many name brands and good buys. There's a huge stock of a line called Sharif, which is one of my favorites (it's also sold at Neiman Marcus). © 212/674-6720.

KLEIN'S OF MONTICELLO
105 Orchard St., between Delancey and Broome sts.

This is the classiest shop on the Lower East Side and one of the best stores in Manhattan. If you're a Barneys regular, this is your kind of place. Klein's is small, chic, and filled with drop-dead gorgeous, elegant, low-key designer clothes that are made for movie stars and high-profile moguls who know how to dress in quiet style. © 212/966-1453.

TG-170
170 Ludlow St., between Houston and Stanton sts.

The hottest rage for the trendies, this shop showcases up-and-coming clothing and bag designers. Some think it's great, but I am too old for this. © 212/995-8660. www.tg170.com.

BROOKLYN

··

Aaron & Jenny's Williamsburg FYI

Don't get confused about where the prime shopping is: East Williamsburg (which is basically Bushwick) has not had the makeover that Williamsburg proper has, and is not very fabulous. In Williamsburg proper, the south side is still slightly seedy; the north side is the hipster hangout and home to chic boutiques. In summer, you'll see outdoor merchants selling their wares along Bedford Avenue as if the street were one giant yard sale.

To get here, take the L train to Bedford Avenue, the first stop in Brooklyn. Exit the subway toward Bedford (not Driggs), and you will be between North 7th and North 8th streets. Bedford Avenue is where it's all happening right now.

BEACON'S CLOSET
88 N. 11th St., near Wythe Ave., Brooklyn.

This is Williamsburg's finest store for vintage clothing and music, with the best selection and the most reasonable prices. The converted warehouse is across the street from the Brooklyn Brewery (home to one of the smoothest pale ales in North America). It's divided into huge men's and women's sections; three racks of T-shirts are organized by color and usually sell for under $10. The used-music selection is also top-notch. There's another location in Park Slope. © **718/486-0816.** www.beaconscloset.com.

BROOKLYN INDUSTRIES
162 Bedford Ave., at N. 8th St., Brooklyn.

BI has some of the biggest indie brands, along with its own in-house designer who creates T-shirts, hoodies, and hats. There's great '70s-looking underwear and pants for the ladies, plus a nice sale section with "Ten-Buck-Tees." This is also the place to buy the ubiquitous shirts and hoodies with BROOKLYN sewn

across them. Also located in SoHo and Park Slope, Brooklyn.
© 718/486-6464. www.brooklynindustries.com.

METAPHORS/PILGRIM (HOME)
195 & 202 Bedford Ave., near N. 6th St., Brooklyn.

Rose Knightly is the owner of these two great shops, Metaphors
and Pilgrim (Home). Both are probably boyfriend-borers, but
have such great stuff that you can let him loose in the Mini
Mall (described below) while you browse. **Metaphors** is a gift
shop that sells items geared toward the progressive: yoga man-
uals, meditation crystals, books on philosophy. There's also
women's clothing and lingerie—most of it absolutely darling,
but very pricey. **Pilgrim (Home)** has some of the cutest housewares in town, like kitschy glasses, olive-oil bottles, and the
largest variety of "alternative" cutting boards that we've ever
come across. © 718/782-0917.

SALVATION ARMY/GRANDMA'S (BEST) KEPT SECRET
176 Bedford Ave., at N. 7th St., Brooklyn.

The Salvation Army on Bedford Avenue was called "Grandma's
Kept Secret" until a few years ago, when the owners realized
their odd word omission and awkwardly added a carat (^) and
the word "best" in small letters to their awning. Perhaps an
effort to amend their original assertion of a hidden grandma,
or of a grandma as a kept woman? Regardless, this store is
home to the absolutely cheapest collection of vintage clothes
you will find in the whole 'burg, plus a sizable array of cheap
furniture. Good finds are usually hidden . . . just like Grandma
once was . . . we think. © 718/388-9249. www.salvationarmy
usa.org.

WILLIAMSBURG MINI MALL
218 Bedford Ave., at N. 5th St., Brooklyn.

This is a conglomerate of cool known locally as the Mini
Mall. Aside from shopping for books, electronics, and clothes,
patrons can check their e-mail, take a yoga class, or sip some

java at the fun sidewalk cafe. One standout is the **Mini Mini Market** (not a typo, folks; let's just call it the MMM), one of the kitschiest clothing shops for blocks. Most of its stock is girl-geared, but it also has a modest selection of men's attire, plus fabulous hats and bags, some sneakers, beauty products, and throwback toys. Two other notables inside the mall are the local wine shop and the local cheese shop, both owned by some of the friendliest people in the 'burg.

Eats

Vera Cruz (195 Bedford Ave., between N. 6th and N. 7th sts.; ✆ 718/599-7914) has souped-up versions of typical Mexican fare; the margaritas are incredible. **SEA** (114 N. 6th St., between Wythe Ave. and Berry St.; ✆ 718/384-8850) serves Thai fusion in a fairy-tale garden setting, accompanied by the ambient music of some of Brooklyn's premier DJs.

DUMBO

This is another of New York's famous acronyms, standing for "Down Under the Manhattan Bridge Overpass." This part of Brooklyn is now less seedy, and the low rents have attracted all sorts of galleries and eats. I was most attracted to it when there was an ABC Carpet & Home outlet; that store has recently closed. **West Elm** (75 Front St., at Main St.), the catalog firm, has moved in, as have other home-furnishings retailers who are attracting the Pottery Barn/Williams-Sonoma set. To get here, take the F train to York Street.

Chapter Eight

....

NEW YORK RESOURCES A TO Z

ACCESSORIES

....

Oh, boy. I could write a whole book just on the accessories available in New York. We'll start with a few orders of business:

- All department stores have accessories departments; most boutiques also sell them. Designer boutiques make their cash flow on fragrance and accessories, since few people can afford the clothes. Can't spring for the dress? Never mind, just buy the scarf.
- For our purposes, accessories include jewelry and fake jewelry. But also see the "Jewelry" section, later in this chapter.
- Shoes and bags have their own sections, too, later in this chapter.
- There has been a recent trend of jewelry stores selling their own lines of handbags—Bulgari, Tiffany, and Lalique are all on the bandwagon.
- The stuff sold on the streets is not only fake, but also may finance terrorists. You never know.

ADD
461 West Broadway, between Houston and Prince sts. (Subway: C or E to Spring St.).

A tiny store packed to the gills with frills that you'll want to touch and try on and own. There are dozens of different brands here, most of which I'd never heard. © 212/539-1439.

BOHKEE
1077 Third Ave., at 63rd St. (Subway: 4, 5, 6, N, R, or W to 59th St./Lexington Ave.).

This is New York correspondent Paul Baumrind's find—he says the one-of-a-kind evening bags are seriously impressive. © 212/319-0707.

LAILA ROWE
1031 Third Ave., at 61st St. (Subway: 4, 5, 6, N, R, or W to 59th St./Lexington Ave.); 424 West Broadway, between Prince and Spring sts. (Subway: C or E to Spring St.). Multiple other locations.

Any shopper worth her copycat Birkin bag knows about the various chains of low-cost accessories shops, such as **Claire's,** that are popular all over the U.S. But it may require a trip to New York to meet the hottest new franchise. Laila Rowe is packed with accessories for the chic, with an ethnic fashion twist and low, low prices. This is not teeny-bopper land: Per the recent trends as we go to press, there's plenty of wood, fake jade, and rhinestone brooches. This is the stuff that looks like it was featured in fashion magazines, only with dime-store price tags. There are over a dozen branches dotted around Manhattan; some are better than others, which gives you reason to visit as many as possible. © 212/66-LAILA. www.lailarowe.com.

LESPORTSAC
1065 Madison Ave., between 80th and 81st sts. (Subway: 4, 5, or 6 to 86th St.).

We're talking about carryalls, totes, and handbags, all great for travel. The range sold in the Madison Avenue shop is always ahead of what they get at discount shops and off-pricers, and some of it is rather chic. You can't beat the prices. There's another shop at 176 Spring St., near West Broadway. © **212/988-6200**. www.lesportsac.com.

MARIKO
998 Madison Ave., between 77th and 78th sts. (Subway: 6 to 77th St.).

Fashion alert! This is one of my best secret finds. I bought the best earrings of my life here. Many swoon for the copies of the most prestigious names in jewelry—yep, copies. Fancy copies. There are 18-karat gold earrings, too, in the $650 price range, darling. Prices even on fakes are not low, but the work is sublime and—dare I say it—somewhat funky. In other words, not reproductions of your average big names—instead, copies of Vedura, Elizabeth Gage, and the like. Very sophisticated. © **212/472-1176**.

OMAR
Madison Ave., at 66th St. (Subway: 6 to 68th St./ Hunter College).

Omar has no real address because he's a street vendor. He sells handbags, ties, scarves, and all sorts of fun things—a cut above the average street merchant. Cellphone: © **917/361-7576**.

RALPH LAUREN EYEWEAR
811 Madison Ave., near 68th St. (Subway: 6 to 68th St./Hunter College).

To further prove that Ralph has conquered the world, note the just-opened-as-we-go-to-press, free-standing eyewear store. © **212/988-4620**. www.polo.com.

RENE
1007 Madison Ave., near 77th St. (Subway: 6 to 77th St.).

The lower Madison Avenue location of this store's two branches is across the street from Mariko (listed above), so you can kill two birds with one faux diamond. The upper Madison shop, near 93rd Street, is larger, but I prefer the 77th Street store, where René herself is often behind the counter.

Like Mariko's stock, René's is very chic, though not as flashy. You'll see jewelry made with semiprecious stones: earrings in the just-under-$500 price range, as well as copies of famous collections for $100 to $250. You'll get good value for your money here. Note the chic handbags, very well made but not inexpensive. © 212/327-3912.

SERMONETA
609–611 Madison Ave., near 58th St. (Subway: 4, 5, 6, N, R, or W to 59th St./Lexington Ave.).

International travelers know the Sermoneta name from Italy; this is one of the best glove manufacturers in the world. It has just opened its first U.S. store at a time when Steve Martin's movie *Shopgirl* has put an emphasis on gloves—and fashion has merged the practical with the whimsical. Cashmere-lined gloves cost about $60. © 212/319-5946. www.sermoneta gloves.com.

VBH
940 Madison Ave., between 74th and 75th sts. (Subway: 6 to 77th St.).

This place looks like an art gallery or a branch of the San Francisco retail store Gump's—everything in the store is for sale, although the specialty is leather goods. It's all sleek and expensive and worthy of a movie set. © 212/717-9800. www. vbh-luxury.com.

ZITOMER
965 Madison Ave., near 75th St. (Subway: 6 to 77th St.).

Zitomer's next-door annex is filled with accessories of all kinds—even pet accessories. The look is sort of Euro-glitter. There is a new member of the Zitomer family, **ZChemists,** at

40 W. 57th St. Its accessories department is not as good right now, but the store is still new and could improve. ✆ **212/ 737-5560.** www.zitomer.com.

ACTIVE SPORTSWEAR & SPORTS GEAR

I refuse to list every major active-sportswear chain in Manhattan. However, some specialty retailers are fit for a (sporty) king.

If you need to make a quick purchase, there are branches of the chain **Sports Authority** at 845 Third Ave. (near 51st St.) and 636 Sixth Ave. (near 19th St.). Also note that the various athletic-shoe companies have snazzy shops, such as **Niketown,** 6 E. 57th St. (near Fifth Ave.).

ADIDAS
610 Broadway, at Houston St. (Subway: B, D, F, or V to Broadway/Lafayette St.).

This German athletic brand is back in style—it even got Stella McCartney to design a line. The new store will knock your socks off (bring Peds). ✆ **212/529-0081.** www.adidas.com.

BILLABONG
1515 Broadway, between 44th and 45th sts. (Subway: 1, 2, 3, 7, N, Q, R, or W to Times Sq./42nd St.).

The first U.S. store for this Australian brand of surfer clothes; its skateboard division is also represented. ✆ **212/840-0249.** www.billabong.com.

BURTON
106 Spring St., at Mercer St. (Subway: R or W to Prince St.).

Skiwear and snowboard gear for the with-it crowd. ✆ **212/966-8068.** www.burton.com.

EASTERN MOUNTAIN SPORTS
591 Broadway, at Houston St. (Subway: B, D, F, or V to Broadway/Lafayette St.; or R or W to Prince St.).

Part of a large chain of active outfitters, EMS has one of its largest stores on the edge of SoHo. You can get all your ski-wear, fishing gear, and hiking supplies at this one-stop sporting-goods mart. There's another location at 20 W. 61st St., near Broadway. © **212/966-8730.** www.ems.com.

ORVIS
522 Fifth Ave., at 44th St. (Subway: B, D, F, or V to 42nd St./Bryant Park).

If L.L. Bean came to Manhattan, he would probably check into Orvis. Orvis is famous for its fishing supplies, but also sells gift items (such as fishy ties), dog accessories, and chic fishing clothes that are rather suitable for weekending in the country or for visiting Balmoral. © **212/827-0698.** www.orvis.com.

PARAGON SPORTS
867 Broadway, at 18th St. (Subway: 4, 5, 6, L, N, Q, R, or W to 14th St./Union Sq.).

This sporting-goods supermarket is near Union Square and part of the new Lower Broadway hoopla. It's the kind of store you whirl through with a shopping basket—it truly has everything you can imagine. © **212/255-8036.** www.paragonsports.com.

PATAGONIA
101 Wooster St., between Prince and Spring sts. (Subway: C or E to Spring St.; or R or W to Prince St.).

Though technical products for specific sports make up most of the inventory here, this status brand also sells stylish active clothing for men, women, and kids. There's another branch at 426 Columbus Ave., near 81st Street. © **212/343-1776.** www.patagonia.com.

BEAUTY & BEYOND

See chapter 9 for beauty resources.

BIG NAMES IN FASHION

Manhattan is packed with showcase shops that feature the creations of the world's top designers. For those who shop in these stores, the names, the faces, the looks, and the prices stay more or less the same. Therefore, I list only addresses for the sources in this section.

Please note that many of these designers have recently opened or are in the process of opening stores in SoHo. Also note that because of the amount of available real estate, the big names have been moving around like mad. Since the last edition of this book, almost a dozen shops have moved, and many stores that haven't moved have expanded or re-created themselves. For instance, thought you knew everything about Ferragamo? Be sure to check out the way the shop has been redone. (*Tip:* The quickest way to see a lot of brand names is always at a department store.)

American Big Names

Some of the big names listed below are described elsewhere in the book; others are such ubiquitous brands that no explanation is needed.

ANNA SUI
113 Greene St., between Prince and Spring sts. (Subway: R or W to Prince St.).
℗ **212/941-8406.** www.annasui.com.

CALVIN KLEIN
654 Madison Ave., at 60th St. (Subway: 4, 5, 6, N, R, or W to 59th St./Lexington Ave.).
© 212/292-9000. www.calvinklein.com.

DANA BUCHMAN
65 E. 57th St., near Park Ave. (Subway: 4, 5, 6, N, R, or W to 59th St./Lexington Ave.).
© 212/319-3257. www.danabuchman.com.

DIANE VON FURSTENBERG
385 W. 12th St., near Washington St. (Subway: A, C, E, or L to 14th St./8th Ave.).
© 646/486-4800. www.dvf.com.

DKNY DONNA KARAN NEW YORK
655 Madison Ave., at 60th St. (Subway: 4, 5, 6, N, R, or W to 59th St./Lexington Ave.).
© 212/223-3569. www.dkny.com.

420 West Broadway, near Spring St. (Subway: C or E to Spring St.; or R or W to Prince St.).
© 646/613-1100. www.dkny.com.

DONNA KARAN
819 Madison Ave., near 68th St. (Subway: 6 to 68th St./ Hunter College).
© 212/861-1001. www.donnakaran.com.

MARC JACOBS
163 Mercer St., between Houston and Prince sts. (Subway: R or W to Prince St.).
© 212/343-1490. www.marcjacobs.com.

385 Bleecker St., near Perry St. (Subway: A, C, E, or L to 14th St./8th Ave.).
© 212/924-6126. www.marcjacobs.com.

403 Bleecker St., at W. 11th St. (Subway: A, C, E, or L to 14th St./8th Ave.).
© **212/924-0026.** www.marcjacobs.com.

RALPH LAUREN
867 Madison Ave., at 72nd St. (Subway: 6 to 68th St./ Hunter College).
© **212/606-2100.** www.polo.com.

888 Madison Ave., at 72nd St. (Subway: 6 to 68th St./ Hunter College).
© **212/434-8000.** www.polo.com.

380 Bleecker St., near Perry St. (Subway: A, C, E, or L to 14th St./8th Ave.).
© **212/645-5513.** www.polo.com.

381 Bleecker St., near Perry St. (Subway: A, C, E, or L to 14th St./8th Ave.).
© **646/638-0684.** www.polo.com.

379 West Broadway, near Broome St. (Subway: C or E to Spring St.).
© **212/625-1660.** www.polo.com.

ST. JOHN
665 Fifth Ave., at 53rd St. (Subway: E or V to 5th Ave./ 53rd St.).
© **212/755-5252.** www.stjohnknits.com.

European & Japanese Big Names

You will probably recognize most of the names on this who's-who-of-international-fashion list.

AKRIS
835 Madison Ave., near 69th St. (Subway: 6 to 68th St./Hunter College).
© **212/717-1170.** www.akris.ch.

ALEXANDER MCQUEEN
417 W. 14th St., near Ninth Ave. (Subway: A, C, E, or L to 14th St./8th Ave.).
℗ **212/645-1797.** www.alexandermcqueen.com.

A/X ARMANI EXCHANGE
645 Fifth Ave., near 51st St. (Subway: E or V to 5th Ave./ 53rd St.).
℗ **212/980-3037.** www.armaniexchange.com.

568 Broadway, at Prince St. (Subway: R or W to Prince St.).
℗ **212/431-6000.** www.armaniexchange.com.

129 Fifth Ave., at 20th St. (Subway: R or W to 23rd St.).
℗ **212/254-7230.** www.armaniexchange.com.

Time Warner Center, 10 Columbus Circle (Subway: A, B, C, D, or 1 to 59th St./Columbus Circle).
℗ **212/823-9321.** www.armaniexchange.com.

BALENCIAGA
542 W. 22nd St., between Tenth and Eleventh aves. (Subway: C or E to 23rd St.).
℗ **212/206-0872.** www.balenciaga.com.

BALLY
628 Madison Ave., at 59th St. (Subway: 4, 5, 6, N, R, or W to 59th St./Lexington Ave.).
℗ **212/751-9082.** www.bally.com.

BOTTEGA VENETA
699 Fifth Ave., between 54th and 55th sts. (Subway: E or V to 5th Ave./53rd St.).
℗ **212/371-5511.** www.bottegaveneta.com.

BURBERRY
9 E. 57th St., between Fifth and Madison aves. (Subway: N, R, or W to 5th Ave./59th St.).
℗ **212/407-7100.** www.burberry.com.

131 Spring St., near Greene St. (Subway: C or E to Spring
St.; or R or W to Prince St.).
© 212/925-9300. www.burberry.com.

CELINE
667 Madison Ave., near 61st St. (Subway: 4, 5, 6, N, R, or
W to 59th St./Lexington Ave.).
© 212/486-9700. www.celine.com.

CHANEL
15 E. 57th St., between Fifth and Madison aves. (Subway:
N, R, or W to 5th Ave./59th St.).
© 212/355-5050. www.chanel.com.

139 Spring St., at Wooster St. (Subway: C or E to Spring St.;
or R or W to Prince St.).
© 212/334-0055. www.chanel.com.

737 Madison Ave., near 64th St. (Subway: 6 to 68th St./
Hunter College).
© 212/535-5505. www.chanel.com.

CHLOE
850 Madison Ave., at 70th St. (Subway: 6 to 68th St./
Hunter College).
© 212/717-8220. www.chloe.com.

CHRISTIAN DIOR
21 E. 57th St., between Fifth and Madison aves. (Subway:
N, R, or W to 5th Ave./59th St.).
© 212/931-2950. www.dior.com.

COMME DES GARÇONS
520 W. 22nd St., near Tenth Ave. (Subway: C or E to
23rd St.).
© 212/604-9200.

D&G
434 West Broadway, between Prince and Spring sts. (Subway: C or E to Spring St.; or R or W to Prince St.).
© 212/965-8000. www.dolcegabbana.it.

DOLCE & GABBANA
825 Madison Ave., near 68th St. (Subway: 6 to 68th St./ Hunter College).
© 212/249-4100. www.dolcegabbana.it.

EMANUEL UNGARO
792 Madison Ave., at 67th St. (Subway: 6 to 68th St./ Hunter College).
© 212/249-4090. www.ungaro.com.

EMILIO PUCCI
701 Fifth Ave., near 54th St. (Subway: E or V to 5th Ave./ 53rd St.).
© 212/230-1135. www.emiliopucci.com.

24 E. 64th St., between Madison and Fifth aves. (Subway: F to Lexington Ave./63rd St.).
© 212/752-4777. www.emiliopucci.com.

EMPORIO ARMANI
601 Madison Ave., between 57th and 58th sts. (Subway: 4, 5, 6, N, R, or W to 59th St./Lexington Ave.).
© 212/317-0800. www.emporioarmani.com.

410 West Broadway, at Spring St. (Subway: C or E to Spring St.; or R or W to Prince St.).
© 646/613-8099. www.emporioarmani.com.

ERMENEGILDO ZEGNA
663 Fifth Ave., between 52nd and 53rd sts. (Subway: E or V to 5th Ave./53rd St.).
© 212/421-4488. www.zegna.com.

ESCADA
715 Fifth Ave., near 55th St. (Subway: N, R, or W to 5th Ave./59th St.).
© **212/755-2200.** www.escada.com.

ETRO
720 Madison Ave., near 64th St. (Subway: 6 to 68th St./ Hunter College).
© **212/317-9096.** www.etro.com.

FENDI
677 Fifth Ave., near 53rd St. (Subway: E or V to 5th Ave./ 53rd St.).
© **212/759-4646.** www.fendi.com.

GIANFRANCO FERRE
870 Madison Ave., near 71st St. (Subway: 6 to 68th St./ Hunter College).
© **212/717-5430.** www.gianfrancoferre.com

GIORGIO ARMANI/ARMANI COUTURE
760 Madison Ave., at 65th St. (Subway: 6 to 68th St./ Hunter College).
© **212/988-9191.** www.giorgioarmani.com.

GUCCI
685 Fifth Ave., at 54th St. (Subway: E or V to 5th Ave./ 53rd St.).
© **212/826-2600.** www.gucci.com.

840 Madison Ave., near 70th St. (Subway: 6 to 68th St./ Hunter College).
© **212/717-2619.** www.gucci.com.

HERMES
691 Madison Ave., at 62nd St. (Subway: N, R, or W to 5th Ave./59th St.).
© **212/751-3181.** www.hermes.com.

ISSEY MIYAKE
992 Madison Ave., at 77th St. (Subway: 6 to 77th St.).
© 212/439-7822. www.isseymiyake.com.

119 Hudson St., near N. Moore St. (Subway: 1 to Franklin St.).
© 212/226-0100. www.isseymiyake.com.

KRIZIA
769 Madison Ave., near 66th St. (Subway: 6 to 68th St./ Hunter College).
© 212/879-1211. www.krizia.it.

LA PERLA
803 Madison Ave., between 67th and 68th sts. (Subway: 6 to 68th St./Hunter College).
© 212/570-0050. www.laperla.com.

93 Greene St., near Prince St. (Subway: R or W to Prince St.).
© 212/219-0999. www.laperla.com.

425 W. 14th St., near Ninth Ave. (Subway: A, C, E, or L to 14th St./8th Ave.).
© 212/242-6662. www.laperla.com.

LOUIS VUITTON
1 E. 57th St., at Fifth Ave. (Subway: F to 57th St.).
© 212/758-8877. www.louisvuitton.com.

116 Greene St., between Prince and Spring sts. (Subway: R or W to Prince St.).
© 212/274-9090. www.louisvuitton.com.

MAX MARA
813 Madison Ave., at 68th St. (Subway: 6 to 68th St./ Hunter College).
© 212/879-6100.

450 West Broadway, at Prince St. (Subway: R or W to Prince St.).
© 212/674-1817.

MISSONI
1009 Madison Ave., near 78th St. (Subway: 6 to 77th St.).
© 212/517-9339. www.missoni.it.

NICOLE FARHI
10 E. 60th St., between Fifth and Madison aves. (Subway: N, R, or W to 5th Ave./59th St.).
© 212/223-8811. www.nicolefarhi.com.

NICOLE FARHI/202
75 Ninth Ave., near 16th St. (Subway: A, C, E, or L to 14th St./8th Ave.).
Combination eatery and clothing/home-decor shop.
© 646/638-0115. www.nicolefarhi.com.

PLEATS PLEASE ISSEY MIYAKE
128 Wooster St., at Prince St. (Subway: R or W to Prince St.).
© 212/226-3600. www.pleatsplease.com.

PRADA
45 E. 57th St., between Park and Madison aves. (Subway: 4, 5, 6, N, R, or W to 59th St./Lexington Ave.).
© 212/308-2332. www.prada.com.

724 Fifth Ave., near 56th St. (Subway: E or V to 5th Ave./ 53rd St.).
© 212/664-0010. www.prada.com.

841 Madison Ave., at 70th St. (Subway: 6 to 68th St./ Hunter College).
© 212/327-4200. www.prada.com.

575 Broadway, near Prince St. (Subway: R or W to Prince St.).
© 212/334-8888. www.prada.com.

SALVATORE FERRAGAMO
655 Fifth Ave., at 52nd St. (Subway: E or V to 5th Ave./ 53rd St.).
© 212/759-3822. www.ferragamo.com.

124 Spring St., near Greene St. (Subway: C, E, or 6 to Spring St.).
© 212/226-4330. www.ferragamo.com.

SONIA RYKIEL
849 Madison Ave., near 70th St. (Subway: 6 to 68th St./ Hunter College).
© 212/396-3060. www.soniarykiel.com.

STELLA MCCARTNEY
429 W. 14th St., between Ninth and Tenth aves. (Subway: A, C, E, or L to 14th St./8th Ave.).
© 212/255-1556. www.stellamccartney.com.

VALENTINO
747 Madison Ave., at 65th St. (Subway: 6 to 68th St./ Hunter College).
© 212/772-6969. www.valentino.it.

YOHJI YAMAMOTO
103 Grand St., at Mercer St. (Subway: 6, A, C, E, J, M, N, Q, R, W, or Z to Canal St.).
© 212/966-9066. www. yohjiyamamoto.co.jp.

YVES SAINT LAURENT
3 E. 57th St., near Fifth Ave. (Subway: N, R, or W to 5th Ave./59th St.).
© 212/980-2970. www.ysl.com.

855 Madison Ave., near 71st St. (Subway: 6 to 68th St./ Hunter College).
© 212/988-3821. www.ysl.com.

BOOKS

....

In addition to the choices below, there are the big chains: **Barnes & Noble,** with scads of locations including a popular outlet opposite Union Square, 33 E. 17th St. (© **212/253-0810;** www.bn.com); and **Borders,** which has four stores in Manhattan including one in the Time Warner Center, 10 Columbus Circle (© **212/823-9775;** www.bordersstores.com). Among my favorite large—but still independent—bookstores is **Coliseum,** which visitors should note has moved to 11 W. 42nd St., between Fifth and Sixth avenues (© **212/803-5890;** www. coliseumbooks.com).

BAUMAN RARE BOOKS
535 Madison Ave., between 54th and 55th sts. (Subway: 6 to 51st St.).

Bauman's is one of the foremost resources for serious collectors willing to spend big money for pristine first editions. Titles include everything from Milton's *Paradise Lost* (1669) to a signed copy of Harper Lee's *To Kill a Mockingbird* (1960). © 212/751-0011. www.baumanrarebooks.com.

BOOKS OF WONDER
16 W. 18th St., between Fifth and Sixth aves. (Subway: 4, 5, 6, L, N, Q, R, or W to 14th St./Union Sq.).

You don't have to be a kid to fall in love with this charming bookstore, which served as the model for Meg Ryan's shop in *You've Got Mail.* © 212/989-3270. www.booksofwonder.com.

DRAMA BOOK SHOP
250 W. 40th St., between Seventh and Eighth aves. (Subway: A, C, or E to 42nd St.).

Leading authority for books on all performing arts—not just the theater. © 212/944-0595. www.dramabookshop.com.

RIZZOLI BOOKSTORE
31 W. 57th St., between Fifth and Sixth aves. (Subway: N, R, or W to 5th Ave./59th St.).

This clubby Italian bookstore is the classiest—and most relaxing—spot in town to browse art and design books, plus quality fiction, gourmet cookbooks, and other upscale titles. © 212/759-2424. www.rizzoliusa.com.

STRAND BOOK STORE
828 Broadway, at 12th St. (Subway: 4, 5, 6, L, N, Q, R, or W to 14th St./Union Sq.).

Something of a New York legend, the Strand is worth a visit for its staggering "18 miles of books" (revised from the previous 8 miles) as well as its extensive inventory of review copies and bargain titles at up to 85% off list price.

I am not overwhelmed easily (in a store, anyway) . . . but this place makes me dizzy. It's unquestionably the city's best book deal—almost nothing is marked at list price—and the selection is phenomenal in all categories (there's even a rare-book department on the third floor). Still, you'll work for it: The narrow aisles mean you're always getting bumped; the books are only roughly alphabetized; and there's no air-conditioning. Nevertheless, it's a book-lover's paradise. © 212/473-1452. www.strandbooks.com.

TASCHEN
107 Greene St., between Prince and Spring sts. (Subway: R or W to Prince St.).

I am always amazed by Taschen stores for their combination of incredible architecture, high style, and fabulous lifestyle books—which very often are not overly expensive. I simply don't know how they do it. © 212/226-2212. www.taschen.com.

BOUTIQUES

....

ANN AHN

961 Madison Ave., between 75th and 76th sts. (Subway: 6 to 77th St.).

This is the kind of small Madison Avenue boutique that you might pass without ever knowing that it is the "in" place for Upper East Side ladies who like the Euro-Asian-artsy-hippie-boho look—and are willing to pay $500 and up for classic trousers, jackets, and shrugs. Many one-of-a-kind pieces are classics in their own way, since they're so unique. The look here is something like that offered by the designer Eskandar, but more into fiber arts with an emphasis on texture. © **212/288-6068.**

CALYPSO

815 Madison Ave., near 68th St. (Subway: 6 to 68th St./ Hunter College).

Originally from the bijou island of St. Barth's, with a French accent *(bien sur),* Calypso has consistently been able to take resort chic and turn it into an urban trend. Aside from clothes, there are some accessories and, of course, signature scents. The brand-new flagship just opened in the old Versace space on Madison; there's also a branch at 935 Madison Ave. (near 74th St.), plus locations in trendy areas such as the Meatpacking District (654 Hudson St.), SoHo (424 Broome St.), and Nolita (280 Mott St.). See p. 245 for Calypso Home. © **212/585-0310.** www.calypso-celle.com.

DARYL K

21 Bond St., between Lafayette St. and Bowery.

Daryl Kerrigan was considered the It Girl of her time, yet without explanation she closed down her SoHo shop. Good news for those left naked in the dark: Sheeeee's baaaack. There are only about 25 styles created each season; cult followers stand in line to get them. Barneys Co-Op also sells the line if you

can't get to this downtown boutique. ✆ **212/529-8790.** www.
darylk.com.

DOSA
*107 Thompson St., between Prince and Spring sts. (Subway:
C or E to Spring St.).*

I fell for this line at Bergdorf Goodman, so even if you aren't
heading all the way downtown, you won't be out of luck. On
the other hand, if you're into the rich hippie-dippy look with
jewel-tone silks and cottons, fluid chic, and slightly ethnic
droop, you may want to head directly here. ✆ **212/431-1733.**

EDGE*NYNOHO
*65 Bleecker St., between Broadway and Lafayette St. (Sub-
way: B, D, F, or V to Broadway/Lafayette St.; or 6 to
Bleecker St.).*

This NoHo spot is less a boutique and more a market or a happening—a large space selling the work of new designers trying to get noticed. EDGE*nyNOHO is the place to be seen or
to tell your friends you've discovered. ✆ **212/358-0255.** www.
edgeny.com.

RUEHL
*370 Bleecker St., near Charles St. (Subway: 1 to Christopher
St./Sheridan Sq.).*

I'm gonna break some of my ruehls—I mean, rules—here and
explore a new chain that is on its way to becoming a multiple. There are only around seven of these stores in the world,
with this one being the sole location currently in Manhattan.
Ruehl is a new division of Abercrombie & Fitch, geared to older,
more grown-up, and more well-off clients. Sort of the over-
30-but-I'm-hip crowd. ✆ **212/924-8506.** www.ruehl.com.

YASO
*62 Grand St., near West Broadway (Subway: C or E to
Spring St.; or 1 to Canal St.).*

I am particularly fond of luxurious droopy drape and ethnic chic, so I have been shopping here for well over a dozen years. This is a total-look kind of store, with some home furnishings and accessories along with clothing. © **212/941-8506.**

BRIDAL

All department stores have bridal departments, though many young women today prefer alternative retail—buying wholesale from the bridal suppliers in the Garment District, going to the Filene's Basement bridal sale (p. 287), checking out the Vera Wang once-a-year sale (usually in Feb), and so on. See p. 152 for more information.

ADRIENNES
156 Orchard St., near Rivington St. (Subway: F or V to 2nd Ave.).

The bride is a little bit funky, a little bit rock 'n' roll—or perhaps she wants to work with a designer and have a lot of input in the creation. Dresses tend to be simple and elegant and priced under $5,000. © **212/228-9618.** www.adriennesny.com.

B&J FABRICS
525 Seventh Ave., at 38th St. (Subway: 1, 2, 3, 7, N, Q, R, or W to Times Sq./42nd St.).

See p. 165 for the listing for this store. The fabric for Carolyn Bessette Kennedy's wedding gown came from B&J. © **212/354-8150.** www.bandjfabrics.com.

KLEINFELD
110 W. 20th St., near Sixth Ave. (Subway: F or V to 23rd St.).

Among the biggest tidbits in New York retail is the new Manhattan store recently opened by this Brooklyn bridal icon.

Many area brides make the trek here for the selection. Sometimes there are price breaks; other times the prize is a trunk show or a chance to work with a designer and to modify a design to suit. An appointment is required. © 646/633-4300. www. kleinfeldbridal.com.

MICHAEL'S
1041 Madison Ave., between 79th and 80th sts. (Subway: 6 to 77th St.).

This famous resale shop sells used wedding gowns in addition to a range of other clothing. See p. 306 for full listing. © 212/ 737-7273. www.michaelsconsignment.com.

VERA WANG
991 Madison Ave., at 77th St. (Subway: 6 to 77th St.).

America's most famous name in fancy-schmancy wedding gowns. By appointment, m'dear. If you're planning way ahead, there's a warehouse sale in a downtown hotel once a year, usually in February (look in *New York* magazine for the exact date). Wang has recently extended her empire and now makes everything from fragrance to shoes to jewelry. A new store, **Vera Wang Maids,** 980 Madison Ave., third floor (© 212/628-9898), has been created for the bridesmaids. © 212/628-3400. www.vera wang.com.

CASHMERE

....

Cashmere is difficult to buy at discount because there are so many tricks to the quality—you may pay a low price, but you'll get exactly what you paid for. You'll do better to pay more and get the best possible quality. If you take care of your cashmeres, they will last you a lifetime—or longer. I still wear a sweater of my mother's that is easily 50 years old.

Keep in mind that Italian cashmere is the best, followed by Scottish. Don't buy Chinese cashmere unless you like cheap thrills. Note that the big English brands usually sell Scottish cashmere.

The thought that anyone would walk into a cashmere store and pay regular retail is a joke to me. I'd buy during a sale period, of course! Or I'd use my regular discount sources, be they off-pricers or discounters. But pay full price? Eeeeek! When is the best time to buy cashmere, my dear? July, of course. That's when it's on sale and mere mortals get hot flashes when they think of it.

Big Names

A crop of cashmere specialty stores (mostly Italian) has opened on Madison Avenue. In no way does the $99 cashmere special at Lord & Taylor compare to the cashmere that's sold in these stores. Some of these places sell more than cashmere—in fact, they have to, just to stay in business. I once bought my husband a bathing suit at Malo! Since the big-name makers sell different versions of basically the same thing, I merely list them below.

MALO
*814 Madison Ave., at 68th St. (Subway: 6 to 68th St./
Hunter College).*
℗ **212/396-4721.** www.malo.it.

MANRICO
*804 Madison Ave., near 67th St. (Subway: 6 to 68th St./
Hunter College).*
℗ **212/794-4200.** www.manrico.com.

N. PEAL
*5 W. 56th St., between Fifth and Sixth aves. (Subway: F to
57th St.).*
℗ **212/333-3500.** www.npeal.com.

TSE
*827 Madison Ave., at 69th St. (Subway: 6 to 68th St./
Hunter College).*
✆ **212/472-7790.**

Discounters

You can expect to find off-price cashmere at any of the local
off-price stores (p. 284) or area outlet malls (p. 292). The
major department stores often have cashmere promotions or
special sales as well. The store below offers promotional prices
year-round.

BEST OF SCOTLAND
*581 Fifth Ave., near 47th St., 6th floor (Subway: B, D, F, or
V to Rockefeller Center).*

The words "cashmere" and "discount" do not really go hand
in hand. Prices are not low, and there is little here for less than
$100, but if you like quality cashmere and those shawls with
the little ruffles, this is your chance to buy at a slightly better
price. ✆ **212/644-0403.** www.bestofscotlandnyc.com.

CHIC & SIMPLE

There is a trend in New York for women with money and style
to avoid the big stores and concentrate on a single source or
two that can supply simple yet perfect style and maximum service. The type of clothing that these women buy is classically
chic—always refined, simple, elegant, and practical. Much of
it is in the **Armani** style, but streamlined, and the palette is almost
always monochromatic. These items are not inexpensive.

I've listed **Eileen Fisher** (p. 94) in this text about five million times; she offers the baggier and less expensive version of
this look. If you're an Eileen Fisher fan, the outlet stores in Secaucus (p. 295) and Woodbury Common (p. 297) are worth the
drive.

ANNE FONTAINE

687 Madison Ave., near 62nd St. (Subway: 4, 5, 6, N, R, or W to 59th St./Lexington Ave.).

This French chain now has several shops in Manhattan. Fontaine began by doing only white shirts and blouses, but now also sells black—everything from sporty to dressy. Other locations are at Rockefeller Center (610 Fifth Ave., near 49th St.) and in SoHo (93 Greene St., near Prince St.). © **212/688-4362.** www.annefontaine.com.

BLANC DE CHINE

673 Fifth Ave., at 53rd St. (Subway: E or V to 5th Ave./ 53rd St.).

Armani meets Shanghai Tang in classic, tailored Chinese-inspired clothing for men and women. There's some home styles, too. Prices are up here: Expect to pay at least $500 for a blazer. (You'll never regret it.) Stores are popping up in all major shopping cities—try London and Beijing as well as hometown Hong Kong. © **212/355-1682.** www.blancdechine.com.

CP SHADES

60 Grand St., between West Broadway and Wooster St. (Subway: C or E to Spring St.).

I consider this line the poor gal's Eileen Fisher and a friend of anyone who likes the Armani palette of soft pastels. You'll find droopy, comfy clothes in tones that are nice but neutral. I am personally a big CP Shades fan. I especially go nuts during sales. The look is a little too bohemian for normal workdays in Manhattan, but it's great for weekends or suburbia. © **212/226-4434.** www.cpshades.com.

SHEN NEW YORK

1005 Madison Ave., between 77th and 78th sts. (Subway: 6 to 77th St.).

This is the place for sublime, body-skimming, simple elegance in gorgeous fabrics. I saw a fluttery, lightly layered, froth-of-chiffon sleeveless top that was the whisper of everything I've always wanted to be. It was almost $200, but this is where you put your money when elegance is all you believe in. If I could afford it, I'd shop nowhere else. ☎ **212/717-1185.**

CHILDREN

Shopping for kids in Manhattan is a bit of a Catch-22: You have to be crazy to spend time in New York shopping for kids, but you'd be crazy not to think about it because there are so many great places. So think carefully. If price, or the combination of price and acceptable style, is your main concern, then the truth is that you can do better through catalogs and at suburban discounters. If you want to splurge, however, that's another story. Welcome to a city where people spend $200 for a pair of party shoes for their kids.

I am assuming that you have chains such as **Gap Kids** and **Baby Gap** in your neck of the woods; if not, they are great fun, and sale prices are moderate. Should you be able to hit the outlet malls, please note that **Carter's** has outlets in Woodbury Common as well as the New Jersey malls; these sell not only the Carter's line but also the **Baby Dior** line. See p. 292 for more on outlet stores. In town, the source for discounted kids' everything is **Burlington Coat Factory** (707 Sixth Ave., at 23rd St.), on Ladies' Mile.

A few thoughts to help you:

- All of the big department stores have excellent children's departments.
- The Lower East Side is good for bulk in layette at a 20% discount.
- Madison Avenue is dotted with fine and funky boutiques that sell unusual specialty items that no one has ever seen before (read: very expensive). Check out places like **Au**

Chat Botte (1192 Madison Ave., near 88th St.) for the cat's meow in this genre.

- The area of Madison Avenue from 86th to 96th streets houses many private schools and is therefore jammed with boutiques catering to young ones—many are branches of international big names such as **Bonpoint, Jacadi,** and **Oilily.**
- There are some **Toys "R" Us** branches dotted all over town. Note that Toys "R" Us has closed out its clothing divisions.
- Some of the big names, especially in what I call conservative fashion, make kids' clothes—check out **Brooks Brothers** and **Talbots.** Even **Ralph Lauren** now has a toddler line.
- **Daffy's** (p. 286), the discounter, sells kids' clothes at all of its locations.

GREENSTONES
442 Columbus Ave., near 81st St. (Subway: B or C to 81st St.).

One of the most famous residents of the Upper West Side, Greenstones, thankfully, is not one of those kiddie stores that's as big as a closet with prices as high as a condo. I mean, prices aren't low, but the range of looks is wide, from Chanel-style suits for your young miss to leather bomber jackets. There are almost a hundred different European lines sold here, as well as standard American faves such as OshKosh. Now on the Upper East Side as well, under the name **Greenstones Too** (1184 Madison Ave., near 86th St.). ✆ **212/580-4322.**

KATE SPADE BABY
59 Thompson St., near Broome St. (Subway: C or E to Spring St.).

Tiny shop that Spade must own, since it once housed the launch of other parts of her empire. Now it's turned into a showcase for baby gear, featuring Kate's own creations as well as Euro lines. The real draws are the diaper bags in traditional Spade styles. ✆ **212/965-8654.** www.katespade.com.

MAGIC WINDOWS
1186 Madison Ave., at 87th St. (Subway: 4, 5, or 6 to 86th St.).

Expanded now to include the teenage debutante and party set, this store features mostly dress-up clothes, because the clients all wear uniforms to school. Doesn't everyone? © **212/289-0028.** www.magic-windows.com.

OILILY
820 Madison Ave., between 68th and 69th sts. (Subway: 6 to 68th St./Hunter College).

This is a Dutch chain with stores all over the world and prices that break my heart because I am so attracted to the clothes, the colors, and the look: happy splashy designs, bright mixed patterns, and all the celebration a garment can take. There's children's, women's, and accessories. Best news: There's now an outlet store at Woodbury Common (p. 297). © **212/772-8686.** www.oililyusa.com.

OSHKOSH B'GOSH
586 Fifth Ave., near 48th St. (Subway: B, D, F, or V to Rockefeller Center).

This maker of clothing for tots has been popular in the U.S. for a long time, and almost has cult status in continental Europe. The brand opened a branch in Paris and has now conquered Fifth Avenue with a good-size store crammed with clothes for boys and girls. I find the items expensive and prefer to buy them used, but Europeans will go nuts for the prices here—this line is so pricey overseas that the Manhattan store seems like a bargain basement. © **212/827-0098.** www.oshkosh bgosh.com.

ZITOMER
969 Madison Ave., near 76th St. (Subway: 6 to 77th St.).

Take the elevator from the pharmacy part of this store and go up to little-girl dreamland. Some child actors have admitted that their Oscar gowns come from Zitomer. © 212/737-2016. www.zitomer.com.

DEPARTMENT & SPECIALTY STORES

Things to know:

- Delivery service is available at all stores, but you will be charged for it. Few stores have private delivery service anymore; they usually use UPS or FedEx, except for large pieces of furniture.
- All stores will provide free, simple, gift-wrapping services. Elaborate wrapping costs extra. You can usually get a free shopping bag with handles by asking at customer service or a wrap desk, although stores also have machines that sell outsize shopping bags.
- All stores have buying services, personal shoppers, and translators, as well as clean bathrooms. Many have checkrooms for coats and packages. Most now have spas—now you really can shop till you drop.
- A variety of credit cards are accepted at all stores; some are still pushing their house credit cards and may even offer a 10% discount for purchases made when you sign up for the card. International customers are accepted.

BARNEYS CO-OP
236 W. 18th St., between Seventh and Eighth aves. (Subway: 1 to 18th St.).

This offshoot of Barneys (see below) sells the young, trendy, and really exciting stuff. There are also locations in SoHo (116 Wooster St., near Prince St.) and on the Upper West Side (2151 Broadway, at 75th St.). © 212/593-7800. www.barneys. com.

BARNEYS NEW YORK
660 Madison Ave., at 61st St. (Subway: 4, 5, 6, N, R, or W to 59th St./Lexington Ave.).

Uptown Barneys is a legend. Only visitors and uptown girls shop here, as this store is special beyond special. Barneys has re-created itself as times have changed, and is still one of the most exciting retail properties in Manhattan. Indeed, no shopping trip to New York is complete without a visit to this store. Whether you buy anything or not is meaningless—you must see and touch and feel.

The flagship location is actually two different eight-story stores that connect on the street level. You won't want to miss a square inch. The most exciting part (to me) is Chelsea Passage, the home-design department. I'm also keen on the unique bath products, European favorites that I don't see elsewhere, and cult makeup brands.

Okay, about prices. While a lot of the merchandise is very pricey, a lot of it is not. It all looks expensive, but there are plenty of items, especially accessories, that are moderately priced.

The Madison Avenue store is open daily until 9pm—hours that help make Midtown browsing an evening sport. ✆ 212/826-8900. www.barneys.com.

BERGDORF GOODMAN
754 Fifth Ave., between 57th and 58th sts. (Subway: N, R, or W to 5th Ave./59th St.).

BERGDORF GOODMAN MEN
745 Fifth Ave., at 58th St. (Subway: N, R, or W to 5th Ave./59th St.).

Bergdorf's has had a face-lift, and dramatic things have been done to this store to bring back some of its lost energy. If you haven't been here for a while, do stop in. And drop down under to the newish lower-level beauty floor. My favorite part of the store is still the seventh floor, with a gift department and antiques from Kentshire Galleries; Christmas is a delight.

Every day is a delight, actually. Hours are Monday through Saturday from 10am to 7pm, Thursday evening until 8pm. There's a new restaurant, with a view of the park, on the home-furnishings floor. **Bergdorf Goodman Men** is across the street. © 212/753-7300. www.bergdorfgoodman.com.

BLOOMINGDALE'S
1000 Third Ave., at 59th St. (Subway: 4, 5, 6, N, R, or W to 59th St./Lexington Ave.).

A trip to Bloomie's is a trip to the moon on gossamer wings. You start off filled with energy and excitement, loving everything you see, but as you wear out, you wear down, and suddenly you realize you're lost, the store is difficult to shop, and you can't remember all the departments. *C'est le Bloomie's.* Still, it's one of the best department stores in the world.

You must know the territory or go with someone who does if you like to shop efficiently. Otherwise, just take small doses, always remembering that no one does it like Bloomingdale's, and that's why the store has become a legend in its own time.

I cannot tell you that Bloomingdale's lives up to the hype, but I can tell you that for massive amounts of merchandise and for selection, this store is possibly the best in town. Plus, the designer boutiques are excellent, and second markdowns can make you very happy.

Some tips: The store has many entrances: You can enter from Lexington Avenue, even though the official street address is Third Avenue. There's also a subway stop right under Bloomie's. At press time, a new restaurant has opened. And finally: A smaller branch of the store has opened in SoHo, at 504 Broadway, between Spring and Broome sts. © 212/705-2000. www. bloomingdales.com.

HENRI BENDEL
712 Fifth Ave., near 56th St. (Subway: F to 57th St.).

From a merchandise point of view, this store has changed dramatically and is a little less exclusive and less chic than it once was. Visually, Bendel's is still fun to stare at and shop, although you may not really buy much.

Prices vary from outrageous to quite moderate. The makeup department is good—Bobbi Brown and M.A.C. cosmetics as well as Chanel and a few big brands, plus the store's own famous brown-and-white-striped logo travel cases. Bendel's does good windows, has a wonderful Christmas tree, and frequently changes the front of the store on the ground floor so you always get a sense of adventure. Be sure to check out the original Lalique windows in the cafe.

Here's one of the best parts—this store does zillions of parties and promotional events, many of which are after-hours. You usually get a goody bag when you attend; at the last event I went to, the goodies even included a $25 gift certificate for any purchase at Bendel's. These events are worth attending; get on the mailing list and party like crazy. © 212/247-1100. www.henribendel.com.

JEFFREY NEW YORK
449 W. 14th St., between Ninth and Tenth aves. (Subway: A, C, E, or L to 14th St./8th Ave.).

I'll spare the comparisons to Barneys or even Colette in Paris. Jeffrey has done some very interesting things. Architecturally, this is a temple of moderne set in contrast to the grunginess of the surrounding district. There's a live DJ most of the time, and the salespeople have been poached from the best stores in New York and are thus fabulous beyond belief.

Jeffrey carries shoes, accessories, some cosmetics, menswear, and several types of women's clothing for just about any look. Although some of the names are also sold uptown, Jeffrey's stock is in keeping with his taste, and I find his taste much more exciting than uptown sensibilities—he tends to be less safe and take more risks.

This is one of the most exciting stores in New York if you know who you are. If you're just browsing and don't have a finely tuned understanding of the ironies of glamour, the store isn't worth the time it takes to get downtown. Let's pray there are enough people who get it to keep this store thriving. ✆ 212/206-1272.

LORD & TAYLOR
424 Fifth Ave., between 38th and 39th sts. (Subway: B, D, F, or V to 42nd St./Bryant Park).

Lord & Taylor is a very old-fashioned, traditional department store—the last of a dying breed. I often wonder how it has stayed in business, yet like a Timex watch, it keeps on ticking.

The store has incredible promotions at the beginning of each season, plus various sales throughout the year. Furthermore, it is not nearly as large as Macy's, so you won't be overwhelmed. Thus, you can often buy new merchandise in pleasant surroundings at a 25% discount. *Tip:* Lord & Taylor prices sometimes beat the outlet deals, and coupon promotions are often run in the *New York Times,* so you may latch onto a deal simply by reading the newspaper each day. ✆ 212/391-3344. www.lordandtaylor.com.

MACY'S
151 W. 34th St., at Broadway (Subway: B, D, F, N, R, Q, V, or W to 34th St./Herald Sq.).

I'm not sure why there are other stores in New York, or the world. And I'm also not sure how anyone can be strong enough to shop the whole store and even grasp what it has. Because it has everything. This is the largest retail store in America—and one of the largest in the world. It's so big you can get a headache here.

Macy's is two buildings joined together, so the front and the back of the place don't necessarily feel related. The designer floor is pretty good; the kids' floor is great; and the selection of anything, from petites to juniors to cute but inexpensive clothes, is vast.

Check out the mezzanine shops, which are often overlooked—the Metropolitan Museum of Art actually has its own little gift shop up here. Don't miss the Cellar, the down-stairs section devoted to housewares and gourmet food. There's a small shopping area in the basement that I find very inter-esting—great New York souvenirs, including ones that can be purchased from a vending machine. © **212/695-4400.** www. macys.com.

SAKS FIFTH AVENUE
611 Fifth Ave., at 50th St. (Subway: E or V to 5th Ave./ 53rd St.).

Even though there may be a Saks in your hometown, try to visit the Saks in New York. It has expanded its space and glitzed up its store in the past few years to sail into the new century with a modern look that I think is just the right size—not too big, not too small.

In fact, if I personally need something and don't have time to try my bargain resources, or if I just want to shop in one department store to get a feel for what's happening in the world of style, I invariably choose Saks. This is my favorite department store in New York because it's easy and conven-ient. There's a wonderful desk on the first floor that provides free sightseeing information. Best of all, the ladies' room is large and clean, and possesses banquettes, tons of phones, a change machine, and everything except a fax machine. You may find me there.

The fragrance department is world renowned as the best in America and is trying very hard to keep that reputation now that Sephora is across the street. Saks has a special deal with most perfume houses, so it launches new fragrances as soon as they come out. The store also has a variety of unique gift and purchase promotions. Discounts are available through the Palace Hotel and the Drake Hotel.

There's a wonderful cafe for lunch, Cafe SFA, as well as the new Chocolate Bar, which serves upmarket chocolate treats. © **212/753-4000.** www.saksfifthavenue.com.

Zitomer
969 Madison Ave., near 76th St. (Subway: 6 to 77th St.).

Since Zitomer now calls itself a department store, who am I to blow against the wind? The former fancy-pants drugstore now sells children's fashions upstairs and accessories (for people and pets) in the next-door store. The doggy bakery is gone, but the selection of dog accessories is strong—Toffee always has fun here and chooses a toy from the bins on the floor, including a Chewy Vuitton purse, a Coco Chewnel squeaky toy, and a rubber French poodle pal. © 212/737-2016. www.zitomer.com.

FABRICS, NOTIONS, TRIMS & MORE

If you have nerves of steel, you might want to wander in the 200 block of West 40th Street, where all the fabric stores are lined up. The most famous of these is B&J Fabrics, but there are dozens of them; you can get a headache in no time at all. It's great fun.

B&J Fabrics
525 Seventh Ave., at 38th St. (Subway: 1, 2, 3, 7, N, Q, R, or W to Times Sq./42nd St.).

They've moved! The new store is slightly larger than the old one, and everything is on one floor. A Garment District icon, this place can be overwhelming, but a good eye can find the best. Though B & J is primarily a fabric resource, it also sells some trims. © 212/354-8150. www.bandjfabrics.com.

Hyman Hendler & Sons
67 W. 38th St., between Fifth and Sixth aves. (Subway: 1, 2, 3, 7, N, Q, R, Q, or W to Times Sq./42nd St.; or B, D, F, or V to 42nd St./Bryant Park).

So fancy, so special, so much a scene of a New York from days past—this is an old-fashioned ribbon broker, now mostly serving the trade. However, anyone can buy. It's like a museum here—you will go nuts over the colors, the quality, and the possibilities. ✆ 212/840-8393. www.hymanhendler.com.

M&J TRIMMING
1008 Sixth Ave., near 38th St. (Subway: 1, 2, 3, 7, N, Q, R, Q, or W to Times Sq./42nd St.; or B, D, F, or V to 42nd St./ Bryant Park).

This branch of M&J specializes in trims only: buttons, gems, feathers, braids, and other trims of all kinds, as well as all other sorts of fun gewgaws. The walls are lined with cards wrapped with yards of trim. If you buy the whole card, you get a 10% discount. This is where to find your Chanel-style braid. ✆ 212/ 204-9595. www.mjtrim.com.

MOKUBA NEW YORK
55 W. 39th St., between Fifth and Sixth aves. (Subway: 1, 2, 3, 7, N, Q, R, Q, or W to Times Sq./42nd St.; or B, D, F, or V to 42nd St./Bryant Park).

This Japanese ribbon resource, with stores in Paris and Tokyo, is in the same geographic location as Hyman Hendler (see above), but a block over—so I am always confused. Ribbons and trimmings freaks should see them both, although Mokuba tends to be very, very expensive. ✆ 212/869-8900. www. mokubany.com.

TENDER BUTTONS
143 E. 62nd St., between Lexington and Third aves. (Subway: 4, 5, 6, N, R, or W to 59th St./Lexington Ave.).

If it's buttons you need, or even cuff links, this small and wondrous shop can occupy you all day. Even if you don't need buttons, you'd need your marbles examined if you didn't stop by. *Tip:* You can buy Chanel-style buttons here, but you can't buy any fake Chanel buttons or the sorts with the interlocking Cs on them. (If you are missing a genuine Chanel button, take the garment to the boutique and they will give you a missing button if they have it in stock.) ✆ 212/758-7004.

FASHION CHAINS & MULTIPLES

Note: Most of these chains have additional locations throughout the city. Go online, check a phone book, or ask your hotel concierge for a complete selection to find the branch most convenient to you or your hotel.

ABERCROMBIE & FITCH
720 Fifth Ave., at 56th St. (Subway: E or V to 5th Ave./53rd St.; or N, R, or W to 5th Ave./59th St.).

Newly arrived in prime real estate on Fifth Avenue (yes, Fendi used to live here) and fresh from a mall near you, Abercrombie & Fitch must feel that it has it made and can now attract international shoppers with its spiffy new flagship. In order to make sure you don't sing a ho-hum song, the company has gone for a lot of drama and a few big-city twists, making the store a sort of nightclub. There's ample space to show off the must-have uniform of high school and college kids: preppy with a touch of cool; fratty with panache. Abercrombie, if you recall, made it back from nowheresville by presenting a catalog that was banned in Boston and other cities. Now the brand is red hot with teens, and the illicit flourishes are part of the marketing scheme. In truth, the store basically just sells jeans—but then again, there's the attitude and a wannabe lifestyle that goes with it all. ✆ **212/381-0110.** www.abercrombie.com.

ANN TAYLOR
645 Madison Ave., at 60th St. (Subway: 4, 5, 6, N, R, or W to 59th St./Lexington Ave.).

This is specialized retailing at its finest, with private-label merchandise now leading the way for a solid career look. There are also weekend looks, accessories, shoes, and a complete fragrance and bath-and-body line. Additional branches are located all around town, but this is the flagship. Call ✆ **800/DIAL-ANN** for other addresses in Manhattan. ✆ **212/832-9114.** www.anntaylor.com.

ANN TAYLOR LOFT
488 Madison Ave., at 52nd St. (Subway: E or V to 5th Ave./ 53rd St.).

LOFT was Ann Taylor's answer to Gap opening Old Navy—it's a less expensive line that mimics the thought of the real line, but at lower prices and lower quality. I am not impressed, but check it out for yourself. There's a LOFT store in every neighborhood these days, including SoHo (560 Broadway, near Prince St.) and Rockefeller Center (1290 Sixth Ave., near 51st St.); call ✆ **800/DIAL-ANN** for other locations. ✆ **212/308-1129.** www.anntaylorloft.com.

BANANA REPUBLIC
626 Fifth Ave., at 50th St. (Subway: B, D, F, or V to Rockefeller Center).

Banana Republic has been a huge hit ever since the company rebuilt its image as the poor person's Ralph Lauren. This place is all brushed steel and marble floors and glorious lighting. Yes, the lighting helps; this store is a shrine. There are about a dozen branches in the city (call ✆ **888/BR-STYLE** for addresses), but if you're visiting from out of town, the flagship store is the one to gawk at. ✆ **212/974-2350.** www.bananarepublic.com.

CLUB MONACO
6 W. 57th St., between Fifth and Sixth aves. (Subway: E or V to 5th Ave./53rd St.).

This Canadian chain is expanding and moving into the limelight due to its purchase by none other than Ralph Lauren. The firm specializes in translating fashion looks into affordable clothing without doing the cheapie trendy thing. New merchandise comes in every month; the turnover is extraordinary. A firm, solid resource for classic yet hip young things. Other locations include: 520 Broadway (near Spring St.), 121 Prince St. (near Greene St.), 160 Fifth Ave. (near 21st St.), and 1111 Third Ave. (near 65th St.). ✆ **212/459-9863.** www.clubmonaco.com.

EDDIE BAUER

578 Broadway, between Houston and Prince sts. (Subway: R or W to Prince St.).

Who would have ever believed that a Seattle-based store famous for its preppy outdoorsy weekend gear could make it in Manhattan? Eddie Bauer has several stores in town, similar to the ones in your hometown mall. It stocks weekend wear as well as work styles for those prepsters who like conservative clothing, gifts and novelty items, and luggage. A few of the stores have sensational home-furnishings departments. © 212/925-2179. www.eddiebauer.com.

FOREVER 21

40 E. 14th St., between Broadway and University Place. (Subway: 4, 5, 6, L, N, Q, R, or W to 14th St./Union Sq.).

A California chain that I liken to the poor man's H&M (see below)—in other words, very trendy clothes at extremely low prices. There's less for the middle-aged mom here than at H&M, but the style is undeniable. My fave: T-shirts that say "Last night's nightmare: I dreamed I was blonde!" *Note:* Do not confuse with **Century 21.** There's another branch at Herald Square, 50 W. 34th St. © 212/228-0598. www.forever21.com.

GAP

With stores too numerous to list, you're likely to see one every few blocks while walking around Manhattan.

If you are British or French, you'll die laughing when you realize how much you've been overpaying for this merchandise. Furthermore, everyone should know that Gap specializes in moving its stock, so it has very good and very regular sales. You'll see stores in every imaginable neighborhood; call © 800/427-7895 to find the location nearest you. www.gap.com.

H&M

640 Fifth Ave., at 51st St. (Subway: B, D, F, or V to Rockefeller Center).

H&M stands for Hennes & Mauritz, a Swedish firm that has taken New York by storm and now has several stores around Manhattan. This one is the flagship, and it's a great source for men's, women's, and children's clothing inspired by the styles on the catwalks. New merchandise arrives every few weeks, sold at very good prices.

In the last few years, H&M has contracted famed designers to do limited-edition collections. Names such as Karl Lagerfeld and Stella McCartney have attracted around-the-block lines and much pushing and shoving for their store debuts. I have not been overly impressed with the designer collections and prefer the regular old workaday stuff.

Besides the Fifth Avenue flagship, other locations include 1328 Broadway (near 34th St.), 435 Seventh Ave. (near 34th St.), 162 E. 59th St. (near Lexington Ave.), 558 Broadway (near Prince St.), and 515 Broadway (near Spring St.). © 212/489-0390. www.hm.com.

J. CREW
347 Madison Ave., at 45th St. (Subway: 4, 5, 6, 7, or S to Grand Central/42nd St.).

There was a time in recent fashion history when J. Crew ruled the world. Things have been difficult lately, maybe because all the preppies have gotten hip. To compete, the brand has gone more lifestyle and now even does bridal. In addition to the Madison Avenue flagship, there are locations at South Street Seaport (203 Front St.), 99 Prince St. (near Mercer St.), 91 Fifth Ave. (near 17th St.), the Time Warner Center (10 Columbus Circle), and Rock Center (near 50th St.) hidden in the rear. © 212/949-0570. www.jcrew.com.

LACOSTE
134 Prince St., near Wooster St. (Subway: C or E to Spring St.; or R or W to Prince St.).

While I am very impressed by the remarkable comeback of this brand with its little alligator logo, I am also horrified that anyone would pay $65 and up for a polo shirt. Great colors, though, and controlled distribution to enhance the value. A teenage must-have. There are other branches at 608 Fifth Ave., near 49th Street; and 575 Madison Ave., near 56th Street. ✆ **212/226-5019.** www.lacoste.com.

OLD NAVY
150 W. 34th St., between Broadway and Seventh Ave. (Subway: B, D, F, N, Q, R, V, W, 1, 2, or 3 to 34th St.).

My goal in life is to take the Old Navy franchise to France and retire as a zillionaire. One look at the new flagship on West 34th Street and you will forget that this brand started life as the cheapie line from Gap. All of the locations are good, but the flagship is one of the best stores in New York. There's a diner in the basement, too. Other locations include SoHo (503 Broadway, near Spring St.) and Ladies' Mile (610 Sixth Ave., at 18th St.). ✆ **212/594-0049.** www.oldnavy.com.

TALBOTS
525 Madison Ave., near 53rd St. (Subway: E or V to 5th Ave./53rd St.).

TALBOTS MENS
527 Madison Ave., near 53rd St. (Subway: E or V to 5th Ave./53rd St.).

Attention, conservatives, preppies, and traditionalists: This New England company has gone from mail order to retail, and now has stores all over the U.S. The twice-annual sales are the times to stock up. Other Manhattan locations include the Upper West Side (2289 Broadway, near 82nd St.) and South Street Seaport (189 Front St.). Besides its new men's line, Talbots also has kids' stores (1523 Second Ave., near 79th St.) and petites' sections. Call ✆ **800/825-2687** to find the location nearest you. ✆ **212/838-8811.** www.talbots.com.

ZARA

689 Fifth Ave., at 54th St. (Subway: E or V to 5th Ave./53rd St.).

This Spanish chain has been hidden in Manhattan for a decade, with a store across the street from Bloomingdale's, at 750 Lexington Ave. Now, with the success of H&M, Zara has come out of the closet to open a flagship right under Liz Arden. The clothes are moderately priced interpretations of more expensive styles for men, women, and children—for weekend and work. More fashion-forward than Banana Republic, but not as hip as H&M. Other stores are in Midtown (39 W. 34th St., near Fifth Ave.), near Union Square (101 Fifth Ave., near 17th St.), and in SoHo (580 Broadway, near Prince St.). © 212/371-2417. www.zara.com.

FOODSTUFFS

There are entire guidebooks written about food resources (and I don't mean restaurants) in New York. Below are some sources that are part of the tourist experience.

Farmers' Markets

The best of them all is the Union Square **Greenmarket** (Broadway, between 14th and 17th sts.), held on Monday, Wednesday, Friday, and Saturday. The best day is Saturday; see p. 106 for details.

In the West Village, the Saturday-only **GreenFlea P.S. 41** flea market with farmers' market is held at Greenwich Avenue and Charles Street. It's nice but not extraordinary. On Sunday, the action shifts to the **GreenFlea M.S. 44** market on the Upper West Side, at Columbus Avenue and 77th Street. A small greenmarket sells fruits, pies, pretzels, and honey—but nothing to write home about. See p. 268 for details on the Green-Flea markets.

Foodie Neighborhoods

If you are a foodie looking for ethnic markets, you'll want to hop onto the E, F, R, V, or 7 train and jump off at Roosevelt Avenue/Broadway in Jackson Heights, Queens, where you'll find a 1-mile stretch of the United Nations of grocery stores. Just prowl Roosevelt Avenue: It'll change from Irish to Filipino to Colombian to Korean.

If you want to stick to Manhattan, an old standby is what I call the Spice Neighborhood (on Ninth Avenue in the upper 40s), which is home to many Italian markets as well as specialty food shops. Browse. Don't overdress. Here you'll find burlap bags laden with spices and coffee beans. And I'm not talking Starbucks, my dears.

With the arrival of several new chefs in Manhattan and the rebirth of the Columbus Circle area as foodie land, note that the largest Whole Foods in the U.S. is now in the Time Warner Center. Also check out the Union Square area, home to another Whole Foods, the city's first Trader Joe's, and the excellent Greenmarket.

Specialty Markets

New York is a city of foodies, and these are the stores that tide them all over.

AMISH MARKET
240 E. 45th St., between Second and Third aves. (Subway: 4, 5, 6, 7, or S to Grand Central/42nd St.).

This is not an Amish-a hamischa market from Pennsylvania as you may be expecting, but a deli and takeout source with a handful of branches around town. It focuses on high quality and is especially a godsend down in Battery Park City (17 Battery Place, near West St.). Also at 731 Ninth Ave. (near 49th St.) and 53 Park Place (near West Broadway). ✆ **212/370-1761.** www.amishfinefood.com.

BALDUCCI'S
155 W. 66th St., between Broadway and Amsterdam Ave. (Subway: 1 to 66th St./Lincoln Center).

A new version of the old neighborhood market, with branches in the 'burbs as well. Yep, Balducci's has taken over the suburban Hay Day stores. A newer location has opened in the West Village, in the grand old New York Savings Bank building at 81 Eighth Ave. (at 14th St.). © 212/653-8320. www.balduccis.com.

DEAN & DELUCA
560 Broadway, at Prince St. (Subway: R or W to Prince St.).

For the uninitiated, Dean & DeLuca is the dean of fancy food markets, the fanciest of the chic purveyors of things imported and sublime. Need I say it's expensive? In addition to a well-rounded selection of everything you might want to eat, to cook, or to take to go, there's some cookware and a few cookbooks. My problem with Dean & DeLuca is that I've seen the same foodstuffs in other markets for a lot less money, and I won't pay outrageous prices for the privilege of being chic. Nonetheless, it's a landmark, an icon, and a statement in food and fashion.

   Besides the original location in SoHo, Dean & DeLuca has additional stores, including one at 1150 Madison Ave. (near 85th St.); and several cafes, such as at 75 University Place (at 11th St.), 9 Rockefeller Plaza (near 49th St.), and the Time Warner Center (10 Columbus Circle). © 212/226-6800. www.deananddeluca.com.

DYLAN'S CANDY BAR
1011 Third Ave., near 60th St. (Subway: 4, 5, 6, N, R, or W to 59th St./Lexington Ave.).

Maybe no one would care if Dylan weren't Ralph Lauren's daughter. Still, this modern candy shop boasts an old-fashioned soda fountain and two floors of penny-candy–style containers filled with all sorts of goodies. You can also purchase ready-made or custom-created gift baskets. © 646/735-0078. www.dylanscandybar.com.

E.A.T. & E.A.T. GIFTS
1062 and 1064 Madison Ave., between 80th and 81st sts. (Subway: 6 to 77th St.).

E.A.T. is another operation from the famous Eli Zabar food family. This creative branch, consisting of a market, a cafe, and a gift shop, is truly super—it's one of the best destinations in Manhattan. The gift shop is really adorable and filled with items in all price ranges. © 212/772-0022. www.elizabar.com.

FAIRWAY
2127 Broadway, near 74th St. (Subway: 1, 2, or 3 to 72nd St.).

This place is great fun. Best for unusual mushrooms, dried fruits, and cheeses, Fairway is a grocery store with so-so regular produce but great exotics. It also carries many imported foodstuffs. Upstairs is an enormous health-food department and a cafe. Prices range from extravagant to very fair. © 212/595-1888. www.fairwaymarket.com.

FAUCHON
442 Park Ave., at 56th St. (Subway: 4, 5, 6, N, R, or W to 59th St./Lexington Ave.).

Fauchon is the French big brand in gourmet food. The retail shop sells products from France, while the tea salon serves plenty of croissants. © 212/308-5919. www.fauchon.com.

ITO EN
822 Madison Ave., near 69th St. (Subway: 6 to 68th St./Hunter College).

Over 30 kinds of green tea from a supplier who has begun to branch into retail; this is the flagship store. © 212/988-7111. www.itoen.com.

JUAN VALDEZ CAFE
140 E. 57th St., at Lexington Ave. (Subway: 4, 5, 6, N, R, or W to 59th St./Lexington Ave.).

I have not listed the multitudes of Starbucks or even the Illy boutique that opens during Fashion Week, but this one I simply cannot resist. Juan Valdez, as you remember, was a fictional character created to represent coffee growers. Now some smart businessmen are trying to cash in on the coffee craze. But wait, it gets better—this brew is marketed toward those who prefer coffee that's not as strong as what is currently sold in cafes and parlors around America. As we go to press, there are Juan Valdez cafes at Times Square, 1451 Broadway (at 41st St.), and 245 Park Ave. (near 47th St.); watch Juan conquer the world. © 917/289-0981. www.friendsofjuan.com.

OLIVIERS & CO.
Grand Central Terminal, 412 Lexington Ave., at 43rd St., at Graybar Passage (Subway: 4, 5, 6, 7, or S to Grand Central/ 42nd St.).

The same man who created the beauty chain L'Occitane founded O&Co., which features olive oil from all over the world, with an emphasis on Mediterranean sources. This place also sells many French foodstuffs. Prices are twice what they are in France, but if you don't mind spending $36 for a tin of olive oil, you won't be disappointed. There are also branches in the West Village (249 Bleecker St., near Carmine St.) and SoHo (92 Prince St., near Mercer St.). © 212/973-1472. www. oliviersandco.com.

TRADER JOE'S
142 E. 14th St., between Third and Fourth aves. (Subway: 4, 5, 6, L, N, Q, R, or W to 14th St./Union Sq.).

This California chain of food stores has finally come to New York in what is fast becoming one of the foodie havens of the city, Union Square. Not as expensive as a lot of gourmet food stores, and funkier in its choices of fresh and frozen foods. © 212/529-4612. www.traderjoes.com.

WHOLE FOODS
4 Union Sq. S., between Broadway and University Place (Subway: 4, 5, 6, L, N, Q, R, or W to 14th St./Union Sq.; Time Warner Center, 10 Columbus Circle (Subway: A, B, C, D, or 1 to 59th St./Columbus Circle).

Whole Foods is an almost California-style health-food store with far more than just organic chicken breasts. It's a virtual department store, and the shoppers are worth picking over also. Note that two of the stores in Manhattan have had a hand in defining new shopping districts—the Time Warner Center and the revival of Union Square. There's also an older branch in Chelsea (250 Seventh Ave., at 24th St.), plus new locations in the works for TriBeCa (at Greenwich and Warren sts.) and the Lower East Side (at Bowery and Houston St). © 212/673-5388 for Union Square; © 212/823-9600 for Time Warner Center. www.wholefoodsmarket.com.

ZABAR'S
2245 Broadway, at 80th St. (Subway: 1 to 79th St.).

For New York food mavens, this has been a stop for every specialty food and takeout item for decades. Some dry goods and cooking equipment are available as well. Not to be confused with Eli Zabar and his similar (but different) food markets. © 212/787-2000. www.zabars.com.

FURS

The fur business has changed tremendously in recent years; things are suddenly looking up. Now that you're ready to come in from the cold, there are plenty of new facts you can snuggle up to.

I am here to state that I believe in ranched fur; I wear both ranched fur and synthetic fur. If you're ready to turn in your good Republican cloth coat, you should be ready for the thrill of your life—Milan and New York are the fur-wearing cities of the world, and New York is the best place to buy and buy well.

Remember that cheap coats, especially those cheap minks and the $995 specials, are made in Asia and are vastly different from a coat made in Europe or the United States. As mother always said, you generally get what you pay for. As fur moves back into the spotlight, it is quality fur, not mass fur, that makes the grade.

The fur union went to hell in a handbasket a few years ago, and ever since then, there has been such deregulation—much like in the airline industry—that anything goes. You must stay on your toes. The only way to make sure you are getting the kind of quality you deserve is to buy from a reputable furrier. And believe me, the markup in the fur business is on less-expensive coats. The markup on fine skins from a superior wholesale furrier is less than 10%. The real savings in a New York fur-buying spree comes in buying a top-of-the-line coat for $5,500 to $7,500 at wholesale.

It gets trickier and trickier to find out what's going on, since most of the big department stores are now advertising and selling what look like awfully nice mink coats in the $2,000-to-$3,000 price range. Because we tend to trust department stores, we have no way of knowing if these coats are cheapies made in Asia and marked up for profit, or really good buys. And not knowing is reason enough to buy wholesale from a furrier you trust—and avoid the big department stores. And while you're at it, also avoid the mass producers and the warehouse sales held in giant coliseums, hotel ballrooms, and stadiums (if you want quality, anyway). Go for a well-known furrier in the district—Seventh Avenue and west on 30th Street.

A fine mink coat costs more than $995, and while it can go for $3,000 to $5,000, the difference between the coat you get for $5,000 from a department store and the coat you get from a private furrier for the same price is monumental.

As I said before, coats made in Asia are usually not as technically well made as coats made in the U.S. Collars are usually not turned as well, sleeves may be set in very tightly, and the skins themselves are not as fine. European skins are also not as fine as American skins. Note that by European, I do not mean Russian (Russian sable is the best of the best). There are only a certain number of minks being ranched in the United States; the rest come from somewhere else, and you need to know where they are coming from.

In terms of what kind of fur to pick, you do have choices, and the choices change every few years because of the demands of fashion as well as what the breeders have in stock. Mink is the most practical fur—it goes everywhere in style and wears the longest. It's also very lightweight. Longhair furs do not wear nearly so well, and certainly are not meant for rugged, everyday wear over a prolonged number of years. They are also decidedly passé, although there is a growing trend to bring back fox. Sheared beaver is a good choice if you aren't buying mink. Shearling coats are big for casual wear and weekends. Aside from mink, beaver, and shearling, there is renewed interest in broadtail, broadtail with sable trim, and especially brown broadtail, which is much harder to find than black. Cashmere coats trimmed with mink or sable are also very in now. Last, but not least, is the category of knitted fur—an invention that came out of Canada and is done with beaver. This is extremely chic, especially in a short-length coat in a fabulous fashion color. A car coat in knitted beaver costs about $3,000 wholesale.

If your education in mink took place years ago, you may be in for a shock. Most of what you thought was important is outdated. The new realities:

- Do not confuse the names of colors with trade names such as Blackglama. Some people will try to tell you that a similar name means the same thing. Blackglama also happens to be very out at the moment, but that's another story.

- Forget all that stuff you learned about "fully let-out skins"—the new trend is called "skin on skin"; it looks more like patchwork.
- If you are looking at fully let-out coats, ask how old they are. The value of a fur coat is directly related to how old it is because the skins dry out each year.
- Dyed fur used to be considered a bad thing—one you pounced upon as a reason not to buy a specific coat. Now it's common, even in natural tones, and is not considered a reason to avoid a sale. Often chemicals (if not dyes) are used to enhance or enrich the color and tone of the natural fur. It's the same thing you do to your hair every 6 weeks.
- Italian hippie looks, inspired years ago by the work of the Fendi sisters, are out—don't invest in them now. Coats are more classic—slimmer and closer to the body. Swing lengths are on the way out. Fringes, studs, flapping tails, and doo-dads are definitely not worth investing in.
- The real news in mink, especially in plucked mink, is color. People considering traditional mink coats think of black and brown shades. Here's the big shocker: Dark is out, light is in. Honey tones are the must-have of the future. Also in: Bright color. Rich color. It's absolutely fabulous.

Please note that semantics are everything in this business; furriers who sell "sheared" mink sell a product that is inferior to "plucked" mink—and don't let anyone tell you it's the same process. Shearing is bad for the remaining fur and breaks down the hide in a way that plucking doesn't. You don't ask, you don't get.

If you are buying traditional mink (not plucked), examine it carefully. Silkiness counts in mink; if the hairs are spiky, long, or coarse, they will wear out. Look at the underfur, which should be dense and thick. A good mink coat should be practically indestructible. Roll it in a ball and watch the hairs jump back. If the coat doesn't perform, jump away from the sale.

Don't forget fur-lined raincoats or the possibility of having your old mink coat made into a fur-lined raincoat, which is what I did. It costs about $3,000: Your old coat is dressed and plucked and pieced together with quilted parts to keep the coat warm but lightweight. Fur collar and cuffs show, while the rest of the fur is inside. You can choose whatever shell you want; I picked an Italian microfiber.

Do not ask a furrier to send an empty box to the home of an out-of-state relative so you can avoid paying New York sales tax. Tacky, tacky.

There are retail stores that sell used furs in Manhattan, and used furs are also sold at upscale charity shops. The problem with a used fur is that you have no idea just how old it is and how it's been cared for. Buy with care. A fur coat loses most of its value in its first few years of life because the skins dry out. The only way to tell what condition a coat is in is to open the seams and have a furrier evaluate the pelts.

Superior Furs

Cheap fur looks great until you put it next to quality fur; then you get the idea that quality pays. If you can afford a quality fur, you'll never be sorry. A superior mink coat will give you 10 to 20 years of superior wear, looking just about as good as new for the first 10 years. A quality mink coat should be female skins, which are lighter than male skins, and wear better. Most mass-produced coats are made of male skins. A quality fur should be ranched in the United States and made in the United States—by someone you trust.

Although there are a half-dozen famous furriers in the Fur District, most of whom take customers with references, I am going to give you the name of only one. This maker is top of the line, has a private showroom, and is not open for browsers—it is interested in people who are actually in the market for a fur coat. You don't have to buy, but the idea is that you don't wander in, touch the furs, and leave. If you want a $2,500 mink coat, this is not for you. If you want a $12,000 mink coat for $5,500 to $7,500, see below for your new best friend.

CORNICHE FURS & LUXURY OUTERWEAR

345 Seventh Ave., at 30th St., 20th floor (Subway: 1 to 28th St.).

To get a quick grasp on how the fur business has changed, note that this old faithful resource now prides itself on "luxury outerwear," though the business is still at the hands of Leonard Kahn. If the name sounds slightly familiar, it could be because Ben Kahn is one of the world's most famous furriers. Leonard Kahn is his nephew.

While Leonard has been in the fur business for decades, the business he is in now is relatively new, and his products are very new and hot; in fact, he is always bragging that they have the youngest team in the business. Their business is mostly wholesale—they make coats for big-name designer labels like Bob Mackie and for department stores (no names, please), but they also sell to some private customers like you and me.

Yes, Leonard will sell you a traditional mink coat or a not-so-traditional mink coat in honey tones that reverses to suede. Yes, Leonard will take your old out-of-fashion mink and turn it into a raincoat or, better yet, pluck it and make it something fabulous. More important, Leonard and his team will now make a silk/micropore shell, or sell you a fur-trimmed cashmere coat, or come up with any number of ways to keep you warm and chic without draping you head-to-toe in minks.

Your options are many: Buy an already made-up coat, design your own coat, or work with Leonard's designers to get a custom coat with products shipped from Europe. If you are a special size, this option is especially convenient. A custom mink coat will be about $8,000 to $10,000, yet the one I've just fallen in love with—a skin-on-skin, light-as-a-feather, honey-colored reversible job that goes to suede on the other side—is a mere $7,500. I'm saving up.

Coats off the rack are less expensive than custom-made, and there are sales. A jacket is less than a coat, of course. A cashmere trench-style coat with a plucked mink collar and cuffs and nutria lining costs about $3,500; a shearling coat ranges from $1,450 on up, depending on quality—the reversible ones cost about $2,250.

Note: Every January there is a sale, and the prices are so low you will weep from greed and delight.

I trust Leonard Kahn 100% and I send you here knowing you will get the best deal in New York. Call for an appointment; serious shoppers only: © 212/564-1735.

HANDBAGS

Even in New York, a woman is first judged by her handbag, then her shoes, and then her hands (watch and manicure). So think about these tips:

- If you're looking for a moderately priced handbag, one of the department stores is your best bet.
- All the big-name European leather-goods stores that carry shoes also sell handbags. These include **Bottega Veneta, Fendi, Ferragamo, Gucci,** and **Prada.** I must say that sale times in these big-name shops may make the goods seem fairly priced.
- For something different, check out the little-known Euro names such as **Anya Hindmarch** (described below).
- All discount sources sell handbags; often they carry name-brand handbags. Try **Daffy's** (p. 286)—especially its location at 125 E. 57th St. (between Park and Lexington aves.)—which often has a good selection of leather goods. **Loehmann's** (p. 288) can be good, too.
- There are a few sources on the Lower East Side that will sell or even order big-name handbags at a 20% discount. I really haven't found it worth the trouble, but many do. **Fine & Klein** (p. 127) is the most famous; it's closed on Saturday.
- During big sale seasons, bags are likely to be marked down 50% . . . except at Vuitton, which never marks down merchandise. If you want a big-name bag and aren't picky about which name, check out **Bergdorf Goodman** or **Saks** during sale season.

- A few upmarket stores sell what look like designer bags without the labels. They usually cost $500 instead of $1,500. Phew.

ANYA HINDMARCH
29 E. 60th St., near Madison Ave. (Subway: 4, 5, 6, N, R, or W to 59th St./Lexington Ave.).

I am conflicted about stores like this—the designs are creative, but the prices are over-the-top, and while I am not against expensive handbags, these are so trendy that they date themselves rapidly. Note that during sales, prices are actually lower than in London. There's a second location in SoHo (115 Greene St., near Spring St.). ✆ **212/750-3974.** www.anyahindmarch.com.

BULGARI
730 Fifth Ave., at 57th St. (Subway: F to 57th St.).

To bring in the young crowd, this store has launched seasonal collections of handbags, mostly in leather. ✆ **212/315-9000.** www. zbulgari.com.

CROUCH & FITZGERALD
400 Madison Ave., near 48th St. (Subway: E or V to 5th Ave./53rd St.).

A new owner has reinvented this store, made it smaller but redirected it, and brought it back as a strong resource for business luggage, travel gear, and tote bags for working women. There's a good combination of name brands mixed among the house brand, which is made in Europe. The emphasis is on the kind of handbags that can contain everything for travel; there's also the **Sherpa Shop** (p. 201) for doggy accessories. ✆ **212/755-5888.** www.crouchandfitzgerald.com.

DOONEY & BOURKE
20 E. 60th St., between Madison and Park aves. (Subway: 4, 5, 6, N, R, or W to 59th St./Lexington Ave.).

Dooney & Bourke—in new digs—is no longer preppy or simple. It has a logo print that is very popular, as well as, every now and then, a leather handbag that is so chic, so stylish, and so hot that I drool thinking about it. The latest fad is logo denim. © 212/223-7444. www.dooney.com.

J. S. Suarez
450 Park Ave., at 57th St. (Subway: 4, 5, 6, N, R, or W to 59th St./Lexington Ave.).

Suarez uses factories in Italy to ship designer-like goods that aren't copies and don't have designer labels. Prices are not low, but they are less than in the big-name stores. This is the most famous discount source in New York for shoes, bags, and small leather goods. Discount is a relative term, however. Frankly, I find the prices very high—about $600 for a leather handbag, possibly more, maybe a little less. Of course, these are the same bags you'd pay double for if they had their designer logos on them. © 212/753-3758.

Kate Spade
454 Broome St., at Mercer St. (Subway: R or W to Prince St.).

Some say she's passé, others say hurray. Whatever your viewpoint, a small empire is definitely being built on "cute" handbags with a preppy-cum-bohemian appeal. Now there's lifestyle looks as well as **Kate Spade Baby** (p. 157). © 212/274-1991. www.katespade.com.

Kieselstein-Cord
132 Prince St., at West Broadway (Subway: C or E to Spring St., or R or W to Prince St.).

From animal-shaped belt buckles to eyewear to handbags with feet, these distinctive (and pricey) designs are now even being copied in Hong Kong. Look for the lizard, frog, or horse-hoof belt buckles as the biggest status symbol this side of a $500 pair of shades. © 212/529-9622. www.kieselstein-cord.com.

LANA MARKS
645 Madison Ave., near 60th St. (Subway: 4, 5, 6, N, R, or W to 59th St./Lexington Ave.).

The bags here begin around $1,000 (more often $4,000–$6,000). They exist as much as financial statements and icons to those in the know as Kleenex and lipstick holders. Styles are classic yet cutting edge. The colors of leather are remarkable; you should go just to stare. ✆ 212/355-6135. www.lanamarks.com.

LULU GUINNESS
394 Bleecker St., near W. 11th St. (Subway: A, C, E, or L to 14th St./8th Ave.).

This British designer creates handbags that are whimsical enough to make you smile—pots of flowers, tiny storefronts, and dress-up minibags for nights on the town. ✆ 212/367-2120. www.luluguinness.com.

TIFFANY & CO.
727 Fifth Ave., at 57th St. (Subway: F to 57th St.).

Yes, this is the same Tiffany & Co. you've come to count on for diamonds by the yard and boxes colored robin's-egg blue. Now it has handbags, too. The really ritzy evening bags cost thousands of dollars, but you can buy a simpler bag, in leather, for around $400 to $500. ✆ 212/755-8000. www.tiffany.com.

HIP & HOT
....

APC
131 Mercer St., between Prince and Spring sts. (Subway: R or W to Prince St.).

With only a few stores in the world, APC is a true cult clothing shop, known for the cut of its basics. (Do not confuse it with **APOC,** which stands for Issey Miyake's "A Piece of Cloth.") ✆ **212/966-9685.** www.apc.fr.

AUTO
805 Washington St., between Horatio and Gansevoort sts. (Subway: A, C, E, or L to 14th St./8th Ave.).

This Meatpacking District shop offers industrial design for the home and office; it's the talk of the town since it gives you some place other than Jeffrey (p. 162) to see when you come to this part of Manhattan. ✆ **212/229-2292.** www.thisisauto.com.

INTERMIX
125 Fifth Ave., near 19th St. (Subway: 4, 5, 6, L, N, Q, R, or W to 14th St./Union Sq.).

Don't let the multiple addresses throw you—this is less a chain than an idea whose time has come: hot stuff from cutting-edge designers in all price ranges. Sizes tend to run small; prices run moderate. Some accessories. Other locations are at 98 Prince St. (near Mercer St.), 365 Bleecker St. (near Charles St.), 210 Columbus Ave. (near 68th St.), and 1003 Madison Ave. (near 77th St.). ✆ **212/533-9720.** www.intermixonline.com.

MAYLE
242 Elizabeth St., between Houston and Prince sts. (Subway: 6 to Spring St.; or R or W to Prince St.).

The trendy one in the family is no longer her dad, Peter. Jane is becoming known not only for her store, but also for her lifestyle. She is often seen with the "in" crowd wearing her snappy designs. ✆ **212/625-0406.**

PUMA BLACK STORE
421 W. 14th St., near Washington St. (Subway: A, C, E, or L to 14th St./8th Ave.).

This Meatpacking District shop features the designer division of Puma, with shoes, clothes, and active sports gear. Considered awesome by those who use words like that. ✆ 212/206-0109. www.puma.com.

SCOOP
1275 Third Ave., near 73rd St. (Subway: 6 to 77th St.).

This place is small and hip and filled with trendy clothing and accessories for fashionistas. There are additional branches in the Meatpacking District (430 W. 14th St.) and SoHo (532 Broadway). ✆ 212/535-5577. www.scoopnyc.com.

THEORY
230 Columbus Ave., near 71st St. (Subway: 1, 2, 3, B, or C to 72nd St.).

No fashionista worth her Jimmy Choos would admit to not knowing the Theory line, this year's flavor of the must-have kind. The clothes are sometimes simple to look at, but the line has a great fit and specializes in fitting tiny women (it goes down to a size 00). If you're going to Woodbury Common (p. 297), don't miss the Theory and Theory Men's outlets. ✆ 212/362-3676. www.theory.com.

JEANS

All department stores carry a bevy of choices, but specialty stores are holding their own in the new- and used-jeans markets, and denim purists are quick to point out that designer jeans pale when compared to **Levi's.** About 50% of shoppers looking for jeans in New York want to buy Levi's; many Europeans come to the U.S. with a list of Levi's style numbers and sizes for friends and family members back home. Unfortunately, they never realize that the choices in denim, throughout the city, are almost endless. Those in the market for Levi's should see the Original Levi's Store, described below.

CHIP & PEPPER
250 Mulberry St., near Prince St. (Subway: 6 to Spring St.; or R or W to Prince St.).

Another L.A.-based jeans company, now open in Nolita to sell you the look. Chip & Pepper does custom jeans that can be created from vintage fabrics. ✆ **212/343-4220.** www.chipand pepper.com.

DIESEL
770 Lexington Ave., at 60th St. (Subway: 4, 5, 6, N, R, or W to 59th St./Lexington Ave.).

This place has Italian jeans known to fit the butt, plus other fashions and trends as well. The superstore near Bloomingdale's has jeans, jeans, and more jeans, including made-to-order pairs. There are downtown flagships, too, at Union Square (1 Union Sq. W., at 14th St.) and in SoHo (135 Spring St., near Greene St.), as well as the Diesel Denim Gallery (68 Greene St., near Spring St.), Diesel Kids (416 West Broadway, near Spring St.), and an outlet store at Woodbury Common (p. 297). ✆ **212/308-0055.** www.diesel.com.

AN EARNEST CUT & SEW
821 Washington St., near Gansevoort St. (Subway: A, C, E, or L to 14th St./8th Ave.).

I buy Lee Slim jeans whenever I can find them and usually for less than $10 a pair. They make me feel 30 years young and look 20 pounds lighter. I have no need for expensive jeans, although I understand the concept.

I can't quite understand paying several hundred dollars for a pair of jeans, let alone even more than that, but I do grasp the idea of denim made to custom-fit and provide just the right lift and give in just the right places. This concept store show-cases the Earnest Sewn line, which was created by the founder of cult brand Paper Denim & Cloth. You can choose the style and the fabric, the thread and all the accessory details; then you're measured, and a pair of jeans is custom-made for you while you wait (several hours).

Note that the store sells more than jeans and is a sort of hangout for the cool in the Meatpacking District; you can sip coffee and read books while you wait for your jeans to be stitched. ✆ **212/242-3414.** www.earnestsewn.com.

LUCKY BRAND JEANS
38 Greene St., between Broome and Grand sts. (Subway: 6 to Spring St.).

Wall-to-wall denim, with other branch stores dotted around town. Also on the Upper East Side (1151 Third Ave., at 67th St.) and near Union Square (172 Fifth Ave., at 22nd St.); there's an outlet at Woodbury Common (p. 297) as well. ✆ **212/625-0707.** www.luckybrandjeans.com.

OMG
678 Broadway, near W. 3rd St. (Subway: B, D, F, or V to Broadway/Lafayette St.; or 6 to Bleecker St.); multiple other locations.

This is like a jeans warehouse for new merchandise. ✆ **212/979-1977.**

ORIGINAL LEVI'S STORE
750 Lexington Ave., near 60th St. (Subway: 4, 5, 6, N, R, or W to 59th St./Lexington Ave.).

Levi's opened its first New York store across the street from Bloomingdale's. The "Original" is a large and excellent shopper's delight. There's another location at 536 Broadway (near Spring St.), plus an outlet at Woodbury Common (p. 297) as well. ✆ **212/826-5957.** www.levis.com.

JEWELRY

....

Jewelry shopping in New York, as in any other place in the world—big city or small—is a matter of trust. The big, fancy jewelers exist not only because their designs are so irresistible, but also because the house has provided years (maybe centuries) of trust. True, every now and then you hear about a trusted jeweler of 50 years going to the slammer for passing off bottoms of Coke bottles as emeralds. But it's rare.

The big-name New York jewelers, whether they are American, South American, or European, have no such scandals attached to them. I'm ready to stake my reputation on their big reputations. That's why I recommend the big stores. Yes, you pay top-of-the-line prices, but you get something very worthwhile: reliability. Never be afraid to walk into a big-name fancy jeweler; you needn't be in the market for a $106,000 bracelet to be a customer. You may find something for as little as $50; surely you will find many choices at $500. How you are treated is a function of how well dressed you are and how you demand to be treated. Some places pride themselves on having a fancy name but being accessible to regular people like us; **Tiffany & Co.** is one of those places. They don't want you to come for breakfast, but they do want you to buy something as a souvenir of your trip to New York.

The reliability of the big jewelers is also related to resale. You can always sell a piece of jewelry made by a status firm, such as **Tiffany, Cartier,** and **Harry Winston.** No matter how old it is, a genuinely fine piece of jewelry from a trusted house is a good investment. It may even appreciate over the years. It will hold value for auction or resale and be the kind of thing your heirs fight to inherit. As my old friend Hans Stern, internationally famous jeweler, explained to me: "Buying from a well-known jeweler is like buying a painting. You are paying for the quality of the art as well as the quality and the reputation of the signature." Some people buy paintings because they like the picture and don't care if it has value; other people go to the big dealers and buy signed works by renowned artists so they can trust their purchase. This is a personal choice.

There is a jewelry district on 47th Street between Fifth and Sixth avenues, and you are welcome to shop there. You may find many wonderful things. The prices will be better than at **Van Cleef,** for sure. However, like all other businesses, insiders run the jewelry business. Strangers off the street can, and do, get taken. Industrial-grade diamonds may be sold to you; and color-enhanced stones may be touted as the best money can buy—irradiated stones will not give you cancer, but they may not be what you had in mind. Dealers know what they are doing; I do not. Consider yourself warned. If you want fun, go to the Diamond District. If you want safety, go to a trusted jeweler.

Tip: It pays to know something about what you are doing, but you can have a perfectly good time and walk away satisfied even if you don't know what you are doing. Remember that fun and big-time investments are two different things.

Faux jewelry is, of course, socially acceptable. It's always been worn, but fewer people used to talk about it, that's all. Almost all important jewels are copied—to fool the burglar. Even Elizabeth Taylor has admitted that there are paste copies of her gem collection. Cheap faux often looks blatantly fake—the gold is too brassy, the gems are lackluster, the fittings are not fine. If you plan on passing off your collection as something related to the crown jewels, choose carefully and pay the extra money. A good fake necklace will probably cost $300; good fake earrings may be $50 to $100. If you want a bad copy of a good watch, they are currently sold on every street corner for about $25. A good eye can see that the watches are too thick to be real. These same watches, by the way, cost $10 on Canal Street, but their reliability is obviously not ensured.

Used and antique jewelry can be bought at auctions, in certain jewelry shops, and in antiques shops. But even earrings from the 1950s are pricey these days, so have a good eye and know what you are buying. For old and used watches, check out **Aaron**

Faber (666 Fifth Ave., near 53rd St.), and **Tourneau** (12 E. 57th St., at Madison Ave.), which has a retro department.

As for contemporary jewelry, sterling silver with semiprecious gemstones is a great look; it's also immensely affordable. Tiffany sells this look, and many smaller boutiques have come to specialize in it. **David Yurman** (729 Madison Ave., at 64th St.) has become famous for his combinations of silver and gold.

Big Names

New York is famous for big-name jewelers, from Americans to international names from around the world. While luxury is more in style than ever before (at least since the Depression), one of the most interesting trends is that these big names are cultivating a younger image and offering affordable items to bring you into the family. **Bulgari** has recently added silks, handbags, and sunglasses to its range and opened a store on Madison Avenue that's meant to be less intimidating than its spiffed-up and really-drop-dead Fifth Avenue rehab. **Hans Stern,** my Brazilian buddy, has turned most of his business over to his sons, who have retooled the Fifth Avenue store and come up with a very kicky gimmick—the rings have stars cut into the undersides of the gold. A dazzling notion! All of New York sparkles a little bit more now that we have more options and a range that suits more budgets.

BULGARI
730 Fifth Ave., at 57th St. (Subway: F to 57th St.).
© **212/315-9000.** www.bulgari.com.

783 Madison Ave., near 67th St. (Subway: 6 to 68th St./Hunter College).
© **212/717-2300.** www.bulgari.com.

CARTIER
653 Fifth Ave., near 52nd St. (Subway: E or V to 5th Ave./53rd St.).
© **212/753-0111.** www.cartier.com.

*828 Madison Ave., at 69th St. (Subway: 6 to 68th St./
Hunter College).*
℗ 212/472-6400. www.cartier.com.

DAVID YURMAN
*729 Madison Ave., at 64th St. (Subway: 4, 5, 6, N, R, or W
to 59th St./Lexington Ave.).*
℗ 212/752-4255. www.davidyurman.com.

HARRY WINSTON
718 Fifth Ave., at 56th St. (Subway: F to 57th St.).
℗ 212/245-2000. www.harrywinston.com.

H. STERN
*645 Fifth Ave., near 52nd St. (Subway: E or V to 5th Ave./
53rd St.).*
℗ 212/688-0300. www.hstern.net.

TIFFANY & CO.
727 Fifth Ave., at 57th St. (Subway: F to 57th St.).
℗ 212/755-8000. www.tiffany.com.

VAN CLEEF & ARPELS
744 Fifth Ave., at 57th St. (Subway: F to 57th St.).
℗ 212/644-9500. www.vancleef.com.

A Discounter

FORTUNOFF
*681 Fifth Ave., at 54th St. (Subway: E or V to 5th Ave./
53rd St.).*

You name it, they've got it—from pearls to diamonds to gold
to precious to semiprecious; from sterling to wear on your ears
to sterling to eat with; and even some modern high-fashion
pieces. But to be frank, I think there's something lacking in these
styles. Maybe the designs are just too ordinary. However, lots
of people shop here for a bargain—and like it.

This store is not as sophisticated as I would like, but it's a good source for discounted basics such as pearls, simple contemporary gold earrings, chains, silverware, and the like. Don't forget to go upstairs. For antique jewelry buffs, look left when you walk in the door for the estate department.

For those who have been working the Diamond District, come with your pen and paper and don't be shy. I was set to buy a pair of seashell earrings (don't ask) at a discount source in the district for $750, which I considered quite good. Then I found a similar pair at Fortunoff for $550. The pair at Fortunoff was not as well made as the pair I wanted, but they made me lose faith in my original jeweler. Don't buy from any no-name jewelry source until you have at least educated your eye and your budget at Fortunoff. © 212/758-6660. www.fortunoff.com.

Midrange Midas

JADED
1048 Madison Ave., near 80th St. (Subway: 6 to 77th St.).

Awash in a sea of jewels, Manhattan also has an ocean of imitations out there. For the rare piece that is part faux and part art (original creations that are not made with precious stones), stop by Jaded, where the designs are private label and the action is uptown. This is the classiest faux in town.

Prices range from $60 to $100 for earrings, but the workmanship is excellent and the pieces are unique. This is the "in" place for the Ladies Who Lunch who want to look fashionable and yet different. If you're looking to make just one Manhattan splurge that defines the essence of New York, this could be the place. © 212/288-6631. www.jadedjewels.com.

K. C. THOMPSON
987 Madison Ave., near 77th St. (Subway: 6 to 77th St.).

This small store is as much like a pastry shop as a jewelry boutique. The insides are bright pink; everything seems to be a bonbon. The jewelry is of the chunky semiprecious school when it comes to most necklaces; there are a few simpler things, but the look makes a statement and is both chic and classic. Prices begin at $1,000, but the average is $2,500. ☎ 212/396-0974. www.kcthompsonny.com.

REINSTEIN/ROSS
29 E. 73rd St., near Madison Ave. (Subway: 6 to 77th St.); 122 Prince St., between Wooster and Greene sts. (Subway: C or E to Spring St.; or R or W to Prince St.).

I think I like this firm because it does a look that is similar to Elizabeth Gage of London; the rings are made of brushed gold in 18 or 22 karat and often have unusual stones in them. The look is sort of neoclassical baroque, although you can also find a more or less traditional gold wedding band inset with little sparkle diamonds. I'm the kind that prefers the white and yellow diamonds, the orange and yellow sapphires, and so on. ☎ 212/772-1901 for uptown location; ☎ 212/226-4513 for SoHo location. www.reinsteinross.com.

Fancy Fauxs

GALE GRANT
485 Madison Ave., near 52nd St. (Subway: E or V to 5th Ave./53rd St.).

Avoid this place at lunch hour, when every other chic woman in New York is trying to buy her fakes. Some of it sparkles a bit too much, but you can get great costume jewelry and some fabulous imitations here. One of my spies was recently in the store, musing over a necklace that might or might not work with a specific dress for an upcoming Important Event. The owner suggested she take the necklace and mark it, then return it to the store to have a new one strung to her exact needs within 48 hours. Now that's service! ☎ 212/752-3142. www.gale grant.com.

MARIKO
998 Madison Ave., between 77th and 78th sts. (Subway: 6 to 77th St.).

See p. 133. ✆ **212/472-1176.**

RENE
1007 Madison Ave., near 77th St. (Subway: 6 to 77th St.).

See p. 133. ✆ **212/327-3912.**

MATERNITY
....

Even when apparel sales were in the dumps, maternity wear was booming. Besides the specialty shops below, check out www.gap.com for Gap's new maternity line.

LIZ LANGE MATERNITY
958 Madison Ave., near 75th St. (Subway: 6 to 77th St.).

This is the most sophisticated of the New York maternity boutiques; she now does a line for Target, too. ✆ **212/879-2191.** www.lizlange.com.

MATERNITY WORKS
16 W. 57th St., between Fifth and Sixth aves., 3rd floor. (Subway: F to 57th St.).

I spotted this store from the street; you will see its ad in the windows above and become desperately curious. It's scary going up, but a good resource for all basics. Prices are very low. ✆ **212/399-9840.** www.maternitymall.com.

MIMI MATERNITY
360 Madison Ave., near 45th St. (Subway: 4, 5, 6, 7, or S to Grand Central/42nd St.).

Offering a more suburban look, Mimi Maternity stores are carefully placed in wealthy residential districts as well as the city's financial districts for working women. Other locations include inside the Destination Maternity flagship (575 Madison Ave., at 57th St.) and on the Upper West Side (2005 Broadway, near 69th St.); call © **877/646-4666** for more addresses. © **212/697-0482**. www.mimimaternity.com.

A PEA IN THE POD
Destination Maternity, 575 Madison Ave., at 57th St. (Subway: E or V to 5th Ave./53rd St.).

This is a chain of moderately priced maternity-wear shops that specialize in fashion, style, and a bit of hip humor for those expecting. The flagship has everything from clothes for work to wedding duds. © **212/588-0220**. www.apeainthepod.com.

MENSWEAR

There's no question that Manhattan is the men's shopping capital of America. Furthermore, it's one of the few cities where there is so much bargain merchandise that even a man who hates to shop will be astonished by the opportunities to save. International businessmen and dignitaries, step this way. Special-size men, turn to p. 206; New York is your place, too.

Almost every man who lives in New York (and many who have just visited) has been to **Barneys** and has an opinion about it. Barneys is surely the most famous men's store in New York. Some men exclaim that they need no other store in Manhattan.

If you still want more, stroll the area I call Men's Mad—Madison Avenue in the mid-40s—where there is a cluster of men's shops (most of them famous names), many of which specialize in conservative business attire. This is where you find your **Brooks Brothers, Paul Stuart, Jos. A. Banks,** and more.

For those willing to go for the gusto and get in some discount shopping, see p. 284.

ALFRED DUNHILL

711 Fifth Ave., at 54th St. (Subway: E or V to 5th Ave./ 53rd St.).

The shop for the man who has everything, can't stand to shop, and wants to drop in at "his" store to fulfill his needs for suits, accessories, and smokes. Very much a private club. © 212/753-9292. www.dunhill.com.

ASCOT CHANG

7 W. 57th St., between Fifth and Sixth aves. (Subway: F to 57th St.).

Ascot Chang is a famous institution in Hong Kong and, indeed, around the world. He is one of the world's best-known and best-loved shirt makers. Now he's come to New York (well, his son has) to open a more conveniently located shop for those who know how comfortable a custom shirt can be. Prices are higher than in Hong Kong, but not unreasonable—you'll pay about $75 for a custom shirt. (It's $30 in Hong Kong.) The shop also has ready-made shirts, as well as made-to-measure; you can choose from about 2,000 fabrics. Women's shirts are not available ready-made as in Hong Kong, but can be custom-ordered. There are also suits, suspenders, ties, tennis togs, and the usual apparel for a well-dressed gent. © 212/759-3333. www.ascotchang.com.

BARNEYS NEW YORK

660 Madison Ave., at 61st St. (Subway: 4, 5, 6, N, R, or W to 59th St./Lexington Ave.).

The Madison Avenue men's store connects to the main part of the store on the first floor only (look for the doorway behind the fragrance counter). You then go up escalator after escalator to layers of men's tailoring, a boxing ring, various health and grooming services, and furnishings. © 212/826-8900. www.barneys.com.

BERGDORF GOODMAN MEN

745 Fifth Ave., at 58th St. (Subway: N, R, or W to 5th Ave./ 59th St.).

I don't know how this store has stayed in business: It is gorgeous and wonderful and special and filled with designer names but, alas, few customers. I think Bergdorf's should just call it a museum and charge admission. This is where the Masters of the Universe shop for the ultimate in power dressing for meetings, weekends, bedroom, boardroom, and even bathroom. Check out the cafe upstairs for a quick bite. © 212/753-7300. www.bergdorfgoodman.com.

BROOKS BROTHERS

346 Madison Ave., at 44th St. (Subway: 4, 5, 6, 7, or S to Grand Central/42nd St.). Also 666 Fifth Ave., at 53rd St. (Subway: E or V to 5th Ave./53rd St.).

It's not that I'm a traditionalist, a conservative dresser, or anything old-fashioned or uptight, but, I'm sorry to say that I don't get it when it comes to the new Brooks Brothers on Fifth Avenue. I mean, I understand it conceptually—a young, modern, hip store to lure in young customers and convert them to a brand that has a reputation for being old-fashioned. Great. It's just that the new store leaves me bored.

Go see for yourself. It carries men's and women's clothing, mostly for the workplace. Note that the clothes and the look are not the same as those at the regular store on Madison Avenue where, thankfully, little has changed.

You can tell a proper Brooks Brothers suit by the square boxy cut, which is why it's a uniform for a certain kind of businessman. The cut is also great on an American body, a large man, or a man with a little extra weight on him.

Brooks Brothers does a steady business in these ultraconservative, always-correct suits, but this is actually a better store for sportswear and casual clothes. It does have boys' and women's departments as well—in fact, it has beefed up the latter in hopes of making a major statement in women's career clothing.

There's also a factory outlet at Woodbury Common (p. 297). © 212/682-8800 for Madison Avenue; © 212/261-9440 for Fifth Avenue. www.brooksbrothers.com.

JOS. A. BANK
366 Madison Ave., at 46th St. (Subway: 4, 5, 6, 7, or S to Grand Central/42nd St.).

This is a Boston retailer with a look that's very similar to Brooks Brothers, but at lower prices. The store isn't very big or splashy, but for conservative dressers looking for traditional clothing, this amounts to almost a price war. © 212/370-0600. www.josabank.com.

PETS

CANINE STYLES
43 Greenwich Ave., between Charles and Perry sts. (Subway: A, C, E, or L to 14th St./8th Ave.).

This small but chic boutique serves cat and dog owners. It's where I found a Statue of Liberty toy and a polka-dot collar for my dog. Oh yes, I think I also bought pet aromatherapy, but don't tell anyone. © 212/352-8591. www.caninestyles.com.

PETCO
860 Broadway, at 17th St. (Subway: 4, 5, 6, L, N, Q, R, or W to 14th St./Union Sq.); multiple other locations.

This is a superstore that sells pets (urrrgh) and tons of pet supplies; you can join its club and save 10% on some purchases. © 212/358-0692. www.petco.com.

THE SHERPA SHOP
Crouch & Fitzgerald, 400 Madison Ave., near 48th St. (Subway: E or V to 5th Ave./53rd St.).

This is the place for fabulous doggy gear—totes and carrying bags and travel items, all at prices around $100 for big and fancy, $50 for small and easy to schlep. The quality of the bags is so high that there is now a cult surrounding them, and the brand name Sherpa is fast becoming generic. The line is also sold in most pet stores and pet chains, but this is the mother shop. Approved by airlines. ✆ 212/755-5888. www.crouchand fitzgerald.com.

SEX TOYS

Sex toys have really come out of the closet in the last year or two. While the Ricky's beauty-supply chain seems to have dropped its Adults Only department, most drugstores now carry a wide range of products and even toys. What's more, designer sex toys are now readily available, along with a new range of condoms and accessories designed specifically for women and called Elexa, made by the friendly guys who brought us Trojans (if you're shy, you can buy online at www.cvs.com).

CONDOMANIA
351 Bleecker St., between Charles and W. 10th sts. (Subway: 1 to Christopher St./Sheridan Sq.).

Believe it or not, this store has great gift ideas, even souvenirs from New York. While the main, uh, thrust, is on condoms, there are many unique and adorable gift items. "Plastics, Benjamin, plastics." ✆ 212/691-9442. www.condomania.com.

MYLA
20 E. 69th St., near Madison Ave. (Subway: 6 to 68th St./Hunter College).

This is a British import; I will not comment on the address except to say that expensive real estate like this demonstrates the upscale intent of the product line. Lingerie as well as toys are available. ✆ 212/570-1590. www.myla.com.

PLEASURE CHEST
156 Seventh Ave. S., between Charles and Perry sts. (Subway: 1 to Christopher St./Sheridan Sq.).

I got this listing from the TV show *Sex and the City;* so there. ✆ 212/242-2158. www.pleasurechesttoys.com.

SONIA RYKIEL
849 Madison Ave., near 70th St. (Subway: 6 to 68th St./ Hunter College).

This shop is mostly a fashion boutique, but following a trend begun by Sonia's daughter Nathalie, there are also some fancy girl things meant to give lasting pleasure. Ask. ✆ 212/396-3060. www.soniarykiel.com.

SHOES

Shoe stores come in all flavors in Manhattan: department stores (which usually have at least two different shoe departments), boutiques, teenage cheapie shoe stores (just take a look at W. 8th St. next time you're in the Village) and, of course, temples to the athletic shoe.

Entire clothing empires and fashion statements have grown from houses that originally manufactured just shoes and small leather goods (**Ferragamo, Gucci, Prada,** even **Bally**). Note that **Nordstrom,** the Seattle-based department store, is famous for its shoes; there are Nordstrom stores in the suburbs, as well as rumors of one coming to the East Side. I'll keep you posted. In the meantime, you can buy shoes from www.nordstrom.com.

Big Names in Shoes & Leather Goods

Here are some of the best-known places in the city to attire your feet in style:

BALLY
628 Madison Ave., at 59th St. (Subway: 4, 5, 6, N, R, or W to 59th St./Lexington Ave.).
© **212/751-9082.** www.bally.com.

BOTTEGA VENETA
699 Fifth Ave., between 54th and 55th sts. (Subway: E or V to 5th Ave./53rd St.).
© **212/371-5511.** www.bottegaveneta.com.

GUCCI
685 Fifth Ave., at 54th St. (Subway: E or V to 5th Ave./ 53rd St.).
© **212/826-2600.** www.gucci.com.

840 Madison Ave., near 70th St. (Subway: 6 to 68th St./ Hunter College).
© **212/717-2619.** www.gucci.com.

LONGCHAMP
713 Madison Ave., near 62nd St. (Subway: 4, 5, 6, N, R, or W to 59th St./Lexington Ave.).
© **212/223-1500.**

LOUIS VUITTON
1 E. 57th St., at Fifth Ave. (Subway: F to 57th St.).
© **212/758-8877.** www.louisvuitton.com.

116 Greene St., between Prince and Spring sts. (Subway: R or W to Prince St.).
© **212/274-9090.** www.louisvuitton.com.

MANOLO BLAHNIK
31 W. 54th St., between Fifth and Sixth aves. (Subway: E or V to 5th Ave./53rd St.).
© **212/582-3007.**

PRADA
45 E. 57th St., between Park and Madison aves. (Subway: 4, 5, 6, N, R, or W to 59th St./Lexington Ave.).
© 212/308-2332. www.prada.com.

724 Fifth Ave., near 56th St. (Subway: E or V to 5th Ave./ 53rd St.).
© 212/664-0010. www.prada.com.

841 Madison Ave., at 70th St. (Subway: 6 to 68th St./ Hunter College).
© 212/327-4200. www.prada.com.

575 Broadway, near Prince St. (Subway: R or W to Prince St.).
© 212/334-8888. www.prada.com.

SALVATORE FERRAGAMO
655 Fifth Ave., near 52nd St. (Subway: E or V to 5th Ave./ 53rd St.).
© 212/759-3822. www.ferragamo.com.

124 Spring St., near Greene St. (Subway: C, E, or 6 to Spring St.).
© 212/226-4330. www.ferragamo.com.

STEPHANE KELIAN
717 Madison Ave., near 63rd St. (Subway: N, R, or W to 5th Ave./59th St.).
© 212/980-1919. www.stephane-kelian.fr.

158 Mercer St., between Prince and Houston sts. (Subway: R or W to Prince St.).
© 212/925-3077. www.stephane-kelian.fr.

STUART WEITZMAN
Time Warner Center, 10 Columbus Circle (Subway: A, B, C, D, or 1 to 59th St./Columbus Circle).
© 212/823-9560. www.stuartweitzman.com.

625 Madison Ave., near 59th St. (Subway: 4, 5, 6, N, R, or W to 59th St./Lexington Ave.).
℗ 212/750-2555. www.stuartweitzman.com.

Specialty Shoes

BELGIAN SHOES
110 E. 55th St., between Park and Lexington aves. (Subway: 4, 5, 6, N, R, or W to 59th St./Lexington Ave.).

Belgian Shoes are handmade moccasins with a distinctive look that has made them a status symbol. These shoes fit differently from others, so you may be a different size. They either fit you or they don't—mine bit me—and the store will not take returns. Still, many swear by them. ℗ **212/755-7372.** www.belgian shoes.com.

CHRISTIAN LOUBOUTIN
941 Madison Ave., near 75th St. (Subway: 6 to 77th St.).

The darling of Paris tootsies has opened a teeny space in Manhattan, where his wild and witty work is showcased. Don't panic if the shoes in a pair don't match—they aren't supposed to. The red sole is his trademark, which is especially hot when you see a celebrity on a late-night chat show who is swinging her legs so that you can casually see the soles of her shoes. There's a second shop at 59 Horatio St. (at Greenwich St.). ℗ **212/ 396-1884.**

SIGERSON MORRISON
28 Prince St., between Mott and Elizabeth sts. (Subway: 6 to Spring St., or R or W to Prince St.).

For the Manolo crowd. Another location is devoted to handbags, right around the corner at 242 Mott St. (at Prince St.). *Tip:* These catch-me-if-you-can high heels and mules go up to size 11. ℗ **212/219-3893.** www.sigersonmorrison.com.

Tod's
650 Madison Ave., at 60th St. (Subway: 4, 5, 6, N, R, or W to 59th St./Lexington Ave.).

Tod's does stylish flat and driving shoes; they are handmade and last forever. I would pay anything for mine because they are the only shoes I can walk all day in. Tod's now has many styles, including its first pair of high heels and a line of sport shoes called Hogan (which has its own store at 134 Spring St., at Wooster St.). It also does handbags, and will even custom-engrave your own initials into your shoe. Hot damn. I have found that there is a universal uniform among chic women who sport jeans, Tod's, a good watch, and an expensive handbag. Just do it. ✆ 212/644-5945. www.todsonline.com.

Moderate to Mass-Market Big Names

You're sure to find something to suit you at one of these stores.

Aerosoles
1250 Sixth Ave., near 50th St. (Subway: B, D, F, or V to Rockefeller Center); multiple other locations.

Tip: Aerosoles has outlet stores around the country, including one at Woodbury Common (p. 297), but prices in the outlets are the same as in the stores and the catalog. The only difference: At the outlet, you get the second pair of shoes at half price. There are locations in every neighborhood, including Union Square (12 E. 14th St.) and the Upper East Side (150 E. 86th St., near Lexington Ave.); call ✆ 800/798-9478 for other addresses. ✆ 212/307-6465. www.aerosoles.com.

DSW (Designer Shoe Warehouse)
40 E. 14th St., near University Place (Subway: 4, 5, 6, L, N, Q, R, or W to 14th St./Union Sq.).

See p. 286. ✆ 212/674-2146. www.dswshoe.com.

GALO

895 Madison Ave., at 72nd St. (Subway: 6 to 68th St./Hunter College).

Classic comfy shoes sold at several locations, including 1296 Third Ave. (at 74th St.) and 825 Lexington Ave. (at 63rd St.). ✆ 212/744-7936. www.galoshoes.com.

NINE WEST

750 Lexington Ave., near 59th St. (Subway: 4, 5, 6, N, R, or W to 59th St./Lexington Ave.); multiple other locations.

This mall standby is everywhere in New York, including SoHo (577 Broadway, near Prince St.), Union Square (115 Fifth Ave., near 19th St.), and Rockefeller Center (1258 Sixth Ave., near 50th St.); call ✆ 800/999-1877 for other addresses. ✆ 212/486-8094. www.ninewest.com.

STEVE MADDEN

540 Broadway, near Prince St. (Subway: R or W to Prince St.).

Funky women's and men's footwear, with a few locations around town. Call ✆ 888/762-3336 for addresses. ✆ 212/343-1800. www.stevemadden.com

UNISA

701 Madison Ave., near 62nd St. (Subway: N, R, or W to 5th Ave./59th St.).

Reasonably priced sandals, flats, mules, and pumps—and even the espadrilles you may recall from the '80s. ✆ 212/753-7474. www.unisa.com.

VIA SPIGA

692 Madison Ave., near 62nd St. (Subway: 6 to 68th St./Hunter College); 390 W. Broadway, between Broome and Spring sts. (Subway: C or E to Spring St.).

Italian-made shoes at decent prices. © 212/871-9955 for the Madison Avenue location; © 212/431-7007 for the SoHo location. www.viaspiga.com.

SHOPPING CENTERS

....

The big malls are in the metropolitan areas outside of Manhattan. In New York City, all you used to get in terms of a mall was several floors of retail space in an office complex—such as "The Market" at Citicorp or "The Atrium" at Trump Tower. Both are boring. Don't laugh, but the best of the mall-like spaces in Manhattan, up until very recently, was Rockefeller Center. That's all changed with the introduction of the mall at the Time Warner Center, on Columbus Circle. Read on.

575
575 Fifth Ave., at 47th St. (Subway: B, D, F, or V to Rockefeller Center).

This is the poor person's Trump Tower, in the not-so-shabby neighborhood of Fifth Avenue and 47th Street. A small branch of **Ann Taylor** anchors this shopping plaza.

MITSUWA MARKETPLACE
595 River Rd., Edgewater, New Jersey.

Okay, I admit it—this is a ringer. But it's so much fun that you must give it a little consideration. Mitsuwa Marketplace is in New Jersey, where everyone who craves a mall should be going. But wait, this is no mall or ordinary shopping center. It's a small strip village that is totally Japanese!

The largest store is a supermarket that includes eateries, and a row of shops sells cosmetics and gift items as well as clothes. The supermarket, which also carries some American items, has a combination of Japanese goods that you can't find in too many other places. Definitely check out the section devoted to Japanese rice steamers, teapots, and so on. The packaging alone will make you nuts with glee. This is a shopping and artistic adventure if ever there was one.

You can drive from Manhattan (the complex is almost right under the George Washington Bridge), you can take a ferry from Eleventh Avenue and 34th Street in Manhattan to the Port Imperial ferry terminal and get a taxi there, or you can catch the $2 Mitsuwa shuttle bus across the street from the north exit of the Port Authority Terminal on West 42nd Street. ⓒ 201/941-9113. www.mitsuwa.com.

PIER 17 PAVILION
South Street Seaport, Fulton and South sts. (Subway: 1, 2, or 3 to Fulton St.).

This is actually part of the South Street Seaport complex, and if you are just wandering happily around the area, you will probably discover it for yourself. But if you aren't paying much attention, or if the crowds are too dense, you might not realize that besides the Faneuil Hall–like South Street Seaport complex, and the short stretch of street-level shops on Fulton Street, there is an additional building along the water next to the lightship *Ambrose* that is really a mall on its own. It's complete with escalators and a branch store of many of the major chains in America—like **Sharper Image, Express, Foot Locker,** and others. ⓒ 212/732-8257. www.southstreetseaport.com.

ROCKEFELLER CENTER
Fifth Ave. to Seventh Ave., from 47th to 51st sts. (Subway: B, D, F, or V to Rockefeller Center).

On rainy days, you can make your way across Midtown underground if you know how to work the city of halls and shops that lies beneath Rockefeller Center. This is more than a mall; it's a village.

Besides fast-food restaurants and a few nice eateries, there are food markets, party stores, candy shops, newsstands (with great magazine selections), and many service-related businesses—banks, a post office, travel agencies, FedEx, and men who shine your shoes—all underground. Most of the stores are not anything you haven't seen before.

Aboveground is quite another story—one of New York's revolutions in retail happened right here. A tiny avenue of storefronts leads to the Christmas tree and the ice-skating rink (in season) at Rockefeller Plaza, as well as a spacious branch of the **Metropolitan Museum of Art Store.**

Around the corner, on Rockefeller Plaza, there's a small branch of gourmet-food purveyor **Dean & DeLuca,** which features a coffee bar and snacks to eat in or take out. This place is especially hot since hanging out in front of the studio for NBC's *Today* show has become such a popular activity. © 212/ 332-6868. www.rockefellercenter.com.

TIME WARNER CENTER
10 Columbus Circle (Subway: A, B, C, D, or 1 to 59th St./ Columbus Circle).

I like this mall, also referred to as the Shops at Columbus Circle, for all the wrong reasons—I like it simply because it's there and it has changed the face of New York. It is not a good mall, however; it has no soul and surely no warmth and, on top of that, it has an odd layout. But the **Whole Foods** on the lower level is indeed fabulous (and fabulously crowded; go during off hours). There are mostly big-name designer shops and upscale restaurants here, with a few of the everyday names you need on a regular basis, like **Sephora** for makeup (though not a great one) and a large **Borders** for books and music. © 212/ 823-6300. www.shopsatcolumbuscircle.com.

TRUMP TOWER ATRIUM
725 Fifth Ave., at 56th St. (Subway: F to 57th St.).

The problem with the Trump Tower is that everybody wants to see it, but nobody thinks they can afford anything in there—so little actual shopping is going on while the mobs come and go. Donald Trump has gone on to other adventures, but still gets a lot of mileage out of his luxury tower, which has apartments in addition to the stores. The atrium space is Glitz City, with five levels (complete with lots of marble and brass) devoted to retail. Many stores are branches of famous names, such as **Asprey,** the London purveyor of fine goods.

SPECIAL SIZES FOR MEN

BARNEYS NEW YORK
660 Madison Ave., at 61st St. (Subway: 4, 5, 6, N, R, or W to 59th St./Lexington Ave.).

Barneys has one of the most complete ranges of clothing sizes in New York. It also does alterations on the premises. The famous warehouse sale (p. 110) has plenty of selection in all size ranges, too. See p. 160 for more about Barneys. © 212/826-8900. www.barneys.com.

ROCHESTER BIG & TALL
1301 Sixth Ave., at 52nd St. (Subway: B, D, or E to 7th Ave./53rd St.).

Rochester carries hot brand names in large and tall sizes, though I must say that the prices make me shiver—and I found it a better value to have my husband's clothes made to order by our tailor in Hong Kong. But if you like to buy ready-made, there is a very good selection of quality looks and makes here. © 212/247-7500. www.rochesterclothing.com.

SPECIAL SIZES FOR WOMEN

New York is one of the best cities in the world for specialty sizes; most of the department stores have made it their business to stock well-developed petite and plus-size women's wear. Even the store catalogs now feature garments available in a range of sizes. Most designers, retailers, and boutiques want to help you look as elegant as possible, no matter how big or small you may be. In fact, many established names, such as **Anne Klein** (petite and plus sizes) and **Liz Claiborne** (petites only), have special sizes, which are sold at their outlet stores; both brands have outlets at Woodbury Common (p. 297).

If you can get in over a weekend, or can buy wholesale, try 498 Seventh Ave. (at 37th St.) for its showrooms for plus-size women. Also try **Forman's Coats/Plus Sizes** (78 Orchard St., between Grand and Broome sts.), and don't forget that any couture garment can be made to measure.

See the "Maternity" section, earlier in this chapter, for special sizes in that category.

STATIONERY

....

JAMIE OSTROW
54 W. 21st St., between Fifth and Sixth aves. (Subway: R or W to 23rd St.).

Notepaper, invitations, and cards. Clients here order big and bold writing papers that are different enough—and expensive enough—to get other New Yorkers to notice their mail. © 212/675-4650. www.jamieostrow.com.

SMYTHSON OF BOND STREET
4 W. 57th St., between Fifth and Sixth aves. (Subway: F to 57th St.).

This hoity-toity British firm has opened in New York with extremely expensive products, some of them very imaginative. Look for notepapers and diaries, as well as small leather goods and some travel items. If you're British, the must-have gift item is the passport cover. If you're American, you can write old-fashioned thank-you notes on these letter papers and know that all your friends will think you're hot stuff. © 212/265-4573. www.smythson.com.

TEENS

Teen buys include vintage clothing and jeans, cutting-edge street fashion that must be cheap, and lots of accessories, including whatever shoes are of the moment. Also see "Hip & Hot," on p. 186. A few more affordable sources are listed below.

LOUNGE
593 Broadway, at Houston St. (Subway: B, D, F, or V to Broadway/Lafayette St.).

With a live DJ spinning the shopping music, this store is either the poor man's Jeffrey or the hipster's H&M. The clothes are moderately priced and slightly more edgy than what you'd find uptown or in a mass-market chain. Men's and women's as well as shoes and boots; some accessories, too. It's a lifestyle store, dude. ✆ 212/226-7585. www.loungesoho.com.

RUGBY
99 University Place, at 12th St. (Subway: 4, 5, 6, L, N, Q, R, or W to 14th St./Union Sq.).

If you can't beat 'em, join 'em—so none other than Ralph Lauren has launched yet another spin-off: a store on the front yard of NYU that sells the casual look teens and tweens have been wearing and buying from the likes of Abercrombie & Fitch (p. 167). The look has a preppy edge to it, keeping with Mr. Lauren's well-defined style. The physical space is also pure Lauren—men's and women's clothes in a store that is so atmospheric as to almost be a movie set. The disturbing part (to me) is the use of a skull-and-crossbones logo and motif—this does not refer to the serious preppydom of secret Yale society Skull and Bones, but is more of a goth take. Frankly, I'd prefer less goth and more Gotham. ✆ 212/677-1895. www.polo.com.

STRAWBERRY
129 E. 42nd St., at Lexington Ave. (Subway: 4, 5, 6, 7, or S to Grand Central/42nd St.); multiple other locations.

There are scads of these cheapie stores all over town; I usually visit the one at Grand Central because of its size and location. These very inexpensive clothes copy the looks made popular by the biggest names in fashion. Yes, Gucci. A lot of it is definitely junky, but if you are patient and use that eagle eye of yours, you will be rewarded. Other locations include 501 Madison Ave. (near 52nd St.) and 49 W. 57th St. (near Sixth Ave.). ✆ **212/986-7030.**

URBAN OUTFITTERS
526 Sixth Ave., at 14th St. (Subway: F, L, or V to 14th St.).

Urban features boho-chic styles at modest prices, making it a strong source for teens and tweens. There are lots of ethnic fashions and trendsetting styles here. Branches are popping up everywhere, including the Upper East Side (999 Third Ave., near 59th St.), NoHo (628 Broadway, at Houston St.), and the East Village (162 Second Ave., at 10th St.). Call ✆ **800/282-2200** for info. ✆ **646/638-1646.** www.urbanoutfitters.com.

VINTAGE

Vintage clothing has never been more chic, thanks to a steady stream of celebrities who wear vintage—Julia Roberts at the Academy Awards, anyone? Teens wear vintage jeans, models wear vintage slips, fashion editors wear vintage Pucci. In addition to the following listings for vintage men's and women's clothing, see p. 304 for resale shops.

In fact, vintage is so chic that Tiffany Dubin has become a New York celebrity (she's the founding director of **Sotheby's** fashion department) and vintage has become an auction staple. **Doyle New York** (175 E. 87th St., near Lexington Ave.; www.doylenewyork.com) has tried to corner the market, but the bigger-name auction people are indeed moving on in.

Funky Vintage

ANDY'S CHEE-PEES
691 Broadway, near 4th St. (Subway: 6 to Bleecker St.).

Mostly jeans, cords, and tatty T-shirts with some gems in there if you hunt. For the teen and tween crowd. ✆ **212/420-5980.**

DAVID OWENS VINTAGE CLOTHING
154 Orchard St., between Stanton and Rivington sts. (Subway: F or V to 2nd Ave.).

Part of the new Lower East Side, this small store sells men's and women's vintage clothing from the 1940s through the 1980s. ✆ **212/677-3301.** www.davidowensvintage.com.

STELLA DALLAS
218 Thompson St., between Bleecker and W. 3rd sts. (Subway: A, B, C, D, E, F, or V to W. 4th St./Washington Sq.).

Couture and name-brand clothes, especially from the 1930s and 1940s—a big celebrity source. ✆ **212/674-0447.**

WHAT COMES AROUND GOES AROUND
351 West Broadway, between Broome and Grand sts. (Subway: C or E to Spring St.).

This source in the heart of SoHo is a great place for spotting celebs who like to wear vintage. The store has been so successful that it now has a wholesale showroom in TriBeCa, where regular retail customers can also shop; call ✆ **212/274-8340** for an appointment. ✆ **212/343-9303.** www.nyvintage.com.

Expensive Vintage

KENI VALENTI RETRO-COUTURE
247 W. 30th St., between Seventh and Eighth aves., 5th floor (Subway: 1, R, or W to 28th St.).

Knock three times and whisper low. But wait, make sure you've called first for an appointment. This is a secret celebrity resource; serious collectors only. © **212/967-7147.** www.keni valenti.com.

RESURRECTION
217 Mott St., between Prince and Spring sts. (Subway: 6 to Spring St.; or R or W to Prince St.).

Much Pucci. © **212/625-1374.** www.resurrectionvintage.com.

Chapter Nine

....

NEW YORK BEAUTY

Beauty may only be skin deep, but it's a huge business in New York, as it is elsewhere in the world. Well-being has become the new mantra, especially in a city so filled with stress and anxiety.

Stores are battling with one another for the chance to carry the best and newest beauty brands—the odder the better. Day spas are everywhere in New York, be they famous names or neighborhood finds. French hairdressers are celebrities here—actually, all hairdressers are celebrities. Hotels are competing to out-spa one another: The Plaza's spa now boasts Anne Sémonin products from Paris, while The Mark offers Exhale, a well-being studio across the street from the hotel at 980 Madison Ave. Department stores have their own spas (one of the most exclusive is the Estée Lauder spa at Bloomingdale's). Television networks are making reality TV out of plastic surgery, everybody is on Atkins or the South Beach diet, and nobody misses a day at the gym. Quick—where's my spinning class?

No city—not even Paris—has the beauty energy that Manhattan now has thanks to stores and spas from **Avon** to **Bergdorf Goodman** to **Bliss** to **Lush** and beyond. Avon is doing more than just calling on New Yorkers (knock, knock, Avon lady!); it now has a fabulous spa just a few feet from Tiffany & Co. Downtown firms have branches uptown and in Midtown (see Bliss). And the fabulous Lush now has a

New York store. If you don't know about Lush yet, read on, read on.

This chapter incorporates such diverse subjects as cosmetics, hairdressers, bath goods, perfumes, and even spa listings. So light up a Diptyque candle, rub a little Origins energizing oil on your brow, and have your eyebrows threaded while you read on.

THE GEOGRAPHY OF BEAUTY

There are beauty businesses on just about every block of Manhattan; certainly every neighborhood has its own mom-and-pop shops, so to speak. The largest concentration of hip and hot sources is in SoHo, which many people in the industry have nicknamed the Lipstick District.

Upper Madison Avenue has several sources for beauty products, but it's best known for its string of very fancy pharmacies, which carry hard-to-find European brands. Midtown is dotted with the city's major department stores as well as flagships of many specialty stores, including **Banana Republic, Gap,** and **Benetton,** which all offer makeup brands. Midtown also has some of the small specialty multiples such as **Mary Quant, Crabtree & Evelyn, L'Occitane,** and so on, many of which began life in another country (although, despite what you may think, Crabtree & Evelyn is an American firm).

THE BIG NAMES IN BEAUTY

AVEDA
Time Warner Center, 10 Columbus Circle (Subway: A, B, C, D, or 1 to 59th St./Columbus Circle); 509 Madison Ave., at 53rd St. (Subway: E or V to 5th Ave./53rd St.); 456 West Broadway, between Houston and Prince sts. (Subway: C or E to Spring St.); multiple other locations.

This cult fave is a leading brand in aromatherapy, with hair-care and beauty products made from high-quality, all-natural ingredients. Call © **800/644-4831** for more locations; also see the listing below. www.aveda.com.

AVEDA INSTITUTE
233 Spring St., between Sixth Ave. and Varick St. (Subway: 1 to Canal St., or C or E to Spring St.).

Some of the best low-priced gifts in Manhattan ($10–$12) come from this tiny SoHo shop. The Aveda Institute is both a store and a spa, featuring aromatherapy treatments and an array of products for men and women, including various hair cocktails that have been created especially for colored and problem hair. The line is sold in salons around the country, and sometimes you'll see a few items in drugstores. However, if you want to experience the full range of products, including candles, aromatherapy, and makeup, you should hit an Aveda store in New York. © **212/807-1492**. www.aveda.com.

AVON SALON & SPA
Trump Tower, 725 Fifth Ave., at 56th St. (Subway: N, R, or W to 5th Ave./59th St.).

This world-famous brand, which heretofore was only sold door-to-door, suddenly opened a glamorous New York spa and beauty center and introduced new products that are available only here. It's been so successful that more free-standing stores and spas will be opening around the U.S. The Aromatherapy Salt Glow here is fab. Prices are not the highest in the city, but they aren't budget, either. © **212/755-AVON**. www.avon salonandspa.com.

THE BODY SHOP
485 Madison Ave., at 51st St. (Subway: E or V to 5th Ave./53rd St.); multiple other locations too numerous to list.

Just when I say that I'm tired of the line, I find something new to interest me. *Note:* Some Body Shop stores in the U.K. offer spa services; this trend will eventually come over to the U.S. Call © **800/263-9746** for addresses. www.thebodyshop.com.

H2O PLUS
511 Madison Ave., at 53rd St. (Subway: E or V to 5th Ave./ 53rd St.).

This Chicago firm has taken the malls of America by storm. As the name would imply, it sells goodies for the bath—gels, shampoos, travel kits, and more. You can find great gifts (some in the $10 range!) for just about every age, though the kiddie bath toys and products are the best. © **212/750-8119.** www.h2oplus.com.

LUSH
1293 Broadway, at 34th St. (Subway: B, D, F, N, R, Q, V, or W to 34th St./Herald Sq.).

The good news: Lush has arrived in the U.S. and opened a few stores in New York. The bad news: The main shop is in a mall across the street from Macy's and has been created for teenage shoppers. But never mind. In the near future, there will probably be a Lush on every other street corner.

For the uninitiated, Lush makes bath balls that snap, crackle, and fizz when you drop them in water, plus natural beauty products ranging from shampoos to skin creams. Everything is sold deli style—the soaps are in loaves, the products are in refrigerator cases. Not every product is fabulous, but the presentation is adorable and the novelty factor is high. Great gift items, especially if you live in a town that has no Lush. Now then, prices are about $5 per bath ball, which I find expensive, but call me irresponsible. Surely you are paying for the novelty factor and the razzmatazz, of which there is much.

A second location has opened at 2165 Broadway (near 76th St.). Be sure to get a copy of the company newspaper *(Lush*

Times) and check out the website if there is no Lush in your hometown. If you're familiar with the line in the U.K., note that the U.S. version comes from Canada to meet demands of the FDA. © **212/564-9120.** www.lush.com.

ORIGINS

402 West Broadway, at Spring St. (Subway: C or E to Spring St.); Grand Central Terminal, 42nd St. and Park Ave. (Subway: 4, 5, 6, 7, or S to Grand Central/42nd St.); multiple other locations.

While this line of natural-ingredient beauty aids, shampoos, aromatherapy treatments, and cosmetics is also sold in traditional department stores, the Origins store has a wider selection as well as some products that are not available elsewhere.

I love this line and often send out gifts from here. I use Jump Start in my bath when I can afford it (at $25 a bottle, it's a rather big splurge); this aromatherapy product has a tingle that really seems worth the moolah—it makes me giggle and sing in the shower.

Limited items (discounted, of course) are available at Woodbury Common (p. 297) at the Cosmetics Company Store (an outlet for the various Estée Lauder brands such as Origins and Clinique). © **800/ORIGINS.** www.origins.com.

SABON

93 Spring St., between Broadway and Mercer St. (Subway: R or W to Prince St.); 434 Sixth Ave., near 10th St. (Subway: A, B, C, D, E, F, or V to W. 4th St./Washington Sq.); 1371 Sixth Ave., near 55th St. (Subway: F to 57th St.); 2052 Broadway, near 70th St. (Subway: 1, 2, or 3 to 72nd St.).

Sabon means soap and it is *bon.* This Israeli firm has several shops in Manhattan and most likely plans to take over the world, much like Lush. Swanky and sophisticated and a lot of fun— especially good gift headquarters, with its natural products and treatments bespeckled with herbs and flowers. © **866/697-2266.** www.sabonnyc.com.

SEPHORA
555 Broadway, between Prince and Spring sts. (Subway: R or W to Prince St.); Time Warner Center, 10 Columbus Circle (Subway: A, B, C, D, or 1 to 59th St./Columbus Circle); multiple other locations.

Let's start with a short history of this French firm, which was getting innovative on its own and was then bought by LVMH, which turned it into a global power. New stores are popping up in all neighborhoods—making Sephora kind of like a neighborhood beauty supermarket that carries many lines you've never heard of. Yummy. Furthermore, different stores carry different brands—including lines created for black women and even Sephora's own house brand—so you will never get bored.

Note there is a no-gift-with-purchase policy at this chain; gift-with-purchase is reserved for U.S. department stores only. Sephora also refrains from spritzing customers with perfume or, alas, giving out scads of fancy giveaways. You can, however, ask for samples of anything you'd like to test, and these are not the kind of samples you get at department stores—rather, they're fresh samples, straight from the jar, and put in containers for you to take home. © 877/SEPHORA. www.sephora.com.

DEPARTMENT STORES

All department stores have enormous makeup-and-perfume departments, usually on the street floor. **Macy's** has recently expanded its beauty department—still on the ground floor—while **Bergdorf's** has taken the dramatic step of creating a totally new department, not on the ground floor but one floor below.

Saks prides itself on having the largest selection of perfume brands in New York; it carries many scent and makeup lines not found anywhere else. **Bloomingdale's** has one of the best cosmetics departments in the city and often has creative promotional events. It also strives to offer some unknown or little-known brands, such as Isabella Rossellini's Manifesto line of makeup.

It is the specialty stores, though, that really go for the gusto—**Takashimaya, Henri Bendel,** and **Barneys** all carry brands that might not be found elsewhere in the city, even at Sephora. Barneys has been the most competitive about finding new brands and garnering exclusive rights to them—its latest find is a line of skin care called B. Kamins, which has a Maple Treatment Cream for extra-dry skin that is supposed to be the last word.

MAKEUP BRANDS & STORES

Makeup must be almost as lucrative as perfume, since many stores have launched their own makeup lines in the last year or so. **Gap** started with bath and aromatherapy and is going into color cosmetics; so is **Banana Republic.** Meanwhile, **Tommy Hilfiger** has a whole Tommy Girl line of makeup now, sold in his boutiques and department stores such as Macy's.

At the other end of the, uh, spectrum, **Versace** went into color cosmetics before he died—that line is now carried in department stores and at Sephora. Many other big-name designers have color cosmetic lines, too, such as **Giorgio Armani** (the cosmetics are actually made by L'Oreal), **Calvin Klein** and, of course, **Yves Saint Laurent** (visit the renovated YSL boutique to see designer Tom Ford's work). Can Donna Karan be far behind?

The stores and brands described below are specialists in the field of makeup; many of them were created by makeup artists or models.

ALCONE COMPANY
235 W. 19th St., between Seventh and Eighth aves. (Subway: C or E to 23rd St.).

This is a professional and theatrical makeup supply store, as well as a hangout for celebs and those in the know. I am addicted to the **Tuttle** line sold here, not only for on-camera work, but also for those days when I need real help with my skin texture. The store also carries **Trish McEvoy** as well as **IL-Makiage,** an Israeli brand that has cult status in some circles because of its great color. Alcone sells products you can't find in department stores; when you're doing Chelsea or Lower Fifth Avenue, make a point to head over to this source. Your life will change forever. © **212/633-0551.** www.alconeco.com.

FACE STOCKHOLM
110 Prince St., at Greene St. (Subway: R or W to Prince St.); Time Warner Center, 10 Columbus Circle (Subway: A, B, C, D, or 1 to 59th St./Columbus Circle); multiple other locations.

Face Stockholm, from Sweden (duh), began life as the makeup of choice for many a supermodel in the 1980s. The reason that the stars took to the brand is the range of colors that can be bought ready-made. There are more than 100 shades of nail polish and almost 200 shades of lipstick. Everything is out, so you can test it. Once considered a cult brand, it has become so popular that it's now distributed through some of the fancy department stores. © **888/334-FACE.** www.facestockholm.com.

M.A.C.
113 Spring St., between Mercer and Greene sts. (Subway: R or W to Prince St., or C or E to Spring St.); 175 Fifth Ave., near 22nd St. (Subway: R or W to 23rd St.); multiple other locations.

This is a Canadian brand of makeup that is often worn by models. The line has became so enormously chic, and has gathered such a devoted following, that it was snapped up by Estée Lauder. Its products are available at **Henri Bendel** in a totally renovated selling space, at a few other department stores, and at M.A.C.'s own stores (of course).

Ricky's: The Funky Beauty-Supply Store

A small but growing chain of beauty-supply stores that has reached cult status with many in the beauty biz, Ricky's has recently opened some uptown stores as the chain works its way into middle-class accessibility. Ricky's supplies stars, models, the rich and famous—this is the store where the movers and shakers of the beauty world hang out because it's a semi-professional source of supplies and goods.

Ricky's creates its own house line of products and sells wigs, hair accessories, and just about anything else that's fun, funky, and unusual, including body glitter in every color imaginable. This is a must-stop for Halloween products. (**Note:** Ricky's has recently discontinued the Adults Only shopping section.)

It also sells what the business calls "diverted goods." These are legally made name-brand products that the manufacturing company did not want sold at a discount but could not prevent from being released through a middleman. (Well, that's an oversimplification, but you get the idea—they're cheaper than you'd find elsewhere.)

Ricky's is a growing business, with about a dozen branches in Manhattan. The flagship is at 509 Fifth Ave., near 42nd Street (Subway: B, D, F, or V to 42nd St./Bryant Park). Other store locations include 590 Broadway (below Houston St.), 44 E. 8th St. (at Greene St.), 278 Third Ave. (at 22nd St.), 1189 First Ave. (near 65th St.), 988 Eighth Ave. (at 58th St.), and many more.

For a complete list, go to www.rickys-nyc.com. Further note—there is now a store in East Hampton, at 50 Main St. And yes, your grandmother is right: Ricky's has even opened in Florida.

People say that the reason this line is so popular is that the makeup lasts longer on the face (and lips) than other brands; I think the reason it's so popular is that the prices are pretty low and the image is very high. The colors are sublime; I buy a new eye shadow ($14) any time I'm down and out.

Tip: This brand is *muuuch* cheaper than other major U.S. or European brands, yet the quality is top-notch. ✆ 800/588-0070. www.maccosmetics.com.

MARY QUANT
520 Madison Ave., at 53rd St. (Subway: E or V to 5th Ave./ 53rd St.).

If you're old enough to remember Mary Quant as the queen of Carnaby Street in the Swinging Sixties, you already know who she is and what her makeup's about. Now she's come back into style and has opened shops in London, Paris, Tokyo, and New York that sell makeup and some accessories. They say her forte is "color concepts," entire groups of makeup that are color-coordinated—pinks, browns, reds, and so on. While I am big on nostalgia, I tested a few items and wasn't that impressed. I list it for those of you who might want to know whatever happened to this brand. ✆ 212/980-7577. www.maryquant.co.uk.

MISSHA
516 Fifth Ave., at 43rd St. (Subway: B, D, F, or V to 42nd St./Bryant Park).

Here's another Korean newcomer to the Manhattan beauty scene. This one's a total line of cosmetics and beauty supplies at friendly prices. The store is light, bright, and easy to shop; most items cost about $5 each. The target audience is teen or tween, but don't let that stop you. The almost throwaway stuff is great fun to test and play with. A second shop has opened in SoHo at 513 Broadway, near Spring Street. ✆ 212/596-4012. www.missha.net.

SHU UEMURA
121 Greene St., between Houston and Prince sts. (Subway: R or W to Prince St., or C or E to Spring St.).

This Japanese line is carried in some department and specialty stores, so you needn't make the pilgrimage to this one—but it is great fun. There are more shades of cosmetics in this brand than in just about any other line in the world, and there are many pieces of equipment as well. You'll also find a range of skin-care products. Excellent but pricey. ✆ 212/979-5500. www.shuuemura.com.

BATH & BODY STORES

CASWELL-MASSEY
518 Lexington Ave., at 48th St. (Subway: 6 to 51st St., or E or V to Lexington Ave./53rd St.).

Resembling an old-fashioned British chemist shop (pharmacy), Caswell-Massey is best known for its private-label products, which have been going strong for hundreds of years now: George Washington even used its cologne (no. 6). ✆ 212/755-2254. www.casswell-massey.com.

CRABTREE & EVELYN
Time Warner Center, 10 Columbus Circle (Subway: A, B, C, D, or 1 to 59th St./Columbus Circle); 30 Rockefeller Center, near 49th St. (Subway: B, D, F, or V to Rockefeller Center); 520 Madison Ave., near 53rd St. (Subway: E or V to 5th Ave./53rd St.); multiple other locations.

I know this will come as a shock, but here goes: Crabtree & Evelyn is not a British firm, nor is it 100 years old. In fact, it was born in the era of the natural 1970s in New England and has become an international soap-and-jam empire based on the old English look. It has stores in suburban malls everywhere, plus an outlet at Woodbury Common (p. 297).

In my weaker moments, I get this line mixed up with Caswell-Massey; then I remember that George Washington used

Caswell-Massey, and Crabtree & Evelyn is the line that first seduced me into flavored/scented soaps. The history of my life can be traced through my changes in taste, from avocado to almond scents in soaps and creams and lotions. © 800/CRAB-TREE. www.crabtreeandevelyn.com.

FRESH
922 Madison Ave., near 73rd St. (Subway: 6 to 77th St.); 57 Spring St., between Mulberry and Lafayette sts. (Subway: 6 to Spring St.); multiple other locations.

These products are somewhat farm-inspired, made with milk, eggs, honey, and so on. The sugar-cube fizz balls for the bath are a bit pricey but heavenly, and the body salt scrubs may actually be worth $40! New Yorkers from the *Sex and the City* set really eat this stuff up. © 800/FRESH-20. www.fresh.com.

L'OCCITANE
1046 Madison Ave., at 80th St. (Subway: 6 to 77th St.); 510 Madison Ave., near 52nd St. (Subway: E or V to 5th Ave., at 51st St.); Time Warner Center, 10 Columbus Circle (Subway: A, B, C, D, or 1 to 59th St./Columbus Circle); 92 Prince St., near Broadway (Subway: R or W to Prince St.); multiple other locations.

This is one of my favorite French brands in America, offering perfumes, aromatherapy, soaps, candles, makeup, and body products from the south of France. Honestly, I'm not certain how to classify this one, for L'Occitane does it all: It also sells bedding, bathroom stuff, home sprays, and travel kits. If you don't know this brand, please sniff your way over and inhale deeply. There's an outlet at Woodbury Common (p. 297), too.

Note that L'Occitane is connected by lineage and some moneymen to **Oliviers & Co.**, an olive-oil firm, so the stores are often next door to each other. © 888/623-2880. www.loccitane.com.

Lush
1293 Broadway, at 34th St. (Subway: B, D, F, N, R, Q, V, or W to 34th St./Herald Sq.).

See p. 221. ✆ **212/564-9120**. www.lush.com.

Perlier Kelemata
436 West Broadway, at Prince St. (Subway: C or E to Spring St.).

Although Perlier sounds French, this is actually an Italian firm. It has a cosmetics line (Harmonia) as well as bath goods (Perlier) and Kelemata skin-care products, which happen to be great. While the Perlier line is best known for its honey products, the ones made with vanilla are also sublime. ✆ **212/925-9999**. www.perlierusa.com/perlier.asp.

Whole Body at Whole Foods
260 Seventh Ave., at 25th St. (Subway: 1 to 23rd St.).

Check out the **Whole Foods** organic market and then pop into adjacent **Whole Body** for natural bath, body, and beauty products. Some lines are a tad underground, while others are famous in Europe and otherwise hard to find in New York, like **Dr. Hauschka**, a German brand that is all the rage in London. (Try the rose oil on your cuticles.) ✆ **212/924-9972**. www.wholefoodsmarket.com.

PHARMACIES WITH A TWIST
....

Boyd's
968 Third Ave., at 58th St. (Subway: 4, 5, 6, N, R, or W to 59th St./Lexington Ave.).

Boyd's regulars, please note this new address. Others, pay attention: Boyd's is a cornucopia of delight. The store has a remarkable selection, including many European brands not commonly found in the U.S. The prices are high, but boy, is it fun to browse here. It's almost a department store of health and beauty aids, hair gizmos, accessories, perfumes, and every imaginable beauty product—which you can play with and test to your heart's content. This is my favorite place for wandering around dazed.

Boyd's offers free delivery within the city and will ship worldwide. There's now a West Side store, too, at 309 Columbus Ave. (near 75th St.). © **212/838-6558.** www.boydsnyc.com.

CLYDE'S
926 Madison Ave., near 74th St. (Subway: 6 to 77th St.).

This is an uptown and slightly more posh version of Boyd's; I like how fancy it is. The store is spacious and low-key, and will appeal to those who don't like to search every nook and cranny to find what they want. © **212/744-5050.** www.clydes onmadison.com.

CONCORD CHEMISTS
485 Madison Ave., at 52nd St. (Subway: B, D, F, or V to Rockefeller Center).

This is an unusual drugstore: It has many Euro lines of makeup and beauty treatments, some accessories, and a few brands of gunks and goops that are hard to find. I used to work in the office building above the store, so I have been dropping in for years (it's near Saks and Burger Heaven) and working with a woman named Ana Medina for skin care. She gives me zillions of samples and tells me to test them and then come back to purchase—it's a soft sell, which I appreciate, and the brands she has are not found elsewhere. © **212/486-9543.** www. concord-chemists.com.

JANET SARTIN INSTITUTE
500 Park Ave., near 58th St. (Subway: 4, 5, 6, N, R, or W to 59th St./Lexington Ave.).

Before day spas were common—in fact, before I even had blemishes—Janet Sartin was one of the most serious specialists in skin care. Call ahead for an appointment, or just drop in to stock up on products. ✆ **212/751-5858. www.sartin.com.**

KIEHL'S
109 Third Ave., at 13th St. (Subway: 4, 5, 6, L, N, Q, R, or W to 14th St./Union Sq.).

This pharmacy is old-fashioned in the most yummy sense of the word; you can actually feel the tradition in this place. Kiehl's offers the kind of ambience other stores can only try to copy. Its products are created from knowledge based on hundreds of years of customer feedback and satisfaction. Okay, so the store is only 150 years old, but you get the point.

Kiehl's goods have become the rage in Europe, so they make excellent gifts for international visitors to take home. These are the sort of "in" products that show people that you know about the very best in beauty and body and face care. Some department stores and European-style drugstores in Manhattan also sell this line. ✆ **212/677-3171. www.kiehls.com.**

ZITOMER
969 Madison Ave., near 76th St. (Subway: 6 to 77th St.).

Larger and more extensively packed than Boyd's, Zitomer is a virtual department store of great drugstore stuff—it even sells clothing and has a doggy boutique. The store is a bit over-the-top for me, but it's great fun for the first-timer. The merchandise is very similar to what's on the shelves at Boyd's (European brands of toothpaste, deodorant, hair spray, bath bubbles, soap, wrinkle cream), but whereas Boyd's has greater hair-accessory and perfume selections, Zitomer specializes in hard-to-find brands and European skin-care specialties.

This place is possibly more fun than Boyd's—it's twice the size and now has a second store next door. The owners have a clear understanding of who their shoppers are, so they have enlarged and expanded and fooled around with the merchandise mix so that you can find everything you need for a chic life of beauty on the road—or on Upper Madison. © 212/737-2016. www.zitomer.com.

PERFUME & SCENT SHOPS

All department stores, many discounters, and many specialty stores sell perfumes. The listings below are specialty houses known for their own lines of scents.

BOND NO. 9

9 Bond St., between Broadway and Lafayette St. (Subway: 6 to Bleecker St.); 399 Bleecker St., at 11th St. (Subway: 1 to Christopher St./Sheridan Sq.); 680 Madison Ave., near 61st St. (Subway: N, R, or W to 5th Ave./59th St.); 897 Madison Ave., near 73rd St. (Subway: 6 to 68th St./Hunter College).

The NoHo flagship is worth the trip for the decor and ambience alone. Bond No. 9—named after the address of the shop, obviously—is a fragrance line named after various New York neighborhoods, like Park Avenue, Chinatown, and Chelsea Flowers. (The latest, however, is somewhat controversially called the Scent of Peace.) This line is not yet sold in Europe and therefore makes a great gift to take overseas. © 877/273-3369. www.bondno9fragrances.com.

CARON

675 Madison Ave., near 61st St. (Subway: N, R, or W to 5th Ave./59th St.).

Although nothing will ever be as *charmant* as Caron's store on avenue Montaigne in Paris, this new store is great fun, as are the Caron scents, which are largely unknown in the U.S. I wear the one that was created for the first "air hostesses" (in 1947); it's spicy. I used to wear the old version of Fleur de

Rocaille, which is more floral. The line has a lot of history and is considered very sophisticated—so sophisticated, in fact, that regulars bring their own perfume bottles in for refills. If you don't want to be part of the wave of commercial scents being spritzed about and inserted into products, then visit Caron for an old-world alternative. All fragrances come only in perfume—nothing is diluted with *eau*. © **212/319-4888.**

CHANEL
15 E. 57th St., between Fifth and Madison aves. (Subway: N, R, or W to 5th Ave./59th St.).

Yeah, yeah, I know: Chanel is sold in every department store in America. But there is a tiny line of fragrances (about five of them), created by Coco herself, which is sold only in Chanel boutiques around the world. I know this because I wear one of them, Cuir de Russie (Russian Leather), which is spicy and a tad heavy—but I am a woman of a certain age and it's a heady scent. © **212/355-5050.** www.chanel.com.

JAR PARFUMS AT BERGDORF GOODMAN
754 Fifth Ave., between 57th and 58th sts. (Subway: N, R, or W to 5th Ave./59th St.).

Joel Arthur Rosenthal is a French jeweler (formerly of the Bronx) who has made his initials famous among the elite clients who know his Place Vendôme shop. Now he's branching into scent—and Bergdorf's has him. If you're dancing for joy, then you won't mind the price tags that begin at $350 and go up, up and away. © **212/872-2874.** www.jar-parfums.fr.

JO MALONE
949 Broadway, at 22nd St. (Subway: R or W to 23rd St.); 946 Madison Ave., near 74th St. (Subway: 6 to 77th St.); multiple other locations.

This British cult scent heroine merged into the Estée Lauder empire in order to go global; her first store in America rests between an **Origins** and a **M.A.C.**—two of Lauder's other brands. I mention all this because it was actually hard for me to find the shop; it is in the Flatiron Building, but proudly faces Broadway rather than Fifth Avenue.

Malone does not do color cosmetics (yet); rather, she does body treatments, bath products, perfumes, and home scents such as linen sprays and candles. The grapefruit group of products is a nice wake-up call or summer scent. Prices are so high here that it's a shame Malone doesn't produce smelling salts. Still, this is the ultimate New York status gift or insider name to drop. *Note:* The products cost less in London. © 866/ 305-4706. www.jomalone.com.

L'ARTISAN PARFUMEUR
68 Thompson St., near Spring St. (Subway: C or E to Spring St.).

This French specialty perfume maker has just opened its first shop in the U.S. While the brand has been carried in American department stores, this is its first free-standing store here. There are scents as well as potpourri and home fragrances— many nice gift items. You won't get out of here for less than $50. © 212/334-1500. www.artisanparfumeur.com.

PENHALIGON'S
870 Madison Ave., between 70th and 71st sts. (Subway: 6 to 68th St./Hunter College).

This English brand is now expanding around the world. Penhaligon's is old-fashioned yet a cult classic, with fragrance for both men and women. The names of the scents sound like they belong in a Jane Austen novel. What's interesting is that the firm makes colognes, which are water- and alcohol-based, but many people claim they have long-lasting powers. My favorite products come from the new leather-goods line of accessories for travel, bath, and bed. Note that Penhaligon's has bought the Erno Laszlo line of skin care and is relaunching it. © 212/ 249-1771. www.penhaligons.com.

HAIRSTYLISTS

FREDERIC FEKKAI
15 E. 57th St., between Fifth and Madison aves. (Subway: E or V to 5th Ave./53rd St.).

Okay, read my lips: Fred-er-*reeeek,* that's how we say it. If you say Fred-rick, you give yourself away as a hair novice. This multifloor salon offers the works: hair, beauty, and spa treatments, plus a cafe and retail products. I don't find it very calming, but it sure is fascinating. Even though the space boasts an indoor fountain, the models and photographers are what I find so distracting. It's a real trip.

All beauty and spa services are offered; I got hooked on a lavender rubdown here. Call ahead for an appointment—it takes about 3 months to get the master himself to give you a haircut and, thus, a new identity.

Fekkai has expanded into accessories such as headbands (adorable) and handbags (very chic), and has written a book as well. He recently announced plans to open a salon inside the Henri Bendel flagship store on Fifth Avenue. © 212/753-9500. www.fredericfekkai.com

JEAN-CLAUDE BIGUINE
1177 Sixth Ave., near 45th St. (Subway: B, D, F, or V to 42nd St./Bryant Park); multiple other locations.

The theory here is French class that's accessible to the American masses. This is a French chain of hair salons; just walk in for a *coupe* (cut), *le brushing* (styling), or whatever Madame needs, for a minimal fee; appointments are optional. Biguine is a bigwig (yuck, yuck) in France, but has only a few salons here in the States; he also has a new cosmetics line in France that I hope will come to these shores soon. © 212/921-4484. www.biguine.com.

NAIL SALONS

Nail salons are not only located on every other corner in Manhattan, but are found upstairs in town houses as well, where real-estate prices are slightly less expensive. In these places, you can usually get a manicure and pedicure in the $20 range. But there's also a lot of power nail-painting going on, and Ladies Who Lunch would not be caught dead in one of those cheapie neighborhood nail bars; these ladies have their own favorite spots, usually run by nail experts. Many spas, especially hotel spas, also offer nail services.

A couple of mass-market chains are taking over New York. I tested a branch of **Bloomie Nails** (no relation to Bloomingdale's) and adored it, though there was a bit of a high-pressure sell in terms of products and services. I had just arrived in New York and my ankles were swollen from the flight, so I got a manicure, a pedicure, and some sort of leg and foot spa treatment that was heavenly, even though it cost about $65 . . . just for the feet! There are locations all over town; call © **212/675-6016** or go to www.bloomienails.com.

BuffSpa
Bergdorf Goodman, 754 Fifth Ave., between 57th and 58th sts. (Subway: N, R, or W to 5th Ave./59th St.).

I'm sorry, but if this isn't a scene from TV's *Sex and the City*, I don't know what is—socialites and celebs gossiping while getting their toenails painted. Of course, you can have more than a pedicure, but to me, you go here for the scene or to be seen. To book, call © **212/872-8624**.

ElleGee Nail Salon
22 E. 66th St., between Fifth and Madison aves., upstairs (Subway: 6 to 68th St./Hunter College).

This source comes from Janet, who has great nails and insists on healthy treatments—and on patience and attentiveness from the staff. The price is steep ($35 for a manicure), but the location is deep in Madison Avenue shopping country and the services are top flight. To book, call © **212/472-5063.**

HAVEN
150 Mercer St., between Houston and Prince sts. (Subway: R or W to Prince St.).

Another SoHo treat—this spa offers what it calls the Mythic Manicure, which costs $25 and lasts for 2 weeks. To book, call © **212/343-3515.** www.havensoho.com.

RESCUE BEAUTY LOUNGE
8 Centre Market Place, between Grand and Broome sts. (Subway: 6 to Spring St.).

This Nolita nail salon has expanded and now attracts a large client list of celebs who come for the natural aromatherapy treatments. A basic manicure is $20 which, by New York standards, is a good price. This is not one of those salons that specialize in gimmick nails; this is a serious treatment center. To book, call © **212/431-0449.** www.rescuebeauty.com.

SPAS
....

The day-spa business has become so huge that it's hard to know a department store from a spa from a beauty salon these days. **Macy's** (p. 163) has opened a spa area. **Frédéric Fekkai** (p. 236) has full spa services, too; I went for the fake tan once. Many hotels have had spas for a while now—some even offer special jet-lag or shopping treatments to rejuvenate you.

AMORE PACIFIC
114 Spring St., between Mercer and Greene sts. (Subway: R or W to Prince St.).

If you think the best thing we ever got from Korea was the M*A*S*H television series, then you haven't checked out

Amore, a Korean beauty gallery and spa in SoHo. The space feels like a shrine of peace and simplicity; the skin-care line has been tested by mavens who claim it's among the best (it's sold uptown at Bergdorf's). As these things go, the prices are also sublime—about $100 for a 1-hour treatment, which is a bargain in New York. To book, call © **212/966-0400.** www. amorepacific.com.

AVEDA INSTITUTE
233 Spring St., between Sixth Ave. and Varick St. (Subway: 1 to Canal St., or C or E to Spring St.).

See p. 220 for more information. © **212/807-1492.** www. aveda.com.

AVON SALON & SPA
Trump Tower, 725 Fifth Ave., at 56th St. (Subway: N, R, or W to 5th Ave./59th St.).

See p. 220 for more information. © **212/755-AVON.** www.avon salonandspa.com.

BLISS SPA
568 Broadway, at Prince St. (Subway: R or W to Prince St.); 19 E. 57th St., between Fifth and Madison aves. (Subway: N, R, or W to 5th Ave./59th St.); 541 Lexington Ave., at 49th St. (Subway: 6 to 51st St.).

Bliss may be responsible for starting the day-spa craze in New York. The firm became so hot that it was gobbled up by LVMH; it has also morphed into a catalog and website of products. Bliss has clean, modern packaging and offers a look and feel of practical luxury—you feel like you're taking care of yourself, not wasting money or splurging on something silly. The environment is luxe, but the emphasis is on well-being. If you're looking for just the right gift for a bride, or a thank-you to an overworked friend or mom, the gift certificates are considered, uh, bliss. To book at any New York location, call © **212/219-8970.** www.blissspa.com.

CLARINS

1061 Madison Ave., near 80th St. (Subway: 6 to 77th St.);
247 Columbus Ave., near 72nd St. (Subway: B or C to
Columbus Ave.).

Face and body treatments are available at this store-cum-spa, where all the products are from the famed French brand. There's a special program for men, too. To book, call © 212/ 734-6100 for Madison Avenue, or © 212/362-0190 for Columbus Avenue. www.clarins.com.

MASTIC SPA

436 West Broadway, near Prince St. (Subway: C or E to
Spring St., or R or W to Prince St.).

This Greek spa sells products from its retail store, but also offers spa services. There are lines for men and for women, and the shop is very good about giving out samples. The all-natural cures are made with Mediterranean ingredients, be it oils or herbs. Color cosmetics are also available. To book, call © 212/219-3251. www.masticspa.com.

QIORA

535 Madison Ave., near 54th St. (Subway: E or V to 5th
Ave./53rd St.).

Located right in Midtown for the business crowd, this spa is also well positioned for visitors and shoppers alike. Owned by **Shiseido,** the spa offers treatments that combine beauty with instruction on relaxation techniques. To book, call © 212/527-0400.

Chapter Ten

....

NEW YORK HOME

HOME SWEET APARTMENT

For those with gobs of money, it's not hard to get in touch with the great names in interior design and to create digs that should be (and perhaps will be) featured in *Architectural Digest*. I'm usually looking for something less stellar. I did my first apartment in New York with castoffs found at curbside. I still hate to pay full retail price—especially when it comes to home furnishings and decorative items. In fact, I buy a lot of the things for my house in Provence at **T.J. Maxx** (p. 289) and bring them back to France. I'll search out a Target in any suburb, and I *loooove* Kmart style for basics.

If you're going high-end, toss this book aside and ask your secretary to dial a designer. If you do your own decor, are always looking for a deal, and like to mix mass and class, read on for my suggestions and those of Paul Baumrind, correspondent for *Born to Shop New York* and a real live interior designer.

TO THE TRADE

If you are seriously planning a renovation or refurbishment, you must know that the three little words most important to you are no longer "I love you" (or "You look younger"), but "to the trade."

"To the trade" signifies that the business will deal only with the design trade; those designers who wish to work with such firms must register and fill out documentation with their financial and credit history, thus opening an account.

In short, you can try printing up business cards that imply that you are a designer, which may get you into a showroom, but chances are that you won't be able to actually do business with the house until you open an account and establish credit. This can be very tricky, moderately tricky, or easy as pie; it varies from house to house and is usually worth a shot. Since business is worse than crummy these days, there is more latitude, except with the biggest, snobbiest houses.

Once you are able to "buy direct," as they say on the street, you will learn two new favorite words: net and gross. Net is the wholesale price. Gross is what the designer will charge the customer. If you are your own only client, you'll save the difference between net and gross. If you get these two terms mixed up (I do), you will never pass yourself off as a pro when you work the showrooms.

Remember, you still owe the tax man, so don't forget to pay up even when you buy wholesale.

Showroom Etiquette

Assuming you are faking your way through this, here are some step-by-step instructions. First of all, if you do have a friend who is legit, or at least knows the ropes better than you do, you should make a dry run with her or him so that you know how to behave and aren't a nervous Nellie.

In order to make a go of it on your own, please remember:

- **No showroom in the world wants to do business with tourists just in for the day.** Wear proper business clothing;

have well-made business cards; carry a shopping bag, tote, or attaché case for samples; and do not carry a diaper bag. A Polaroid camera is actually okay, as is a digital. Design showrooms will not let you take pictures, but antiques showrooms will.

- **Be warm, friendly, confident, and, above all, professional.** The regulars are well known. You are a newcomer. Walk to the desk, introduce yourself, offer a business card and a handshake (when appropriate), and sign in (if indicated). Explain your needs: "I have a client who asked me to take a look at your line. She's just wild about . . . "

- **Take the provided paper and pencil and write down style names and numbers as you work the boards of samples.** When you go to the desk (this is just like the library), ask about the policy on taking out samples. You will most likely have to register and establish credit to take out a sample. Find out when the sample is due back. Return it on time.

- **Ask about delivery dates.** Contrary to popular belief, a showroom is not a warehouse. The fabric or wallpaper you want is not on a shelf in the back somewhere. It may not even exist yet. Standard delivery is 6 weeks. Some showrooms take less time, and some take more—much more. You are expected to pay for half of the order when you "write paper" (place the order) and then pay the remaining portion upon delivery.

SPECIAL PROMOTIONS & EVENTS

Aside from the goings-on in the D&D (design and decoration) industry, there are a lot of tabletop people who are actually in the gift industry or other aspects of design. Many of them hold sample sales. On weekends before Christmas, a large number of warehouses are open to the public; there are ads in the papers and sometimes flyers handed out on the streets.

REGULAR RETAIL

There's hardly such a thing as regular retail anymore, and the days when a family walked into B. Altman and chose a living-room set are as dead as B. Altman. Nowadays, most department stores do not even have furniture departments.

Mass merchants who offer style and value have inherited the "regular retail" home-furnishings business: namely, **Pottery Barn** and **Crate & Barrel.** Terence Conran is here with the **Terence Conran Shop,** located under the 59th Street Bridge; **West Elm** is the newest contender—a catalog division of Williams-Sonoma that has its first stores in DUMBO and Chelsea. Many Manhattanites are willing to drive to the suburbs to get even better buys; **Ikea** (in Elizabeth, New Jersey) is thriving, as are out-of-the-way outlet stores.

ABC Carpet & Home has become one of the few full-service home-furnishing stores in the city. It's actually one of Manhattan's "showplace" stores, and it's an absolute retail dream. ABC has also created a renaissance in the neighborhood around it.

Most big-name American designers—and many European ones—have gone into the lifestyle business, as have some of the chains. **Banana Republic** has a home-decor department in its Rockefeller Center store, and both **Donna Karan** and **Calvin Klein** sell home style on Madison Avenue. The **Versace** people and the **Dolce & Gabbana** boys have been doing decorative arts for several years now.

There are design concepts that come from Europe and find a place in America; there are copycat firms that charge a lot of money for newly made antiques; there's style, there's wit, there's bad taste—all easily accessible, some easily affordable. But more importantly, now there's good taste that's affordable. And New York will never be the same.

TRENDSETTERS IN HOME STYLE

ARMANI CASA
97 Greene St., between Prince and Spring sts. (Subway: R or W to Prince St.).

Don't let the entryway fool you; this place is very deep and also has a downstairs level. The style here is Zen—not quite Asian, but very minimalist. Besides $50 dishes, there's furniture and now bedding (the latter also sold at Bloomingdale's). ✆ 212/334-1271. www.armanicasa.com.

BAKER TRIBECA
129 Hudson St., at Beach St. (Subway: 1 to Franklin St.).

This large showroom, located in trendy TriBeCa, sells mostly traditional American furnishings. I prefer the stuff upstairs—it's more solid and classic as opposed to the newer and edgier designs on the ground floor. ✆ 212/343-2956. www.baker furniture.com.

B&B ITALIA
150 E. 58th St., between Lexington and Third aves. (Subway: 4, 5, 6, N, R, or W to 59th St./Lexington Ave.).

Modern and moderne, and, as the name says, Italian. ✆ 212/ 758-4046. www.bebitalia.it.

CALYPSO HOME
199 Lafayette St., at Broome St. (Subway: 6 to Spring St.).

The Calypso empire began as ethnic-island ready-to-wear and has expanded into a lifestyle look complete with home store. Located near the original boutique, Calypso Home specializes in tabletop and gift items, plus some furniture. Prices are as varied as the pieces, but the customer is used to paying top dollar for just the right thing. It's perfect, darling, who cares what it costs? ✆ 212/925-6200. www.calypso-celle.com.

FELISSIMO
10 W. 56th St., between Fifth and Sixth aves. (Subway: E or V to 5th Ave./53rd St.).

Felissimo takes up an entire town house, where it sells artsy-fartsy gifts and tabletop goods in the most sumptuous surroundings in town. This place is a gallery of good taste. The dishes are somewhat in the same style as those at Armani Casa; you'll also find linens, paper, candles, and much more. It's a pleasure to indulge your senses in this tranquil space. Try the store's new scent. ☏ **212/247-5656.** www.felissimo.com.

PEARL RIVER MART
477 Broadway, between Grand and Broome sts. (Subway: 6 to Spring St.; or R or W to Prince St.).

I'm not sure that you can call this store trendsetting; it features all sorts of Chinese-style products, many of which are now considered chic and fun decor additions, and which are, at this time in style history, also trendy. This stuff has been around forever, though Pearl River itself has recently moved up the street from Chinatown. The Mao Communist souvenirs are considered cutting edge. You could get inspired here. ☏ **212/431-4770.** www.pearlriver.com.

RALPH LAUREN
867 Madison Ave., at 72nd St. (Subway: 6 to 68th St./ Hunter College); multiple other locations.

There isn't a bigger influence on modern mass design in America than Ralph Lauren and his faux-English, old-world, old-style country looks. To see it all in action, stop by the flagship in the old Rhinelander Mansion on Madison Avenue. There are also Ralph Lauren bedroom boutiques in a few department stores and at ABC Carpet & Home. Much of the big-time home-furnishings line is available to the trade; to get the bed linens at discount, try any of the Ralph Lauren outlet stores outside of the city, such as at Woodbury Common (p. 297). ✆ **212/606-2100.** www.polo.com.

SHABBY CHIC
83 Wooster St., between Prince and Spring sts. (Subway: C or E to Spring St.; or R or W to Prince St.).

If you adore comfy, oversize, upholstered furniture that could have come straight from Grandma's, then you've come to the right source. You can pay a fortune here for mismatched faded chintz or a giant cabbage-rose couch complete with slipcovers and throw pillows. *Tip:* Target now sells a line of home decor by Shabby Chic. ✆ **212/274-9842.** www.shabbychic.com.

TAKASHIMAYA
693 Fifth Ave., near 54th St. (Subway: E or V to 5th Ave./ 53rd St.).

I have raved in other parts of this book about Takashimaya, the elegant Japanese department store. Poke into the atrium, take a look at the French florist's booth, and go upstairs. Make the time—the displays are beautiful and the style is far more country French than Japanese. And, yes, there are a number of affordable items. Well, a few, anyway. ✆ **212/350-0100.**

TIFFANY & CO.
727 Fifth Ave., at 57th St. (Subway: F to 57th St.).

If you're thinking breakfast at Tiffany's, then you should be thinking about the trendsetting tabletop designs for which this store has become famous. In fact, Tiffany has even published a book on its table settings. The store has moderately priced items, so that while the reputation is upscale, just about anyone can afford something or other here. Learn how to mix your flea-market finds with Tiffany delights for the perfectly groomed table. ✆ **212/755-8000.** www.tiffany.com.

THE COMPLETE LOOK FOR THE HOME

Moss
146 Greene St., between Houston and Prince sts. (Subway: R or W to Prince St.).

The sleek store sells a little of everything, with an emphasis on gift items and home style in the quirky and moderne vein. The 7,000-square-foot space is fun, but I don't live and die by Philippe Starck lemon squeezers (though others do). Moss is somewhat like an art gallery—many products have either an edge or black humor in the subtext. ✆ 212/204-7100. www.mossonline.com.

Pearl River Mart
477 Broadway, between Grand and Broome sts. (Subway: 6 to Spring St.; or R or W to Prince St.).

Pearl River is a Chinese emporium of cheap chic. See p. 246 for more. ✆ 212/431-4770. www.pearlriver.com.

William-Wayne & Co.
850 Lexington Ave., at 64th St. (Subway: 6 to 68th St./Hunter College); 40 University Place, at 9th St. (Subway: R or W to 8th St.).

William-Wayne started out downtown as a funky little resource, and then turned rich and famous. One of the stores features wonderful accessories and tabletop items; Paul adores this place because he says it reminds him of my living room. That's a polite way of saying that it's crammed with fun junk, many with animal themes. The other shop has more of a country look and features garden and outdoor furniture. This is one of those New York cutie-pie stores that you just have to see, even if you don't buy anything. ✆ 212/737-8934 for Lexington Avenue; ✆ 212/533-4711 for University Place. www.william-wayne.com.

MASS PLUS CLASS

Perhaps the biggest change on both the social and design scenes in New York is that good design at low prices has not only become readily available, but is almost de rigueur in every economic bracket.

ABC CARPET & HOME
888 Broadway, at 19th St. (Subway: R or W to 23rd St.).

If you've ever doubted that retail is theater, then you haven't been to ABC Carpet. The street-level floor is an emporium of goods, with items for the home, for kids, and for gifts. Upstairs, there are floors devoted to fabrics, linens, and furniture. The thought that this is a discounter pervades, although frankly, I don't think they know the meaning of the word discount here (though there is a great outlet store in the Bronx, at 1055 Bronx River Ave., near Watson Ave.; ✆ 718/842-8772; Subway: 6 to Whitlock Ave.). They do, however, know the meaning of the words style, selection, and serendipity. ✆ 212/473-3000. www. abchome.com.

BED BATH & BEYOND
620 Sixth Ave., at 18th St. (Subway: 1 to 18th St.); 410 E. 61st St., at First Ave. (Subway: 4, 5, 6, N, R, or W to 59th St./Lexington Ave.); 1932 Broadway, at 65th St. (Subway: 1 to 66th St./Lincoln Center).

This national chain was one of Manhattan's first superstores, and its stores are *packed* with sheets, towels, kitchen items, and everything in the world you can imagine. The New York stores are not unlike the suburban branches, except they're even larger and grander. ✆ 800/GO-BEYOND. www.bedbath andbeyond.com.

CRATE & BARREL
650 Madison Ave., at 59th St. (Subway: N, R, or W to 5th Ave./59th St.); 611 Broadway, at Houston St. (Subway: R or W to Prince St.).

Chicago is no second city when it comes to exporting its most famous store to Madison Avenue. Its arrival created almost as much excitement as Barneys did when it opened up here several years back. There's a newer branch in SoHo as well.

Items range from plates to sofas, all chic but mass produced. The look tends to be clean and lean without embellishment—just old-fashioned, simple design in the right colors for the moment. The total lifestyle look seems perfectly designed for the places that New Yorkers inhabit (be they city apartments or country weekend retreats). Plus, the prices are bargains, the displays are great, and the salespeople are friendly. © 800/967-6696. www.crateandbarrel.com.

ETHAN ALLEN
1107 Third Ave., at 65th St. (Subway: 6 to 68th St./Hunter College); 192 Lexington Ave., at 32nd St. (Subway: 6 to 33rd St.); 103 West End Ave., at 64th St. (Subway: 1 to 66th St./Lincoln Center).

This company's reproduction furniture, which has been popular in suburban areas for ages, is now making a big splash in Manhattan. Its large showrooms feature a country and/or colonial look in various woods and veneers; the specialty is complete suites—bedroom, dining-room, and living-room sets. My designer friend Paul and I are both cringing as we tell you this. We'd rather buy from flea markets, but you might like brand-new. Suit yourself. I am compelled to confess that my sleigh bed, bought as a psychological refreshment after my husband died, came from here and I adore it. Sometimes it's not about quality or long-lasting furniture, but the thrill of the piece and the comfort it gives you. © 888/324-3571. www.ethan allen.com.

GRACIOUS HOME

1217 and 1220 Third Ave., at 70th St. (Subway: 6 to 68th St./Hunter College); 1992 Broadway, at 67th St. (Subway: 1 to 66th St./Lincoln Center).

This place has hardware, bed linens, vacuum cleaners, paint, wallpaper, and everything else you could possibly need as you renovate, restore, or redo your home. Prices are in keeping with regular retail in Manhattan, but most people don't mind because of the selection. The newer West Side location is more chic to me (I like the tabletop department), although prices on many items are way beyond me—like $100 a sheet. Still, Gracious Home is sort of an institution. © 800/338-7809. www.gracioushome.com.

HOME DEPOT

980 Third Ave., at 59th St. (Subway: 4, 5, 6, N, R, or W to 59th St./Lexington Ave.); 40 W. 23rd St., between Fifth and Sixth aves. (Subway: R or W to 23rd St.).

The famous suburban home-improvement store has two Manhattan branches. Civilization arrives in Gotham. © 212/929-9571. www.homedepot.com.

IKEA

1000 Ikea Dr. (New Jersey Tpk., Exit 13A), Elizabeth, New Jersey.

Ikea is a Swedish design firm that is famous for its simple, clean-lined, knockdown furniture—that means everything comes in a flat box and you put it together yourself. Prices are also knocked down, and while the furniture won't last a lifetime, it's great for a first apartment or a kid's room. There's free bus service from the Port Authority on weekends; call © 800/BUS-IKEA for details. © 908/289-4488.

JENSEN-LEWIS
89 Seventh Ave., at 15th St. (Subway: 1, 2, or 3 to 14th St.).

This Chelsea source specializes in a modern home look, especially leather and canvas furniture, and is conveniently located near a few other home stores. Very good prices. ☎ 212/929-4880. www.jensen-lewis.com.

RESTORATION HARDWARE
935 Broadway, at 22nd St. (Subway: R or W to 23rd St.).

I wish I could rave about this store the way many people do, but I find the merchandise very bland and so much like Pottery Barn meets Williams-Sonoma with a dash of Archie McPhee that I don't even know how these people stay in business, let alone thrive. Still, it's a popular resource for home stuff. ☎ 212/625-1374. www.restorationhardware.com.

SIMON'S HARDWARE
421 Third Ave., at 29th St. (Subway: 6 to 28th St.).

Paul (resident interior designer for *Born to Shop New York*) gives us this professional source where anyone can shop; it specializes in knobs, handles, and pulls for cabinets, doors, and more. ☎ 212/532-9220. www.simonshardwareandbath.com.

SMITH & HAWKEN
394 West Broadway, near Spring St. (Subway: C or E to Spring St.).

Smith & Hawken began as a catalog company and now has stores stretched across America. It sells stylish garden and home style with a touch of the green thumb. ☎ 212/925-1190. www.smithandhawken.com.

TERENCE CONRAN SHOP
407 E. 59th St., at First Ave., under 59th St. Bridge. (Subway: 4, 5, 6, N, R, or W to 59th St./Lexington Ave.).

The point of this store is to be more cutting edge than Crate & Barrel, but not too expensive. I admit that I am often confused between the offerings from Crate & Barrel and Conran's, though I know that the latter believes it is trendier. The Conran Shop also has a greater mix of merchandise, such as luggage, lifestyle gadgets, foodstuffs, and gifts. ✆ **212/755-9079.** www.conran.com.

WEST ELM
112 W. 18th St., between Sixth and Seventh aves. (Subway 1 to 18th St.); 75 Front St., at Main St., Brooklyn (Subway: F to York St.).

The good news is that New Yorkers have another resource in West Elm, and it's fun to discover DUMBO (though the ABC Carpet outlet there has recently shuttered). The bad news is that the Manhattan branch isn't very large—and the look is just a slightly dressed-up and woodier Ikea. Owned by Williams-Sonoma, the West Elm catalog firm is just now opening up brick-and-mortar stores. I didn't want you to think I was asleep at the wheel, but frankly, hand me the NoDoz. Aside from furniture for urban apartments, the store also sells tabletop and bedding. ✆ **888/922-4119.** www.westelm.com.

BIG NAMES IN TABLETOP

Go to the following stores for classics in crystal, porcelain, and more.

BACCARAT
625 Madison Ave., at 59th St. (Subway: 4, 5, 6, N, R, or W to 59th St./Lexington Ave.).
✆ **212/826-4100.** www.baccarat.fr.

BERNARDAUD/LIMOGES
499 Park Ave., at 59th St. (Subway: 4, 5, 6, N, R, or W to 59th St./Lexington Ave.).
© 212/371-4300. www.bernardaud.fr.

CARTIER
653 Fifth Ave., near 52nd St. (Subway: E or V to 5th Ave./ 53rd St.).
© 212/753-0111. www.cartier.com.

CHRISTOFLE
680 Madison Ave., at 62nd St. (Subway: 4, 5, 6, N, R, or W to 59th St./Lexington Ave.).
© 212/308-9390. www.christofle.com.

DAUM
694 Madison Ave., near 62nd St. (Subway: 4, 5, 6, N, R, or W to 59th St./Lexington Ave.).
© 212/355-2063. www.daum.fr.

LALIQUE
712 Madison Ave., near 63rd St. (Subway: 4, 5, 6, N, R, or W to 59th St./Lexington Ave.).
© 212/355-6550. www.lalique.com.

TIFFANY & CO.
727 Fifth Ave., at 57th St. (Subway: F to 57th St.).
© 212/755-8000. www.tiffany.com.

TRENDSETTERS IN TABLETOP & GIFT ITEMS

Don't forget museum gift shops for excellent and sophisticated tabletop items and gifts.

ADRIEN LINFORD
1339 Madison Ave., at 94th St. (Subway: 6 to 96th St.); 927 Madison Ave., near 74th St. (Subway: 6 to 77th St.).

Paul says that much of the merchandise here—gifts, tabletop, and rich-lady necessities—is also at Barneys. Items are often inventive and always chic. Much of the merchandise is the sort that comes from Vietnam but is identified as chic without being thought of as a souvenir. © **212/426-1500** for 94th Street; © **212/628-4500** for 74th Street.

AGATHA RUIZ DE LA PRADA
135 Wooster St., between Houston and Prince sts. (Subway: R or W to Prince St.; or C or E to Spring St.).

If there's only one Prada in your style lexicon, it's time to learn about this Spanish designer who does bright, hot colors and a very distinctive style that is possibly best loved by the young. The SoHo store—her first in the U.S.—has furniture, kitchenware, housewares, rugs, and bedding. Prices are moderate to low. You get a lot of wham for your buck here, but will you still love yourself in the morning? © **212/598-4078.** www.agatharuizdelaprada.com.

THE APARTMENT
101 Crosby St., near Prince St. (Subway: R or W to Prince St.; or 6 to Spring St.).

Talk about concept stores—this SoHo fun spot is set up like a real apartment, with fun, funky, and minimalist merchandise appropriately displayed in room sets. Don't miss the bathroom—the stuff in there is for sale, too. © **212/219-3661.** www.theapt.com.

AUTO
805 Washington St., between Horatio and Gansevoort sts. (Subway: A, C, E, or L to 14th St./8th Ave.).

Like an art gallery, Auto has a whole lifestyle selection of fashion, beauty, and home items that you might want to stare at but may be afraid to touch until you relax, look around, and see the humor. Do your wackiest gift shopping here. © 212/229-2292. www.thisisauto.com.

BARNEYS NEW YORK
660 Madison Ave., at 61st St. (Subway: 4, 5, 6, N, R, or W to 59th St./Lexington Ave.).

A marvelous store and a boon to Madison Avenue, but most of all, a fabulous gift and tabletop resource. Don't miss Chelsea Passage. © 212/826-8900. www.barneys.com.

BERGDORF GOODMAN
754 Fifth Ave., between 57th and 58th sts. (Subway: N, R, or W to 5th Ave./59th St.).

The seventh floor is the only stop you'll need to make if you want to get a quick survey of elegant choices for your home: beautiful china, linens, and stationery, plus nooks and crannies filled with the best-bought wonders of the world—from hand-painted dinner napkins sprinkled with gold dust to Venetian glass swizzle sticks. Kentshire Galleries has a shop here for antiques. © 212/753-7300. www.bergdorfgoodman.com.

JOHN DERIAN
6 E. 2nd St., between Second Ave. and Bowery. (Subway: 6 to Bleecker St.; or F or V to 2nd Ave.).

Don't be afraid of the neighborhood (just take a taxi)—fear instead the damage you can do to your credit rating here. Feast your eyes; feast your heart. This decoupage artist began selling plates to Bergdorf's and now has an empire of tabletop items and assorted other wares. It's truly an art form and the man is a genius, though an expensive genius. **John Derian Dry Goods,** the annex at no. 10, focuses more on linens and home furnishings. *Tip:* Sometimes you can find copies of his cut-and-paste items at Anthropologie for less moola. ✆ **212/677-3917**. www.johnderian.com.

Mackenzie-Childs
14 W. 57th St., between Fifth and Sixth aves. (Subway: F to 57th St.).

This small design firm from Vermont sells hand-painted everything. Anyone who has ever dreamed of coming to New York to see the best of American talent has got to step into this place to soak up the glory. You probably can't afford to buy more than a doorknob. But what a doorknob! ✆ **212/570-6050**. www.mackenzie-childs.com.

"REAL PEOPLE" TABLETOP

The only resource you really need for tabletop items, whatever your budget, is **Crate & Barrel** (p. 250). But if you're looking for a few other resources, well, New York's got more. And the more the merrier.

Fishs Eddy
889 Broadway, at 19th St. (Subway: 4, 5, 6, L, N, Q, R, or W to 14th St./Union Sq.).

See p. 106 for the dish on all the dishes at Fishs Eddy. If you're into restaurant supply and funky styles, this is a great stop. Prices are fair; style is high. The two uptown locations have closed, but Fishs Eddy's new designs can now be found at Gracious Home stores. ✆ **877/347-4733**. www.fishseddy.com.

Fortunoff
681 Fifth Ave., at 54th St. (Subway: E or V to 5th Ave./53rd St.).

Similar to, but not really a discounter . . . yet with a reputation for brands at a price; plus some estate pieces in jewelry and tabletop. Check out silver, china, dishes, other tabletop items, and even Swatch watches—this a good place to see it all, to register for it all, or to drool over it all. ✆ **212/758-6660.** www.fortunoff.com.

MICHAEL C. FINA
545 Fifth Ave., at 45th St. (Subway: B, D, F, or V to 42nd St./Bryant Park.).

All major china, crystal, and silver lines are discounted here— Lenox, Wedgwood, Spode, Noritake, and more. The jewelry counter is boring, but the gift shopping is tremendous fun. On a price-by-price basis, Fina may not always offer the best deals in the world, but for $15-to-$25 wedding gifts, look no further. ✆ **212/557-2500.** www.michaelcfina.com.

PIER 1 IMPORTS
71 Fifth Ave., at 15th St. (Subway: 4, 5, 6, L, N, Q, R, or W to 14th St./Union Sq.).

The imports here are from all over the planet and certainly hail from the world of inexpensive. It's a one-stop supermarket of wicker for your beach house or first apartment. You may find the Manhattan stores a little jazzier than many suburban branches, offering a bit more in the way of gift items rather than big pieces. ✆ **800/245-4595.** www.pier1.com.

POTTERY BARN
600 Broadway, near Houston St. (Subway: R or W to Prince St.); 127 E. 59th St., between Lexington and Park aves. (Subway: 4, 5, 6, N, R, or W to 59th St./Lexington Ave.); 1965 Broadway, at 67th St. (Subway: 1 to 66th St./Lincoln Center).

Whenever I need Christmas gifts in the $10 range, this is my first destination. Aside from the holiday specialties, you'll find a host of plates and platters, candlesticks, linens, and furniture. Add it to the resource list for beach homes and first apartments. ✆ **888/779-5176.** www.potterybarn.com.

SUR LA TABLE
75 Spring St., at Crosby St. (Subway: R or W to Prince St.).

Sur La Table is the wonderful tabletop-and-cookware resource that started out in Seattle's Pike Place Market. Now it's in SoHo and giving Williams-Sonoma a run for its money. ☎ 212/966-3375. www.surlatable.com.

WILLIAMS-SONOMA
110 Seventh Ave., at 16th St. (Subway: 1, 2, or 3 to 14th St.); Time Warner Center, 10 Columbus Circle (Subway: A, B, C, D, or 1 to 59th St./Columbus Circle); 121 E. 59th St., between Park and Lexington aves. (Subway: 4, 5, 6, N, R, or W to 59th St./Lexington Ave.); 1175 Madison Ave., at 86th St. (Subway: 4, 5, or 6 to 86th St.).

This cooking-oriented chain continues to pump out housewares, trendy must-haves for entertaining, and even its own cookbooks. Fancy cookware, gourmet foodstuffs, and tabletop items are the specialties. ☎ 877/812-6235. www.williams-sonoma.com.

BIG NAMES IN LINENS

FRETTE
799 Madison Ave., near 67th St. (Subway: 6 to 68th St./ Hunter College).

Frette sells fine and fancy Italian linen. It has also introduced a lingerie line, so you have something to wear between its fancy sheets. ☎ 212/988-5221. www.frette.com.

OLATZ
43 Clarkson St., near Hudson St. (Subway: 1 to Houston St.).

Oh my, Olatz—that's all I can say. I am not the kind of girl who spends $700 on a tablecloth. Neither am I married into the high worlds of art and entertaining and style and Cuban

hot-cha-cha. Still, it's fabulous to visit. ✆ **212/255-8627.** www.
olatz.com.

PORTHAULT
*18 E. 69th St., between Fifth and Madison aves. (Subway: 6
to 68th St./Hunter College).*

The most expensive beds in America are probably dressed in
Porthault prints from France—a set of king-size sheets with
standard pillowcases is well over $1,500. Every January, there's
a half-price markdown spree. I know some women who treat
themselves to one pillowcase a year; as time goes by, they
amass a delightful mélange of Porthault prints, which they mix
with white sheets (always a style classic) and American quilts—
the look is stunning. ✆ **212/688-1660.** www.dporthault.fr.

PRATESI
*829 Madison Ave., at 69th St. (Subway: 6 to 68th St./
Hunter College).*

More fine Italian linen. A basic sheet set does cost more than
$1,000 (but of course); then again, that's less expensive than
Porthault. Pratesi has numerous styles that are suitable for the
man who doesn't want to sleep in a bed of roses. Sales are held
in January and July. ✆ **212/288-2315.** www.pratesi.com.

SCHWEITZER LINEN
*1132 Madison Ave., near 84th St. (Subway: 4, 5, or 6 to
86th St.); 1053 Lexington Ave., near 75th St. (Subway: 6 to
77th St.); 457 Columbus Ave., near 81st St. (Subway: 1 to
79th St.).*

Schweitzer Linen carries only the high-end lines of major sheet
companies (like the Royal Collection or the Versailles Collection) and European sheets made to look like even more expensive European sheets: The only Porthault look-alikes I've ever
seen come from this firm. It caters to a well-off local crowd that

wants top-of-the-line quality, subtle prints, and the European look. Schweitzer also does custom work. © 800/554-6367. www. schweitzerlinen.com.

OFF-PRICE BED LINENS

Most of my bed linens come from either **T.J. Maxx** (p. 289) or **Century 21** (p. 290) . . . or the **Pratesi** outlet in Italy. In fact, the thought of paying regular retail makes my nose itch. The department stores often have good sales, though. In addition, many specialty stores have their own look and their own home-style departments. Also, if you make the trek to the Lower East Side, you may see newer styles than you'd find in off-price stores, though at a mere 20% off regular retail.

While the Lower East Side is trying to transform itself more into a home-style area than a discounter's paradise, and many resources have moved out, you can still count on **Harris Levy** (278 Grand St., between Forsyth and Eldridge sts.) for 20% off on bed linens.

European shoppers, take note: Bed sizes in the U.S., U.K., and continental Europe are different—know what you are doing! Sheet sizes are frequently marked in centimeters as well as inches, so look at the small print.

KITCHEN CONCEPTS

BODUM
413 W. 14th St., between Ninth and Tenth aves. (Subway: A, C, E, or L to 14th St./8th Ave.).

This Danish brand has trendy kitchen items at fair prices. A visit to Bodum is a good way to stock a kitchen, see the Meat-packing District, and make a pit stop at the store's cafe. © 212/367-9125. www.bodumusa.com.

BRIDGE KITCHENWARE CORPORATION
711 Third Ave., at 45th St. (Subway: 4, 5, 6, 7, or S to Grand Central/42nd St.).

Calling all cooks! This is the favorite address—note that it's a new location—of professional chefs in Manhattan. Whatever kitchen utensils you may need, this place will have them. © 212/688-4220. www.bridgekitchenware.com.

BROADWAY PANHANDLER
477 Broome St., at Wooster St. (Subway: C or E to Spring St.).

This housewares store seems ordinary enough at first, but it has become a local legend. Check out the selection of Wilton cake supplies and professional equipment for fancy baking. Also known for great prices on kitchen equipment. © 212/966-3434. www.broadwaypanhandler.com.

THE CONTAINER STORE
629 Sixth Ave., at 19th St. (Subway: 1 to 18th St.); 725 Lexington Ave., at 58th St. (Subway: 4, 5, 6, N, R, or W to 59th St./Lexington Ave.).

The Container Store is a good source for organizational home style and for getting started in a new home. Its first Manhattan location, across from Bed Bath & Beyond on Ladies' Mile, makes it easy to shop and compare. A second location has opened near Bloomingdale's. © 888/CONTAIN. www.container store.com.

DEAN & DELUCA
560 Broadway, at Prince St. (Subway: R or W to Prince St.).

This upscale SoHo grocery store, greengrocer, and cookware shop has the beautiful people (and a coffee counter where you can stare at them), the beautiful fruit, and the prices to match.

I love it here and insist that you visit. © **212/226-6800.** www.deananddeluca.com.

BATHROOM CONCEPTS
....

Obviously **Bed Bath & Beyond** (p. 249) is a good place to start for bathroom accessories. Other fine resources include **The Container Store** (p. 262) and discounters like **T.J. Maxx** (p. 289) and **Century 21** (p. 290). If you want to spend more, **Gracious Home** (p. 251) has plenty that will spin your head.

THE APARTMENT
101 Crosby St., near Prince St. (Subway: R or W to Prince St.; or 6 to Spring St.).

See p. 255. © **212/219-3661.** www.theapt.com.

PORTICO HOME
Time Warner Center, 10 Columbus Circle. (Subway: A, B, C, D, or 1 to 59th St./Columbus Circle).

The SoHo store has closed, but Portico remains a good source for fancy bed linens and bathroom chic. The new location in the Time Warner Center will open in 2007. In the meantime, shop online or call © **646/383-4805** to visit the design showroom at 430 W. 14th St. © **877/517-8800.** www.portico home.com.

WATERWORKS
225 E. 57th St., between Second and Third aves. (Subway: 4, 5, 6, N, R, or W to 59th St./Lexington Ave.); 469 Broome St., near Greene St. (Subway: C or E to Spring St.).

When you care enough to have the very best, shop at Waterworks for everything from fixtures to bathroom design elements. Prices are high, but the selection is unique and sophisticated. © **800/998-BATH.** www.waterworks.com.

ELECTRONICS CONCEPTS

....

APPLE STORE
103 Prince St., at Greene St. (Subway: R or W to Prince St.).

The Big Apple now has its own extremely hip Apple Store. There's a Genius Bar upstairs to help you understand tech stuff. What has SoHo come to? *©* **212/226-3126.** www.apple.com.

BEST BUY
60 W. 23rd St., at Sixth Ave. (Subway: F or V to 23rd St.); multiple other locations.

Here's another instance of the suburban big-box chains coming into Manhattan. This branch of Best Buy is in a great part of town (near The Container Store and many off-pricers) and has electronics for the whole family. Other locations are popping up around town; call *©* **888/BEST-BUY** for addresses. *©* **212/366-1373.** www.bestbuy.com.

BROOKSTONE
16 W. 50th St., near Rockefeller Plaza. (Subway: B, D, F, or V to Rockefeller Center).

This is the original big boy's toy and gadget store, with plenty of products to test. There's probably a branch in the mall nearest you. Good source for gifts. *©* **212/262-3237.** www. brookstone.com.

COMPUSA
420 Fifth Ave., at 37th St. (Subway: 6 to 33rd St.); 1775 Broadway, at 57th St. (Subway: A, B, C, D, or 1 to 59th St./Columbus Circle).

CompUSA is a big-box warehouse store, just like in the 'burbs, for computers, software, and supplies. It also does repairs. *©* **800/COMP-USA.** www.compusa.com.

HAMMACHER SCHLEMMER
147 E. 57th St., between Lexington and Third aves. (Subway: 4, 5, 6, N, R, or W to 59th St./Lexington Ave.).

This is the place for gadgets and toys and travel devices and everything that whirrs and whistles and goes bump in the night. There are floors and floors of fun and novelty items—some of them are even practical and worth the money. ✆ **212/421-9000. www.hammacher.com.**

J&R MUSIC & COMPUTER WORLD
Park Row, between Ann and Beekman sts. (Subway: R or W to City Hall.).

The best source for electronics and boy toys—and a homegrown alternative to all the national chains. ✆ **212/238-9000. www.jr.com.**

SHARPER IMAGE
10 W. 57th St., between Fifth and Sixth aves. (Subway: F to 57th St.); multiple other locations.

For the life of me, I can't adequately explain the difference between Brookstone and Sharper Image, except that the gadgets at Brookstone tend to be more health- and relaxation-oriented, while Sharper Image has more technology items and cutting-edge toys. ✆ **212/265-2550. www.sharperimage.com**

SONY STYLE
550 Madison Ave., at 56th St. (Subway: E or V to 5th Ave./53rd St.).

You can play with all the latest toys and gadgets and technology here. You cannot, however, play with the many boys and young men who hang out here. ✆ **212/833-8800. www.sonystyle.com.**

HOME-FURNISHING FABRICS & YARD GOODS

....

Also see the "Fabrics, Notions, Trims & More" section on p. 165 and take a look at the small shops clustered on East 20th and East 19th streets near Broadway (around the corner from ABC Carpet & Home).

PATERSON SILKS
151 W. 72nd St., between Columbus and Amsterdam aves. (Subway: 1, 2, or 3 to 72nd St.).

This place is pretty funky, and you'll need a bit of a sense of humor to shop here. These guys are mass purveyors of fabrics, curtains, slipcovers, and even fashion fabrics. Last time I stopped by, the selection made my skin crawl. After I got used to the stock, though, and adjusted my sights, I realized there were a lot of simple basics at very good prices. Also at 300 E. 90th St., at Second Avenue. ✆ **212/874-9510.**

PIERRE DEUX
625 Madison Ave., near 59th St. (Subway: 4, 5, 6, N, R, or W to 59th St./Lexington Ave.).

This reincarnation of Pierre Deux has far more than fabrics—it's an entire French-country lifestyle shop. It carries Les Olivades printed fabrics and its own custom-made line. (It no longer sells Souleiado.) Also check out the gift and tabletop items. ✆ **212/521-8012.** www.pierredeux.com.

SILK TRADING CO.
ABC Carpet & Home, 888 Broadway, at 19th St. (Subway: R or W to 23rd St.).

This chain has stores in various design centers around the country, but has debuted in Manhattan with its own "boutique" within ABC Carpet & Home. It boasts a stunning selection of silks by the yard from international sources, but also sells ready-made draperies along with some furniture and accessories. © 212/473-3000. www.silktrading.com.

FLEA MARKETS

Just because you buy it at a flea market does not mean it's a bargain—or that the price is any better than in a store. Know your prices and comparative values, and keep in mind that this is alternative retail—vendors may tell you any old hogwash in order to get you to buy. We've heard "antiques" vendors say some outrageous (false) things about their wares. Be careful. You should also know that cash is preferred (especially if you are bargaining), most markets are held on weekends (and some vendors appear on only one of those days), outdoor markets are held "weather permitting" (which means there's no market in a downpour or when it's freezing), and some markets do not operate on the weekend between Christmas and New Year's.

Special-event flea markets, such as the **Pier Shows,** are sensational, especially when money is tight and dealers want to raise cash. Watch the trade newspapers for announcements of these shows and other markets. See below for more on Brimfield, the king of the flea markets.

THE ANNEX/HELL'S KITCHEN FLEA MARKET
W. 39th St., between Ninth and Tenth aves. (Subway: A, C, or E to 42nd St.).

The Annex, the best flea market in New York, got driven out of Chelsea by the neighborhood's own success: The parking lot that it called home was sold to make room for new construction. Now it has relocated and joined forces with the Hell's Kitchen Flea Market. This is one of the best in terms of getting the adrenaline running and the heart pumping fast for a few hours of shopping fun. I must warn you, however, that this place was "discovered" a while ago, so the prices can be very high, and vendors may not know their stuff. The crowd that shops, however, is as much fun as the dealers and the goods. Open Saturday and Sunday from 9am to 5pm. © **212/243-5343.** www.hellskitchenfleamarket.com.

BRIMFIELD ANTIQUE & COLLECTIBLES SHOWS
Brimfield, Massachusetts.

The country's wildest flea market is held three times a year in Brimfield, a small Massachusetts community near Sturbridge Village. About 50,000 people show up for each of the three weeklong events. Thousands of dealers from all over the country come to Brimfield; this is truly the largest flea market in the world. The May fair is the most popular, but all three are worthwhile for antiques dealers, as well as professional shoppers and pickers. If you aren't quick-witted, you'll be trampled to death!

The pros are there when the gates open at 7am and run around like maniacs papering the place with money. I just go for the day and don't do it that way, but you should experiment and find your own style.

Please note that the flea markets are held in several areas in town, and that it really does take most of the week to do this properly, the way a dealer should, so a day trip might be frustrating. The event lasts a week, but most of the various areas are open only for 3 days during each event.

Book motel rooms way in advance if you're staying over. Leave the kids at home. The market is held in May, July, and September; for exact dates, call © **413/245-3436** or **508/597-8155**, or check www.brimfield.com.

GREENFLEA M.S. 44
Columbus Ave., between 76th and 77th sts. (Subway: 1 to 79th St.).

This is a varied market with several parts to it so, as a whole, it's got something for everyone. You'll see a small greenmarket—don't miss the pretzels—and both an outdoor and an indoor portion of the flea market.

The outdoor portion brims with colors, energy, and style. You'll find lots of arts and crafts and, of course, traditional flea-market–esque "antiques." A large percentage of people seem to have just returned from some exotic destination and offer wares from wherever they traveled to (Ecuador, Mexico, Bali). There's also a small amount of new and basic merchandise (socks, underwear, pet needs). Nothing beats a gorgeous day, a hot pretzel, and all this fun.

Inside the school is a jumble of "antiques"—I get claustrophobic from it all. I'm happy enough with the used treasures sold outside; on a pretty day, it seems like a sin to be indoors, and the crowds don't agree with me. Open Sunday only, from 10am to about 5:30pm. ✆ **212/239-3025.** www.greenflea markets.com.

GreenFlea P.S. 41
Greenwich Ave., at Charles St., between Sixth and Seventh aves. (Subway: 1, 2, or 3 to 14th St.).

This schoolyard extravaganza comes complete with greenmarket. It gets going late, so don't arrive before 11am. This is part of the Village's glory. Open Saturday only. ✆ **212/239-3025.** www.greenfleamarkets.com.

AUCTIONS FOR ART & ANTIQUES

There's a war going on in them thar sale rooms, so stay tuned. **Christie's,** hoping to ease past **Sotheby's** and get more business, has lowered the seller's premium. The world waits with bated breath to see who sneezes next.

For buying art, antiques, collectibles, or fancy junk, auctions are a good training ground. If you study catalogs, go to viewings, eavesdrop on conversations, and attend enough auctions, you'll become knowledgeable not only in the art of auctioning, but also in the nuances of the items you collect and of those who also collect them.

There are two types of auction houses: big-time and fun-time. They never get the same kinds of lots, though each big-time house has a more casual division.

Things go to auction for two reasons: One, a collector has decided to give up a piece or pieces of his or her collection; or two, a collector has died and the estate needs to liquidate the assets. Country auctions are usually the best places to find over-looked pieces. These auctions are advertised in local papers as well as in *Antiques and the Arts Weekly,* published by the Bee Publishing Company (© 203/426-3141; www.thebee.com). If you're looking for something more serious to keep you up on the latest auctions, get a subscription to *Art + Auction,* a glossy magazine dedicated to those who care.

Previews (also called viewings or exhibitions) are very important and occur the week before the auction. During the auction, there is no time to think or change your mind; you must know ahead of time if you are going to bid on a piece, and you can even send in a sealed bid or fax your bid ahead of time.

During previews it is important to think about the following questions:

- Are there provenance papers on the item (which give the history of ownership)? All quality pieces of furniture and art will have them.
- What is the condition of the item? How many repairs have been done to the legs? Can you tell if anything has been replaced? Has the piece been refinished recently, and if so, by whom? Can you ask the owner for details? Usually the answer to this last question is "No." In this case, you might consider hiring a consultant to look at the piece for you.
- Can you guarantee authenticity? Provenance papers help, of course. I need not tell you about all the fakes that have gone through the auction houses. Quality houses will authen-ticate as best they can, but even they get fooled sometimes.

Authentications will be found in the catalog listing. If nothing is listed, ask why. Very often the auction house cannot risk giving a guarantee unless there is no question as to the origin of the item. I once attended an auction where the auctioneer asked the artist to stand up and authenticate her work of art in person.

Once you leave the preview, take the catalog home and read the fine print. Everything you need to know about how the auction will be run and what the house is responsible for handling is in the front or back of the catalog.

Check to see if the piece you will be bidding on is "subject to reserve." "Reserve" is the minimum price for which the piece will be sold. It is a confidential price known only to the auction house and the owner of the piece. However, it is important for you to know if you will be bidding against a set price, as sometimes the piece will be taken off the block if the reserve is not met. Sometimes the house will bid on behalf of the consignee (the person who is auctioning the item) to meet the reserve.

Tucked into the catalog, or on the final pages of the book, will be a list of prices for the lot numbers that show what a similar item went for at a previous date, or what the house estimates the sale price to be. This can give you an idea of where to expect the bidding to fall. Or it might not. One of the reasons that auctions are so much fun is that you never know what will happen.

Once you have done your homework and decide to attend the auction to bid on one or more "lots," there are a few more details:

You may be asked to register when you arrive at the auction house. If the auction involves high-stakes items and you are going to be bidding above $10,000, bring credit references with you. Once you have registered, you will be given a "paddle" with your bidding number on it. This number corresponds to your registration. During the auction, names are never used. Lots are assigned to the highest bidder's number.

Don't be shy when bidding. If the auctioneer can't see your paddle, you will lose out on the bidding. Everything you've heard about sneezes, flicks of the wrist, or eyebrow arching is nonsense. While some people bid in a subtle motion, everyone does know what's going on—even if paddles aren't being used.

If you can't be present at the auction, you can name a representative to bid for you, or be on the phone with a member of the auction-house staff. It is also possible to bid by mail. Absentee bid forms are published in the auction catalog, or can be obtained from the auction house by mail.

When figuring price, don't forget to add in the auction-house commission and the tax. Ask ahead of time what the auction house will be taking as its cut. If you thought the price you bid was the price paid, welcome to the cruel world of auctions. The auction house gets from 10% to 20% of the sale price. If you are bidding on a large item, figure in the cost of delivery also. The auction houses all have services to help you get the item home, but they are not free.

Payment will be requested at the time of the sale, unless you have an account with the house or have arranged ahead of time to be invoiced. All large auction houses preregister bidders and check references.

Payment for goods will be asked for in U.S. dollars. Although you will see prices being quoted on the currency board in many international currencies during the bidding, it is merely for the convenience of the international clientele, so that they can compare the price in dollars with the price in their own currency. On small items, you can often pay with American Express, Visa, or MasterCard.

If you are planning on shipping your purchase out of the country, be sure to obtain an export permit from either the auction house or whatever department of antiquities applies—the auction house will tell you. As in European countries, some items may not be exportable. Check with a U.S. Customs expert in this area.

You will be expected to take possession of your purchase within 3 working days. After that time, you will be charged a storage fee.

Read the Thursday Home section of the *New York Times* for listings of weekly events. Also check ads in the Friday *Times* and, perhaps, the Saturday *Times*.

If you are observing but aren't planning to buy, you may be a tad nervous. Relax. You're welcome here, even if you don't bid. Dress like you own a bank, and you'll be fine. Admission to a big-time event is always by catalog (the catalog admits two)—pay for the catalog at the desk before the preview, right before the actual auction, or subscribe. Prices range from $2 to $25.

Many big-time auctions are star-studded events and may be black tie. A collection of important jewels, by the way, does have a viewing, but the bidding is done with slides on a screen, as if it were home-movie night. Remember to keep your cool when the really big rocks are screened. Previews are far more casual than auctions; you may even attend in jeans, as long as you are wearing Gucci loafers with them. It is better to go to the preview, but it's not imperative if you are not planning on buying. You will see the items at much closer range at the preview, and you can touch many of them. This is a no-no during the auction.

Should you plan to buy for the first time in the big time, you may want to walk through it all at an auction that is not yours, just to get the lay of the land. After all, there's no reason to be intimidated or unduly nervous when you will have enough on your mind spending your trust fund on a piece of canvas and oil paint.

CHRISTIE'S
20 Rockefeller Plaza, at 49th St. (Subway: B, D, F, or V to Rockefeller Center).

Christie's is a British firm; Sotheby's is based in the U.S. People who shop big-time auctions do not prefer one house to the other; they merely choose the auction they are interested in. Both houses will treat you and your money with equal charm or disdain, depending on your money and your manners. Call to request a catalog. © **212/636-2000**. www.christies.com.

DOYLE NEW YORK
175 E. 87th St., between Lexington and Third aves. (Subway: 4, 5, or 6 to 86th St.).

Doyle's tries to acquire some unusual items not seen in the other houses; it's not quite as intimidating to me as the big-timers. The house has important auctions and must get your attention if you are a serious shopper, even though snobs will tell you it just isn't Christie's. © **212/427-2730**. www.doylenew york.com.

PHILLIPS
450 W. 15 St., between Ninth and Tenth aves. (Subway: A, C, E, or L to 14th St./8th Ave.).

Phillips is an international auction house of the same caliber as Christie's and Sotheby's. It is able to acquire lots of good-quality items, some with incredible pedigrees, representing centuries of ostentatious buying or conservative wealth poured discreetly into fabulous collections. © **212/940-1200**. www. phillips-dpl.com.

SOTHEBY'S
1334 York Ave., at 72nd St. (Subway: 6 to 68th St./Hunter College).

Sotheby's is the world's "other" famous auction house, leading the ranks along with Christie's. It publishes a catalog for all sales, national and international. You can subscribe to the catalogs that deal only with your collecting mania (painting, pre-Columbian, furniture, and so on), which is a wonderful way to keep up with the international market in your area.

Sotheby's experts are available for consultation to both buyers and sellers. (Other auction houses also provide this service.) If you have a piece of art that you think is worthy of being put up for auction, you can make an appointment to bring it in or have an expert visit you. I've fallen in love with a few of the Sotheby's experts; they know their stuff and are really fun to be with—especially when you share a common interest.

Sotheby's **Arcade Auctions** are for those of us who can't yet afford an Old Master. These sales are well within the affordable range and often involve surprise packages. Sotheby's also has sidewalk sales, when it marks down its unsold items. Look in the newspaper for an announcement of these sales; it'll be the most fun you've had in years. © 541/312-5682. www. sothebys.com.

SWANN GALLERIES
104 E. 25th St., between Park and Lexington aves. (Subway: R or W to 23rd St.).

Specialists in books and paper goods, movie posters, and ephemera, this upstairs location is low-key and funky. **Tepper Galleries** is at street level; and no, I'm not mixed up—Swann is upstairs, so take the elevator. You'll be thrilled when you get there. © 212/254-4710. www.swanngalleries.com.

HOITY-TOITY ANTIQUES: THE UPPER EAST SIDE

The Upper East Side is home to the best of the best. If you are looking for a Ming vase, Empire chairs, a Federal hutch, or a Louis sofa, and have a well-endowed checkbook, look no further. These shops are superb in both quality and selection. The owners are knowledgeable and willing to help you find what you are in search of. They will also authenticate and help you ship.

Most hoity-toity shops are specialists; many require an appointment and are not even open to the public. (I haven't listed any of those, thank you.) Seek and ye shall find; shop and ye shall spend. If you are buying, dress however you please. If you are browsing, please look the part and dress up in respect for the artworks and the dealers.

NEWEL GALLERIES
425 E. 53rd St., between First Ave. and Sutton Place. (Subway: 6 to 51st St.).

This one is in a category by itself and is one of those "Gee, Toto" kinds of places. They do not have one of these in your hometown, no matter where you come from (unless you're from Manhattan). Shocking and wonderful and weird and fabulous and incredible and not to be believed and—well, you just have to go see this for yourself: Newel is an antiques resource of extraordinary proportions. Many pieces are for rent; all are one of a kind. You have to experience the six floors of warehouse space here to appreciate Newel's unusual nature. This is theater. This is what you came to New York for. Closed on weekends. ✆ **212/758-1970.** www.newel.com.

NOT QUITE HOITY OR TOITY, BUT FANCY

In the last few decades, East 60th Street in the 200 block has been many things. Lately, the area has become home to a large number of antiques shops selling mostly Continental antiques, not of the Lord-Rothschild-is-pleased category, but far above the flea-market and garden variety. There are almost two dozen dealers here, so the best thing to do is just walk and wander. Begin at no. 207 and make your way east—a few shops are open to the trade only.

And Don't Forget

MANHATTAN ART & ANTIQUES CENTER
1050 Second Ave., between 55th and 56th sts. (Subway: 4, 5, 6, N, R, or W to 59th St./Lexington Ave.).

This place houses about 100 dealers selling this and that. I have bought here and used to come here often; now I prefer tag sales and flea markets, but this is still fun. These are professional dealers, and they know what they've got. © 212/355-4400. www.the-maac.com.

NOT-SO-FANCY ANTIQUES

You don't have to grow up in Versailles to want to buy antiques. Even if your budget is limited, you can still find enough selection and enough specialty items to make a trip to the markets worthwhile. Recent college grads and young professionals, take note: You can have your cake and eat it, too.

Enjoy Madison Avenue and the East Side and all the gilt trips you can stand, but take your checkbook when you travel to 12th Street or to Brooklyn—these are the areas where designers go to nose through lots of stuff, hoping to find hidden jewels. The shoppers wear blue jeans or are properly dressed professionals, although Brooklyn on a weekend is decidedly laid-back.

Atlantic Avenue, Brooklyn

Many of the antiques shops that could no longer pay the rent in Manhattan have moved to Atlantic Avenue. The street is incredibly long and houses many, many antiques stores of varying quality and price range. From Manhattan, take the F train to Bergen Street. Walk back along Smith Street and turn right onto Atlantic after 3 blocks. On weekends, there's a flea-market–like affair set up by dealers for locals.

The greatest concentration of antiques shops starts at Hoyt Street and continues along Atlantic Avenue for about 10 blocks.

University Place

Located between the Village, SoHo, and the nether regions of Lower Manhattan, University Place is a street that's just filled with the fun kind of antiques shops that I love to prowl. University Place starts right below 14th Street and ends at Washington Square Park; it creates its own little neighborhood, bounded by Broadway, which at this point in its life is now on the East Side.

University Place, along with the little side streets between Fifth Avenue and Broadway, is not the home of the $35 bed frame, but this is where affordable furniture can be yours. You should know your market if you are spending a lot of money or think you have a serious piece; otherwise, just enjoy.

If this sounds like I've just told you about the funkiest little yet-to-be-discovered part of town ever created, think again. Some very sharp dealers have already moved down here and are slowly creating a gentrified zone connected to the renewal of the entire Fifth Avenue area between 23rd and 14th streets and the Gramercy Park area. The area is so well combed by dealers that the diamonds get ferreted out very quickly. You may be forced to make do with rhinestones. And if you're the kind who only likes the high and the mighty, honey, this ain't for you. Home, James.

Chapter Eleven

....

NEW YORK BARGAINS

BARGAIN CAPITAL USA
....

New York, with so many retail opportunities, also has a lot of bargain opportunities. Retail has been hard hit by the city's struggle for financial recovery, so everywhere you look, there's a sale or a deal. And this is the town where the slogan "I can get it for you wholesale" is a way of life. So step this way— have I got a deal for you.

If you're visiting from overseas, no doubt you think New York, even at regular retail prices, is indeed a bargain mecca, because compared to Britain or France in terms of regular retail prices, it is. And you haven't even been to Woodbury Common yet. And you probably don't know about Filene's Basement or Loehmann's. If you're British, you probably do know about T.J. Maxx, but maybe not. And you surely have never heard of Century 21. Don't even know to thank Sy Syms and his firm, Syms, in your nightly prayers? Read on, read on.

I urge all international visitors to New York to read this chapter and highlight the good parts. If your English is spotty, get a dictionary. This is the part where I tell you about the *gangas* (that's "bargains" in Spanish—and, yes, it was one of the first words I learned in that language).

SALES

....

You can get a good bargain at any good store, but in New York you get an incredible selection during sale times. Since many department stores carry the same merchandise, you may be able to build your wardrobe as you go from store to store, buying part of an outfit at one store and finishing the look off with a component from another store.

Like all parts of the United States, New York has two big sale periods: Spring and summer merchandise are sold at rock-bottom prices mid-July through August, and fall merchandise goes on sale right after Christmas or in January.

Some stores have cyclical sale periods—they clean house every 60 to 90 days and mark down automatically, with or without big sale announcements. Or, they may have private sales for charge or preferred customers. If a store needs cash, it may host a 1-day sale, with hours from 8am until 11pm (or so), just to bring in as much traffic as possible and boost the bottom line.

Most sales are announced in local newspapers, and some special sales are written about editorially, as in *New York* magazine's "Sales & Bargains" column (also online at www.new yorkmetro.com). Even factory outlets have sales. Sometimes a store runs a coupon ad in the newspaper that corresponds to a sale—you get a 15% or 20% discount with the use of the coupon. This is not as low-rent as it sounds; some of Manhattan's biggest department stores do it regularly, especially around holidays when they want to jumpstart the shopping season.

Sales in New York come in all different flavors. When Chanel runs a sale, it prints an invitation in the *New York Times* telling customers that they can "refresh their wardrobes at reduced prices." How's that for genteel? My friend Polly convinced me that we had to cover the Hermès sale for academic purposes and, oh my, what a fiasco: hand-drawn poster boards on the floor of Hermès with arrows pointing to the upstairs salon; silks in clear plastic garbage bags piled on the floor; ladies' room closed to sale shoppers. Enter this door; exit this door; stand here, Madame; yes, we are sold out of silk scarves; no, Madame, we do not give boxes or gift-wrap sale merchandise.

The conditions of the sale are posted in the store during the sale. Yes, even at the Hermès sales they do this. Some stores specify a no-return policy during sale periods; if an item is not returnable, the clerk must tell you that it is not returnable, and the sales slip must also state this fact.

One final tip about sales: At the American designer stores and department stores, after-Christmas sales take place, well, after Christmas—either the day after Christmas or else right after New Year's. However, the European designer boutiques in New York tend to have their sales much, much later in January—the third or fourth week of the month, to be exact. I mention this because if you are flying to New York specifically to shop the after-Christmas sales, do not assume that December 26 is the magic day. It may in fact be January 26! Also note that the July sales are now held during the last week of June.

NONTRADITIONAL RETAILING

Most New Yorkers depend on various nontraditional methods of retailing to keep up their standard of living: vintage clothing continues to be popular; jewelry and accessories are frequently bought off the street or from markets that sell their low-cost wares off pegboards; and trips are often made to New Jersey for bulk shopping. There are private parties in homes for direct selling, and there are newsletters listing sample sales.

Smart shoppers combine their good clothes and luxury brands with items bought from catalogs, discounters, off-pricers, street vendors, and private sales—and get away with it.

DEPARTMENT-STORE SECRETS

New York is the king of department-store flagships, so even if you have a branch of these stores in your hometown, you owe it to yourself—and your bottom line—to visit the Manhattan location. With-it department stores have mouthwatering colors, ambience, entertainment, and cachet, in addition to great markdowns (they're often able to offer their shoppers a kind of value not seen elsewhere). You'd be surprised at just what kinds of bargains and treats you may find in New York's department stores.

Besides offering fantastic sales, look to department stores to offer promotions and customer services you just can't find elsewhere. A large department store once gave away a second strand of pearls to customers who bought one strand (a Mother's Day promotion), and cosmetics and perfume gift-with-purchase deals and giveaways are commonplace. The big thing now is the bonus—bring in a coupon to get a free product, turn in your old lipstick and get a free new one, and so on. There might not be a free lunch in New York, but there certainly are free makeovers. Extras are everywhere you turn in department stores.

When it comes to bargains, remember that department stores have to unload merchandise just like every other retailer does. They do this through the rather old method we all love best: sales. But when the sale merchandise isn't all sold, what happens to it? It does not go to retail heaven. Usually it goes back to the warehouse, to be held for the annual department-store warehouse sale—or to the factory outlet. Yep, department stores now have factory outlets. They are all located outside of Manhattan, out of respect for regular retail, but they aren't hard to get to, so read on.

Note: If you are not experienced at negotiating department-store sales, ask a salesperson for help. There are often additional markdowns off the last ticketed price, which may be hard to discern.

TIPS FOR BARGAIN-BASEMENT SHOPPING

Here are some tips for shopping the bargain basements:

- Remember that bargain basements may or may not have new merchandise. Some get their goods at the beginning of the season; others don't get new items until traditional stores have dumped their unsold merchandise. Old merchandise is always less expensive than new merchandise.
- Look for damages.
- Know the return policy before you buy.
- Try everything on; actual sizes may be different from the marked sizes.
- If you are shopping in a chain, understand that another branch of that chain will have some of the same merchandise and some different merchandise; the better the zip code, the better the choices. Along the same lines, different factory outlets can have entirely different merchandise in exactly the same time frame.
- Expect communal dressing rooms and sometimes-primitive conditions.
- Be prepared to check your handbag and/or your shopping bags. Security can be offensively tight at bargain basements.
- Remember that few bargain basements will mail packages for you.

Shop a department store before you go to a bargain basement so that you know what kinds of prices to look for. At various well-known bargain basements (all listed in this book), I saw the same designer blouse on the same day for several different prices that covered a range of more than $100. The Saks Fifth Avenue price was $230. I then saw the blouse at different outlets for $180, $163, $142, $109, and $93. It is impossible to know which bargain is the very best bargain when you are shopping, but try to do a little homework first.

Also know that department-store prices can be competitive with outlet prices. Try this experience on for size: I was shopping at my beloved Filene's Basement, where I found a truly fabulous, stunning skirt by a Belgian designer for the Filene's Basement price of $49. A sensational bargain. But wait: The Neiman Marcus price tag, still attached, showed all the markdown prices that Neiman's had used in order to sell this little skirt. The last price on the floor at Neiman's was $51! While both prices are great bargains, there ain't much margin here, and department-store prices, very frequently, are as good as it gets.

Some bargain basements just don't have bargains. Let the shopper beware.

DISCOUNT STORES & OFF-PRICERS

So what's the difference between a discounter and an off-pricer? The discounter sells some current brand-name merchandise and some private-label merchandise at a 20%-to-25% discount off prices that you'd find in department stores. The off-pricer sometimes sells current merchandise that is gleaned from a warehouse closeout, but often sells older merchandise at a deeper discount.

Just for comparison's sake, remember that sale prices in any department store are 20% to 50% off. The big difference is that the department store offers the sale price after the merchandise has been on the floor for a while. The discounter starts off with the "everyday low price."

Discounters may also have merchandise made for them, specifically created by designers to be sold at low prices—Target is famous for this, but Loehmann's used to sell clothes made by the big brands that you couldn't differentiate from designer clothes unless you compared the two pieces.

Target and **Kmart** are two of the more famous discounters. **Filene's Basement, Century 21, T.J. Maxx,** and **Daffy's** are off-pricers. I actually think that **Loehmann's** functions as both. As we go to press, there is no Target store in Manhattan. However, there are Target stores outside of New York, as well as frequent Target promotions and temporary stores in New York City.

Off-pricers offer the most savings. These stores can be smaller and less fancy than discounters, or as big as a warehouse and very nicely decorated. Have you been to **Century 21** lately? The Manhattan store was redone after the September 11, 2001, terrorist attacks, and is as fancy as any department store. Century 21 has also redone its store in Brooklyn.

Easy Access: These Stores Are Everywhere

CONWAY

1333 Broadway, at 35th St. (Subway: B, D, F, N, R, Q, V, or W to 34th St./Herald Sq.); 11 W. 34th St., between Fifth and Sixth aves. (Subway: B, D, F, N, R, Q, V, or W to 34th St./Herald Sq.); 201 E. 42nd St., at Third Ave. (Subway: 4, 5, 6, 7, or S to Grand Central/42nd St.).

Conway has many different branches and parts to it; to get the real flavor, you must shop at the giant store on Broadway, near Macy's. The other stores are ordinary and bland, but not this one: It's a real Turkish bazaar (albeit air-conditioned), with tables piled high with merchandise—out-of-season; discontinued, unloved styles; and designer overruns. This branch is the souk of your dreams, but you have to like the jumble. This is not Bendel's. This is a bargain basement in the truest sense of the word; all it lacks is basement space. Only for the strong-hearted!

There are actually more than five different branches in the same neighborhood. If you like cheap clothes for your kids, inexpensive towels for summer camp, or discounted household goods, you just might have a good time here. International shoppers get a discount when they show their passports to the cashier. © 212/967-3460 for Broadway flagship.

DAFFY'S

335 Madison Ave., at 44th St. (Subway: 4, 5, 6, 7, or S to Grand Central/42nd St.).; 125 E. 57th St., between Park and Madison aves. (Subway: N, R, or W to 5th Ave./59th St.); 1311 Broadway, at 34th St. (Subway: B, D, F, N, R, Q, V, or W to 34th St./Herald Sq.); 1775 Broadway, with entrance on W. 57th St. (Subway: A, B, C, D, or 1 to 59th St./Columbus Circle); 462 Broadway, at Grand St. (Subway: R or W to Prince St.).

I always check out this source in homage to past bargains and as a tribute to my Gypsy soul—I just can't pass up the idea of a bargain. Daffy's does get some names sometimes, and you can do rather well for yourself. I especially like the idea that one of the branches is almost next door to the Four Seasons.

The store on Madison, though not the biggest, is convenient for Midtown shoppers. The East 57th Street store is the fanciest and easiest to shop. The West Side store, near Macy's, is a many-level splendor inside a mall: It is truly overwhelming. And I am not overwhelmed easily. That branch—and the one at Broadway and West 57th—are my least favorite. Although the old store on Lower Fifth Avenue has closed, there's a brand-new location in SoHo.

Like all the places listed in this section, it's very much hit-or-miss at Daffy's. © **212/557-4422** for Madison Avenue location. www.daffys.com.

DSW (DESIGNER SHOE WAREHOUSE)

40 E. 14th St., near University Place (Subway: 4, 5, 6, L, N, Q, R, or W to 14th St./Union Sq.).

This is an enormous space devoted not only to shoes for men, women, and kids, but also to accessories and gift items. There are tons of brands (and a handful of really, really big-name brands—such as Pucci). Note that this is in the same building as a branch of Filene's Basement. © **212/674-2146.** www.dsw shoe.com.

FILENE'S BASEMENT

4 Union Sq. S., near University Place (Subway: 4, 5, 6, L, N, Q, R, or W to 14th St./Union Sq.); 620 Sixth Ave., at 18th St. (Subway: F or V to 14th St.); 2222 Broadway, at 79th St. (Subway: 1 to 79th St.).

Filene's Basement stocks overruns and unsold designer goodies, from shoes to underwear, for men and women. It has departments for petites, plus sizes, and some home style (not much). The Boston stores are better, but that doesn't mean you should ignore the New York branches (heaven forbid). It just means that New York can be spotty; you have to get lucky. I just bought an Alberta Ferretti evening skirt for $299. There's also a good selection of Jones New York.

Announcement: The New York stores now participate in the bridal sale—a total madhouse with a heap of wedding gowns at rock-bottom prices, usually $99 each for dresses worth up to $10,000. So here's the deal: You wait in line, then you race in and grab *any* gown. Then you can trade with other people if you want. The sales are usually in February and November and are announced on the website.

Note that the new Union Square store is atop DSW, while the Sixth Avenue location is in the same building as T.J. Maxx, so you can get two birds with one credit card. © 212/358-0169 for Union Square location. www.filenesbasement.com.

FORMAN'S

82 Orchard St., near Broome St. (Subway: B or D to Grand St.); 560 Fifth Ave., near 46th St. (Subway: B, D, F, or V to Rockefeller Center); 59 John St., at William St. (Subway: A, C, J, M, Z, 2, 3, 4, or 5 to Fulton St.).

Forman's is one of the oldest and most established discount sources in Manhattan; for decades it was famous for its stores on the Lower East Side. While it still has a store there, the company has changed its approach and opened stores in many key shopping districts—even on Fifth Avenue!

Forman's carries brands like Ellen Tracy, Ralph Lauren Polo, and so on, and sells petites, coats, some accessories, and other items. Forman's also stocks a lot of Jones New York, a brand I like and often buy. This brand's trousers go for $119 in department stores. If you can find them at Loehmann's, they sell for $89. At Forman's, they cost $109—a mere $10 discount off the department-store price. This is not impressive, but it's something.

Sometimes there are end-of-season sales, when bargains get better, so it's always good to check. Those on the mailing list also receive postcards announcing special discounts and deals. *Note:* All Forman's stores are closed on Saturday. © 212/228-2500 for Orchard Street location.

LOEHMANN'S
101 Seventh Ave., at 16th St. (Subway: 1, 2, or 3 to 14th St.).

I've found that the quality of shopping at Loehmann's has improved enormously in recent years; either I've gotten lucky or things are looking up. Now I come here as a first stop in my downtown discovery tour of bargains.

The store is clean and modern—and crammed with merchandise, so that racks bulge and items sometimes droop onto the floor. You might want to go first thing in the morning when you have lots of energy to explore. Loehmann's sells men's and women's accessories and designer stuff. On my last visit, I was shocked by how many French brands were on hand—brands that as an American shopper I probably would not have known. Not that status is everything, but I got things at a fraction of their Paris costs.

The store has a very aggressive promotional policy, so you may be rewarded with coupons for further shopping dates, including discounts during the week of your birthday. © 212/352-0856. www.loehmanns.com.

T.J. Maxx
620 Sixth Ave., at 18th St. (Subway: F or V to 14th St.).

This off-pricer sells a little of everything—clothing for men, women, and children; underwear; shoes; luggage; home accessories; and bed and bath products. It even carries some big-name designers every now and then. My favorite finds here have been home items, dishes, picture frames, and gifts in the $10-to-$15 price range. For serious clothing, you have to be lucky—although there are clothes in all sizes and styles. © 212/229-0875. www.tjmaxx.com.

Slightly Out-of-the-Way

Aaron's
627 Fifth Ave., between 17th and 18th sts., Brooklyn (Subway: M or R to Prospect Ave.).

A sign near Aaron's, a Brooklyn bargain basement that is worth the trip a thousand times over, says: IF YOUR HUSBAND ISN'T IN THE BUSINESS.

You do need to be organized to get to Aaron's, but it's far more worthwhile than the Lower East Side and certainly simpler than renting a car and driving to an outlet mall in the 'burbs. Don't mind that it's 20 to 30 minutes away on the subway; it's worth the trip. The Brooklyn subway station is clean and non-threatening, and the 1-block walk from station to store is safe and simple. You may have hot flashes, though, when you get inside: The amount of stuff is a little overwhelming.

Aaron's has about 10,000 square feet of clean, well-lit space with neat racks and handwritten signs that identify many of your favorite designers. The variety of names ranges from the traditional (Jones New York), to the expected, to the big-time (Adrienne Vittadini). Clothes I've never seen discounted elsewhere are sometimes carried here. Stock is kept in the back, so if you don't see your size, ask, and it will be brought forward. The sales help is nice; no one is too pushy.

The tags are marked down 20% to 25% off regular retail, which might not be the bargain of the century, but there is a lot of stock and selection. Often, there are even further discounts.

The store opens at 10am, which makes it a good first stop. Leave your hotel at 9:30am and avoid rush-hour traffic. Aaron's charges $5 to send a large package out of state; its refund policy is posted.

Directions: Take the M or R train to Prospect Avenue in Brooklyn, which will put you at Fourth Avenue and 17th Street. Then walk 1 block east to Fifth Avenue. It's easy, and you can't miss it. © **718/768-5400.** www.aarons.com.

CENTURY 21

22 Cortlandt St., between Church St. and Broadway (Subway: R or W to City Hall or Rector St., until Cortlandt St. reopens in 2007).

Words fail me and my palms get sweaty when I think about Century 21. There is no question that this is one of the best bargain resources in New York. Though the merchandise in the Manhattan store was damaged during the 9/11 attacks on the World Trade Center, the building's structure was left quite intact and the store has been back in business for several years now.

Century 21 sells name brands at discounts—and, my friends, what names! I've seen some heavy-duty designers (Armani, Lacroix, Prada, Sonia Rykiel, Tod's) that I've never spotted at Filene's Basement or anywhere else. The store sells men's, women's, and children's clothing; linens; shoes; luggage; small electronics; and name-brand perfumes and cosmetics. Prices, for the most part, are 40% lower than retail; they range from 25% to 75% off, depending on the item.

The women's underwear selection is pretty good, and there is a small department for plus sizes. The shoe department separates out the Tod's from the rest. I am addicted to designer sunglasses, which I buy here for about $50 a pair. You can get European designer ties for $40 to $50 each (saving about $70 per tie), and you can even snag Annick Goutal perfumes. The perfumes and cosmetics are not discounted, but Century 21 has an incentive system so that the more you buy, the larger the gift coupon you get for use on any item in the store.

Besides its department store in Lower Manhattan, Century 21 has a recently refurbished store in Brooklyn in the middle of real-people neighborhood Bay Ridge, with a separate home-style store behind; it's at 472 86th St., between Fourth and Fifth avenues (© **718/748-3266**; Subway: R to 86th St. in Brooklyn). There are also locations in New Jersey and Long Island. © **212/227-9092**. www.c21stores.com.

LOEHMANN'S (THE BRONX)
5740 Broadway, at 236th St., Bronx (Subway: 1 to 238th St.).

Note that this listing is for out-of-the-way locations; the Loehmann's on Ladies' Mile, in Manhattan, is listed on p. 288. There is also a branch in Sheepshead Bay, Brooklyn, at 2807 E. 21st St., at Shore Parkway (© **718/368-1256**).

Naturally, you've heard of Loehmann's and probably shopped in one of its many stores, but this location is its flagship, housed in a former ice-skating rink in a lovely section of the Bronx called Riverdale-Kingsbridge. You can't miss the structure: Its domed roof is easily spied from afar. While this Loehmann's is nice, it's not immensely different from the Loehmann's in your own neighborhood, and might not be worth the trip if you are visiting from out of town. However, I have found designer clothes in this store that weren't in other branches. Impossible to know.

The store itself is clean and spiffy, complete with benches for husbands to sit on and the Back Room, where the big-name designer collections are housed. There are other bargain shops, off-pricers, and discounters nearby, so you can make a day of it.

Directions: To get here by subway, take the 1 to 238th Street. Exit onto Broadway and walk 2 blocks south. By bus, take the regular BX no. 9 to West 236th Street (at Broadway); the

Liberty Lines express bus BMX no. 1 (which runs along Third Ave. in Manhattan) to West 239th Street; or the BMX no. 2, which runs up Sixth Avenue in Manhattan, to the same stop in the Bronx.

By car from the West Side: Drive north on the Henry Hudson and exit at West 239th Street. It's probably easier to go from the East Side by taking I-87 North (Major Deegan Expwy.), exiting at West 230th Street or Van Cortland Park South (W. 240th St.); then heading west a block or two to Broadway. Call for more specific directions. © 718/543-6420. www.loehmanns.com.

Just for Men

ROTHMAN'S
200 Park Ave. S., at 17th St. (Subway: 4, 5, 6, L, N, Q, R, or W to 14th St./Union Sq.).

The old Harry Rothman's on Fifth Avenue is gone. This store, on Park Avenue South, is run by Harry's grandson. There's quite a little collection of discount stores on this block, which makes it convenient for women to shop while men take in the glories of the reincarnated Harry's, which sells discounted big-name designer clothes and suits. It has a wide variety of sizes, so any man can find the right fit. This store is near the Greenmarket and all the excitement at ABC Carpet & Home and Ladies' Mile, so you can't afford to miss it. © 212/777-7400. www.rothmans ny.com.

FACTORY OUTLETS

The factory-outlet business has become so attractive (that means profitable) that many makers are overproducing perfect merchandise for their outlet stores. This capitalizes on the designer's well-known name and expensive advertising campaign, which has already been paid for, and reaches a totally different segment of the market, so it doesn't compete with the traditional retailers.

The prices in factory outlets are usually the same as at discount stores or department-store sales—20% to 25% off regular retail. A dress that has a $100 price tag usually sells for $79 at an outlet. But it can sell for $50, and certainly will be marked down as the season draws to a close. The discount may vary on a per-item basis, since irregulars should be less expensive than overruns.

Outlets may or may not offer a better deal than off-pricers. Generally speaking, an off-pricer has better bargains than an outlet store, unless you hit a sample sale or special promotion. On the other hand, if you have the opportunity to spend a day at Woodbury Common, an entire city of outlets, you may indeed do all the shopping and saving you might ever crave.

There are several factory-outlet villages in the greater New York area that offer different types of shopping to the eager public. I feel very strongly that no trip to New York could be called a proper shopping excursion without a visit to at least one of the outlet malls. If you're going to only one, there is no doubt in my mind that it should be **Woodbury Common;** it's both easy to get to and easy to shop.

A few general outlet survival tips:

- Wear comfortable shoes—you'll do a lot of walking.
- Carry high heels in a tote bag if you need them to get the right look for clothes you may try on.
- If possible, avoid bringing young children with you.
- Go with a friend, and share the driving if you've come a long way. You will be exhausted at the end of the day, so reserve enough energy to deal with the drive back. This kind of shopping is more fun with a friend, anyway.
- Drive if you can; it's worth the price of a rental car. I once saw bargains at the Eileen Fisher outlet that were so great that the trip more than paid for itself. Bring friends and share the cost of the rental.

- Know that weekends are very crowded; a weekday visit is preferable if possible.
- Read the carefully posted signs about return policies before you buy. The rules vary from store to store, but most warehouses allow returns within a 7-day period.
- Sign up on mailing lists if you want. Each warehouse has a mailing list and will honor out-of-state addresses, although it may not send to addresses outside of the U.S.
- If someone is carrying an interesting shopping bag, ask questions. Discount shoppers love to help others.
- Do not assume a bargain or a best-price-in-town price tag.

JERSEY GARDENS
651 Kapkowski Rd., off the New Jersey Tpk., Exit 13A, Elizabeth, New Jersey.

Jersey Gardens is a relatively new mall that sprang up near Newark Airport and existing superstores like Ikea. The reason that designers, manufacturers, and retailers are fighting it out now is that the mall is very, very attractive and is drawing traffic from regular retail—several other Jersey malls report that business is down 20% in some categories, and they are furious.

This mall has more than a million square feet of shopping, which includes a mix of outlets and value-oriented stores as well as restaurants and diversions to keep the whole family dizzy. In fact, it's more amusement park than outlet village.

Most of the architecture is hot and spiffy, though some of the outlets are the bare-bones type. The style of the mall reminds me of properties run by the Mills Corporation, which does not happen to own this mall. In total, there are 201 stores (as opposed to the 220 in Woodbury Common); all are indoors.

Among the tenants are several department-store outlets, such as **Off 5th Saks Fifth Avenue Outlet** and **Neiman Marcus Last Call**. There are also off-pricers like **Daffy's** and **Filene's Basement**. For main-street brands, there's everything from **Gap** to **Banana Republic**.

Directions: There are shuttle buses from New York's Port Authority and from Newark Airport; the bus service from Manhattan doubles up on weekends, although the crowds do, too. Call New Jersey Transit at © 973/762-5100 for bus departure times.

SECAUCUS OUTLETS
Secaucus, New Jersey.

Secaucus has an industrial zone that's more or less devoted to factory outlets, but it's in no way similar to any outlet village you've ever been to. This is true industrial space, with warehouse units, a few small commercial malls that fit the traditional outlet-mall profile, and free-standing units dotted all over the place—you must shop and drive.

There are a series of showrooms; some of them are 20,000 square feet, new, clean, and well lit. There are no dumps here, but it's all urban sprawl. Of course, that's the point. The area is in constant flux; there is no charm. There are over 100 stores in the area as well as a nearby regional mall, the **Mall at Mill Creek,** which is a normal mall, not an outlet center.

Tip: When you arrive, pick up the free magazine for the area, which will help orient you with what's new or what's where—it also has coupons in it.

Here are some basics:

- The outlets are separated into two main areas: **Harmon Cove** (20 Enterprise Ave.) and **Outlets at the Cove** (45 Meadowlands Pkwy.). I suggest you start at Harmon Cove because it's a mall and it has an information booth. When I visited, the woman at the information booth was filled with ideas and tips; she gave out free coupons and knew what was happening throughout the entire area, not just in her little mall. For the skinny on the Secaucus outlets, you can also call © 877/688-5382 or go to www.hartzmountain.com.

- Never, never attempt to go to Secaucus and Flemington (home of **Liberty Village** outlet mall and many other outlet stores) on the same day, unless you are a masochist.
- Know that the distances between the various warehouses are not that huge, but the area is bigger than Disneyland (and much more fun). Be prepared to move your car constantly—at least five or six different times.
- Be aware that stores do move around and change. I couldn't believe the differences since I was here last. The best way to be on top of the changes is to use the free booklet that's given out everywhere. You can also go to www. secaucusoutlets.com for advance planning.
- Know that some venues and sales are seasonal. They are advertised with banners and signs.
- Read the locally printed broadside that is free at your first stop. There's also a map, so you can take some time to plot your day.
- Stores are usually open at least from 10am to 5pm Monday through Saturday, often with later hours on Thursday and limited hours on Sunday; not every store is open on Sunday. Note that hours at the various stores can vary considerably— for example, the Century 21 outlet (yawn) opens at 10am except on Thursday and Sunday, when it opens at 11am. Later Sunday hours you were expecting, but Thursday?
- Try to eat at off-peak hours—there are not enough restaurants around. Or bring snacks. There is a food court in the Harmon Cove mall.
- Yes, Dunkin' Donuts has indeed opened.
- Bring your checkbook—most stores take them and there's no hassle for out-of-state checks. You must have a driver's license and two IDs, though. Traveler's checks are accepted; some credit cards are taken.
- Don't judge a book by its cover. While all the outlets are clean, some of them have decidedly uncute names.
- Be aware that there are kids' clothing outlets, but no toy outlets. If you are bribing your kids into good behavior, bring your own bribery materials.

Eileen Fisher Fans

If you are an Eileen Fisher freak, as I am, know that the outlets are as gorgeous as any store—and are huge and filled with stock! Regular price tags are on the garments, but each grouping has a sign attached to it saying how much to deduct. Worth the trip if you're loading up.

Directions: Take the Holland Tunnel to New Jersey, then Route 1 and Route 9 North to Route 3 (this takes only a few seconds); take the Meadowlands Parkway exit. You'll sort of dead-end; follow signs thereafter.

Call ✆ **800/626-RIDE** for New Jersey Transit bus information and routes from New Jersey and Manhattan's Port Authority.

Weekends away: Die-hards who need serious shopping time can book a room at any of a dozen local hotels. **Crowne Plaza Meadowlands** (✆ **201/348-6900**) has a room-and-breakfast deal for $99 and provides a free shuttle to the outlets. This deal is good for 1 night only and must be reserved in advance, subject to availability.

WOODBURY COMMON
498 Red Apple Court, Central Valley, New York.

Woodbury Common has changed so dramatically in the last few years that I don't know where to begin. Since it will continue to evolve, take a Xanax and dream of renting a golf cart to get around this enormous village-mall. The additions at Woodbury make it so exciting that it cannot be compared to its sister malls in New Jersey, or anywhere else. It has more high-end stores than those others, and *oui,* the only **Chanel** factory outlet in the world. This is, hands down, the king.

If you are an international visitor to the United States, you'd better take notes or videotape—your friends at home just won't believe this place. Bring your station wagon, bring your van, bring your pals. And for heaven's sake, bring your credit cards.

I guess the most important thing I should do is warn you that the area is now too big to do in a day, so you might want to consider spending a night nearby. If you get overwhelmed easily, do research when you arrive so you can hit the places that interest you the most.

Visually speaking, Woodbury Common is the most attractive of the outlet villages. Its core is a fake colonial village, and each shop (you enter from outdoors) is a different pastel shade—it's so cute that you may want to move in. The new additions are not as cute as the center part. They aren't uncute, they're just more economically built. With the new additions, the village has grown a little wild—it sprawls here and there and you could do well with a golf cart to get to all the outlets. Consider moving your car once or twice, although this is impossible on weekends and could be impossible any day— the later in the day it gets, the harder it is to find a parking space.

There are 220 outlets in the village, including many big-name shops like **Armani, Barneys, Brooks Brothers, Burberry, Calvin Klein, Coach, Cole Haan, Crate & Barrel, Dior, Ellen Tracy, Ferragamo, Frette, Gucci, J. Crew, Joseph Abboud, Loro Piana, Neiman Marcus Last Call, Off 5th Saks Fifth Avenue Outlet, Samsonite, Space (Prada, Miu Miu), Theory, TSE, Tumi,** and **Versace.**

Stop by the information center for a free map and newspaper upon arrival. You may want to join the VIP Shopper Club (www.premiumoutlets.com/vip). There are several clean restroom stations scattered around the mall. Of course, there are places to have coffee or a bite. What they really need is a hotel on the premises.

Directions: The drive is easy (on a gorgeous highway) and beautiful almost any time of the year, especially autumn. It takes approximately 1 to 1½ hours from Manhattan. Hop on the

New York State Thruway (I-87) and get off at Exit 16. Almost immediately after going through the tollbooth, you will see the mall to your right.

If you are visiting from Connecticut, not Manhattan, you may wonder about the best route because of the limited number of bridges across the Hudson River. Again, it depends on which part of Connecticut you are coming from, but I saved a half-hour by using the Tappan Zee Bridge in my drive from Fairfield County.

You can also get here via **Gray Line** (© **800/669-0051** or 212/397-2620), which operates buses from the Port Authority, at 42nd Street and Eighth Avenue. There are several morning buses and afternoon/evening return buses each day; all riders get a discount coupon booklet. The cost is about $37 per person.

Hours are usually daily from 10am to 9pm, except for some holidays. © **845/928-4000**. www.premiumoutlets.com/woodburycommon.

STREET MERCHANTS

The street merchants in Manhattan are really best for beads and trinkets—and should only amuse you, not take your shopping budget. In good weather, there's someone at every other corner selling a small selection of something: watches, sunglasses, handbags, books, pearls, ties, sweaters, and so on. In bad weather, there are folks selling things like umbrellas, gloves, and scarves.

The quality of all this merchandise is suspicious, but if you take it with a grain of salt, you may find that the shoe fits. The umbrella will last long enough to get you through the storm, the pearls won't turn, and the watches may work for quite some time.

Street hawking, especially of fake or counterfeit merchandise, is essentially illegal, so most hawkers are on the lookout for the police and will roll all of their merchandise into a ball and be gone in less than 30 seconds should anyone look at them suspiciously. Street hawkers are abundant or scarce depending on the police presence at any given time. They try to work popular areas and to attract visitors—Fifth Avenue in Midtown boasts a fair number; Sixth Avenue in the Village (near Bleecker St.) and Lower Broadway (near Astor Place) are other good places to find street merchants. I've also noticed that there are more folks out on the streets on weekends than on weekdays.

When I really need something fake, I simply pop onto the subway and go to Canal Street, where prices and selection are superior.

Counterfeits & Imitations

If you're talking street merchandise, you have to be thinking of the most nontraditional retailing ploys of them all: counterfeit. Or stolen. Or merely "lost." The watches are no doubt counterfeit, while the sweaters may have just gotten "lost" from their original warehouse. It's so hard to keep track of all those trucks, you know.

There is some room for debate as to when an item becomes a counterfeit, a copy, or a knock-off, and at what point it's illegal. If the intent is to defraud the true maker, the item is a counterfeit. Thus, all those $25 Gucci, Rolex, Dunhill, and Cartier watches that street merchants sell are counterfeits. It is illegal to sell them and probably illegal to buy them. There are waves of fashions in fakes—Chanel fakes are harder to find these days, while Dolce & Gabbana fakes are the rage. Coach is also hot.

Most brand names that are sold on the street are frauds, so look carefully at the way the signatures are made. Some Gucci fakes look like Gucci from afar, but careful inspection reveals that those aren't even Gs in the pattern. That's not a fake. It's an attempt to take advantage of your bad eyesight or inattention to detail. But it's legal.

New York does not have the sophisticated counterfeits that can be found in Italy or Bangkok—most U.S. fakes scream "fake" and are just for fun. A few of them are cute enough as joke presents, even though they don't really look that much like the real thing when you inspect them carefully. I would never, ever give a fake and attempt to carry it off as the real item. Blatantly fake merchandise is rather easy to spot. It looks cheap, feels cheap, and may even smell cheap. Good copies take a more practiced eye:

- Know what the real thing looks and feels like.
- Know if the real maker even has the same style. Those phony Chanel-style sunglasses sold on Canal Street? Sure, they look cute, but as it turns out, Chanel sunglasses don't even come in that particular style! See those silly Chanel-style earrings that are studs for pierced ears? Chanel does not manufacture studs. And so on.
- Check the weight of the goods (good watches are very thin these days, for example), the texture of the fabrics, the lining, the stitching, the make of the label, the way the trademark is made. Real Ray-Ban sunglasses not only say Ray-Ban on them (as do the fakes), but also have little RB initials smoked into the lens near the temples. This is difficult or impossible to fake. Most big-name designer goods have the name of the firm etched into the mold for the hardware. It says Gucci or Hermès right in the brass. Fixings and hardware are good clues to fakes, even in terms of quality, if not in terms of engraving.
- Ask if the product comes with an ID card. Ho, ho, ho. Real designer goods now come with their own credit card–like ID card, some with a serial number. Even a tie at Prada comes with such an animal. They don't have ID cards in the Prada-style bags sold on Canal Street.

If you are purposely choosing an imitation, consider the light in which your fake will be shown. If all your friends have the real thing, and you are wearing the fake out to brunch, you'd better believe that sooner or later someone will discover your secret. However, if you are making a one-time appearance at the Oscars, or if your gemstone will be seen only by candlelight, no one will know the difference unless you tell. Do remember, however, that high-quality fakes are not cheap, and that inexpensive fakes always look fake.

SAMPLE MADNESS & SPECIAL SALES

A few designers and manufacturers keep their samples of items in an archive. They lend these clothes out to friends or family (many of the evening clothes you see photographed in society pages are loaners), but they do not sell them. Other designers figure that any amount of cash they can bring in is worthwhile, and realize that the cost of storing decades' worth of samples can get to be exorbitant. What to do? Have a sample sale! New York is home to so many sample sales these days that there's a monthly newsletter or two announcing them; New Yorkers are very proud of this only-in-New-York facet of the city lifestyle.

Once you have ventured forth to your first sample sale, you may find yourself a victim of "sample madness." You end up going to sample sales and buying things you don't need and may not even want—you just get carried away by the prices and the fun.

Many sample sales require cash, though some of the big ones take credit cards. Note that some sample sales are held in boutiques (**Eileen Fisher, Norma Kamali, Dolce & Gabbana**), corporate offices (**Fendi**), private parties or shindigs for best customers or fashion elite (**Chanel, Yves Saint Laurent**), or hotels (**Vera Wang**). Others are held at FIT or the Parsons School of Design in their auditoriums (**Escada**); still others take place at Chelsea Market (**TSE**).

Sample Savvy

To get lots of details on sample sales, subscribe to the *S&B Report* (it stands for "Sales & Bargains"). Note that the subscription rate goes up every year; a subscription presently costs $75 a year for the online version and $124 for the print version. What you get in return is a monthly booklet with names, addresses, and short descriptions of what's for sale. For information, call © 877/579-0222. You can buy a single issue for $10 if you visit only once a year. You can also visit the website (which does have e-commerce!) at www.lazarshopping.com.

If you don't want to subscribe, or if you are in town for just a few days but still want to get in on the action, try these tips:

- Walk down Broadway or Seventh Avenue near the Garment District, and you will more than likely be given handouts touting a variety of sample sales.
- The best way to find a special sale or a sample sale is simply to ask. Call your favorite designers, especially in April and October, and ask, "Do you sell samples or extra stock to the public?" If the answer is no, you might next ask, "Do you have a factory outlet where you sell samples or extra stock?" It never hurts to ask.
- Read the local events magazines like *New York* (www.new yorkmetro.com) and *Time Out New York* (www.time outny.com). Both announce many sales; *New York* has totally redone its shopping coverage, and bargain announcements and many sales are now listed each week.
- *Fashion Update* is a publication that competes with the *S&B Report;* call © 718/377-8873 for details. Or go to **TopButton. com,** a free resource with thousands of sale listings. Then there's the **Bargain Hot Line** (© 212/540-0123), which charges $2 for the first minute and 75¢ for each additional minute.
- Watch advertisements in the *New York Times* for the latest sales; pay close attention around gift-giving seasons. Almost all big sample sales are advertised.
- Sign up for mailing lists, and ask about future shows.

And while you're at the sale, remember these tips:

- Try to avoid the lunch-hour crush; get there when the doors open if possible.
- Whenever possible, try it on.
- Don't give a sample-sale gift to someone in a box from a real department store. The items are usually coded with a red x on the tag, so that people can't return them to the department store for full price.
- Don't buy something just because it's cheap.

USED MERCHANDISE

People often put perfectly good pieces of furniture out on the street for garbage collectors to haul away. Honest. I happen to have pieces of furniture that were rescued from the curbs of New York City.

Also, many people give their cast-offs to charity to get a tax deduction for the donation. Scads of thrift shops and charity-related stores sell previously worn merchandise. I happen to like the **Posh Sale** (p. 310) because of the high quality of the designer merchandise. I must note, though, that some of my younger friends—women ages 25 to 35—tell me that the clothes sold at the Posh Sale are too matronly for them.

Not to worry. These days, used clothing is so chic it's called "vintage"—and even Saks sells it. For the young crowd, there are plenty of East Village sources and even flea markets for vintage. For those who want gently used designer clothes, there are resale shops galore.

Resale Shops

Manhattan's resale shops are a special breed unto themselves, each with its own rules and regulations and secrets. Generally speaking, resale shops pride themselves on fashionable merchandise that is only a year or two (at the most) old. I find that well and good and applaud the notion, but excuse me, how come there are so many Adolfo suits in these stores? Adolfo has been closed for several years, so puh-leeze. All things considered, if you want to wear Chanel, resale is the only way to go. Well, it's not the only way to go, but it's the only way that I can contemplate.

Also note that with the revival of many '60s and '70s fashion looks, it's getting harder and harder to tell vintage from resale. Try both.

DESIGNER RESALE
324 E. 81st St., between First and Second aves. (Subway: 6 to 77th St.).

This place is small, but the clothes are frequently brand-new, and there are indeed designer names to be found. Its occasional color-coded sticker system is a bit unclear, so when you go to pay, the price turns out to be much less than you thought it was. Ask!

Hours are Monday, Tuesday, Wednesday, and Friday from 11am to 7pm; Thursday from 11am to 8pm; Saturday from 10am to 6pm; and Sunday from noon to 5pm. There's a men's branch, **Gentlemen's Resale,** across the street. © **212/734-3639.** www.resaleclothing.net.

ENCORE
1132 Madison Ave., between 84th and 85th sts., 2nd floor (Subway: 4, 5, or 6 to 86th St.).

This store got attention about 30 years ago when it was rumored that Jacqueline Kennedy Onassis was turning in her used clothes here. I had been coming by for years and finding zilch, and then suddenly I hit pay dirt. Would you like to hear about the Yves Saint Laurent Rive Gauche dress for $90? For the last year or so, Encore has been one of my regular sources.

The first floor sells dressy gowns, shoes, and handbags, while the second floor houses more casual items. If you've ever dreamed of interlocking Cs, this could be the start of something big: There are always a few Chanel suits priced from $500 to $750. A Chanel suit at $500 is really an outstanding buy, as the average price for a used Chanel suit is usually higher. (The average price for a new Chanel suit is $4,500, in case you were wondering.)

Open Monday, Wednesday, Friday, and Saturday from 10:30am to 6:30pm; Thursday from 10:30am to 7:30pm; and Sunday from noon to 6pm. © **212/879-2850.** www.encore resale.com.

KAVANAGH'S
146 E. 49th St., between Lexington and Third aves. (Subway: 6 to 51st St., or E or V to Lexington Ave./53rd St.).

This small shop specializes in Chanel and other big names; it has handbags as well as clothing. © **212/702-0152.**

MICHAEL'S
1041 Madison Ave., between 79th and 80th sts., 2nd floor (Subway: 6 to 77th St.).

Over the years, I've personally done better at Encore, but the last time I did some "thrifting" around the city, I had a ball at Michael's and got a whole new wardrobe for about $90—and found nothing at Encore. That's life in the big city. Anyway, this store is close enough to Encore that you can hit both in the same trip.

Michael's has a lot of Chanel: both suits (beginning at $800) and accessories. I saw a pair of red-and-white Chanel slingbacks that I'll never get over as long as I live—they were worthy of a museum. I'm shrinking my feet as we speak. Michael's also has a lot of plain-old regular big-name designer goods that just keep on keeping on. Small sizes will do better than larger. Wedding gowns are now sold upstairs.

Open Monday through Saturday from 9:30am to 6pm, Thursday until 8pm. Closed Saturday in addition to Sunday during July and August. © 212/737-7273. www.michaels consignment.com.

A SECOND CHANCE
1109 Lexington Ave., between 77th and 78th sts., 2nd floor (Subway: 6 to 77th St.).

Located near other great clothing resources, this resale shop has the usual luck of the draw, with some designer names and some midrange names. You may find a Ralph Lauren, Mondi, or Adolfo label, or you may not. The store opens Monday through Saturday at 11am, Sunday at noon. © 212/744-6041. www.asecondchanceresale.com.

Thrift Shops

Stores that specialize in upscale used merchandise consider themselves either resale shops or consignment shops; those that take whatever donations people choose to give in the name of charity are thrift shops, usually run for the benefit of a specific organization. As a result, most schools, hospitals, and disease care and research organizations have their own thrift shops.

By definition, a thrift shop is only as good as you are lucky. It's impossible to review them, since the merchandise comes and goes, and one can never be sure. I've seen that over the years, the thrift shop has become very popular—aside from the young people who are into grunge, there are plenty of well-off middle-class people who are looking for high quality at a worn price.

Do note that prices at these places can be very high, especially if you are used to out-of-town thrift-shop prices. A few basic rules hold true for most thrift shops:

- Many thrift shops take credit cards; few will take checks.
- You can sometimes bargain a little if you buy a lot.
- Most stores open at 11am; Saturday hours may be strange. Few are open on Sunday.

- A lot of thrift shops are located on the Upper East Side; I've grouped together several that make the expedition worthwhile.
- If you are used to the high quality and good prices at stores like Encore and Michael's, you may be turned off after checking out a few thrift shops.

Some thrift shops specialize in home decor, including:

CANCER CARE THRIFT SHOP
1480 Third Ave., at 83rd St. (Subway: 4, 5, or 6 to 86th St.).
© 212/879-9868. www.cancercare.org.

HOUSING WORKS THRIFT SHOP
143 W. 17th St., between Sixth and Seventh aves. (Subway: 1 to 18th St.).
© 212/366-0820. www.housingworks.org.

245 W. 10th St., near Hudson St. (Subway: 1 to Christopher St./Sheridan Sq.).
© 212/352-1618. www.housingworks.org.

157 E. 23rd St., between Lexington and Third aves. (Subway: 6 to 23rd St.).
© 212/529-5955. www.housingworks.org.

202 E. 77th St., between Second and Third aves. (Subway: 6 to 77th St.).
© 212/772-8461. www.housingworks.org.

1730 Second Ave., at 90th St. (Subway: 4, 5, or 6 to 86th St.).
© 212/772-8306. www.housingworks.org.

306 Columbus Ave., near 74th St. (Subway: B or C to 72nd St.).
© 212/579-7566. www.housingworks.org.

MEMORIAL SLOAN-KETTERING CANCER CENTER THRIFT SHOP
*1440 Third Ave., between 81st and 82nd sts. (Subway: 6 to
77th St.).*
© 212/535-1250. www.memorialthriftshop.org.

SPENCE CHAPIN THRIFT SHOP
*1473 Third Ave., between 83rd and 84th sts. (Subway: 4, 5,
or 6 to 86th St.).*
© 212/737-8448. www.spence-chapin.org.

*1850 Second Ave., between 95th and 96th sts. (Subway: 6
to 96th St.).*
© 212/426-7643. www.spence-chapin.org.

SPECIAL-EVENT RETAILING

An event just wouldn't be special if you couldn't buy something, would it? Museums have gift shops, circuses have vendors, and New York City has all sorts of special events that
revolve around the selling of something or other.

The best of these events are charity-related, such as **Seventh
on Sale** (usually held in May—watch the newspapers and
magazines), when designers donate clothing to be sold flea market–style, with income going toward AIDS research. The shoe
industry also does an annual bash, sponsored by QVC.

Some events are food-related—in May, the **Ninth Avenue
International Food Festival** is a big block party that allows you
to roam through throngs of people as you explore a variety of
ethnic-food stands. In Chinatown, there's **Chinese New Year**
in January or February. There are similar festivals in Little Italy,
including September's **Feast of San Gennaro.** Check with your
hotel concierge or *Where* magazine to find out if such events
will be held when you are in town. NYC & Company also puts

together a quarterly list of all special events in Manhattan; check out www.nycvisit.com.

Also investigate traditional charity events: For antiques and furniture, there's the twice-a-year **Seventh Regiment Armory Antiques Show,** at Park Avenue and 67th Street, as well as the Pier Shows.

For clothes, try the **Posh Sale,** a benefit for the Lighthouse for the Blind, also held at the Armory. Twice a year, the great ladies of New York society clean out their closets (designers do this as well) and send their tired, their poor, their wretched excesses to the Posh Sale, where we yearn for them to be free, but will pay $30 to $50 for them. Check www.lighthouse.org for details—there's a sale in both spring and fall. You can also stop by the **Lighthouse Store** (111 E. 59th St., near Park Ave.), a very nice boutique with a combination of types of merchandise. Some are related to large-type or large-size print for those who don't see very well, but many other items are more along the lines of what you would find in a museum store.

SPECIAL VISITORS

For a clothes encounter of the bargain kind, check for magazine and newspaper listings about special visitors from international retailing establishments. The British are particularly adept at flying to New York for a week, taking a suite in a Midtown hotel, and visiting with private customers, to whom they sell at wholesale or rock-bottom British prices.

To become a private customer, one needs only sharp eyes—ads usually run in newspapers or select magazines such as *New York* or *Avenue.* Tailors often employ this method, but so do manufacturers and even entire department stores. A representative from **Harrods** used to come over to sell from the store catalog on a regular basis. Now there's Harrods online for U.S. shoppers.

My tailor from Hong Kong, **W. W. Chan & Sons Tailors Ltd.**, sends a team to New York twice a year; contact sales@ wwchan.com to get on the mailing list. They make both men's and women's clothing.

TRADE-SHOW SHOPPING

Inveterate shoppers usually shun the standard shopping services and go on the prowl themselves, and trade shows are one of their favorite haunts. If you are prepared to do your Christmas shopping in July, your Halloween shopping in May, and your kiddie birthday shopping by the dozen, you can get some great bargains. You'll also save a lot of time in future months when all your friends will be frantic, and you'll be cool as can be.

Manhattan hosts almost 1,000 conventions a year. Not all of these will interest you, but events such as the **Gift Show, Stationery Show,** and **Linens Show** are not only fun to attend (you get a sneak preview of next season's wares), but also fun to shop. On the final day of the show, company representatives will often sell the samples right out of the booths rather than pay to truck the merchandise home. You'll pay wholesale, sometimes less. You may also get a lot of small-time freebies. Trade-show shopping takes organization, storage space, and extra cash resources, but it's the best way to save money and time and still give fabulous gifts.

To shop a trade show:

- Get a list of the week's trade shows from your concierge, a magazine such as *Where,* or NYC & Company.
- Find out the last day of the show and the hours.
- At about 11am on the final day, go to the convention hall and fill out the papers for accreditation. Attendance at a

trade fair may be free, or there may be a charge ($10–$25); either way, you must have some business credentials. This is what business cards are for.

- Your business card should be related to the business of the trade fair whenever possible; it should have some kind of company name rather than anything too cute. Your name should also be on the card. Have other ID, including photo ID. I recently had a very hard time getting into a trade show; they wanted all sorts of extra ID and business letterhead or checkbooks, and so on.

- Be prepared to answer a few innocent questions about your business, such as what you do. Having a gift-buying service or being in the party-planning business are two good entrees to just about anything.

- When you see something that interests you, introduce yourself—with your professional demeanor and company name—and ask if samples are being sold. If the answer is yes, pay in cash. No one wants your check. No one will change a traveler's check. No one has American money for euros. Cash and carry.

- Every now and then, before the last day of the show, you can get a maker to let you buy items for your own use—but you still must meet a minimum order. Sometimes this is only $100. Shipping will be extra.

- Bring heavy-duty shopping bags.

CORPORATE DISCOUNTS

Many regular, traditional retailers offer corporate discounts. **Tiffany & Co.** has one of the most famous corporate plans; if you qualify (you must be incorporated), you can get a discount (usually 10%) on all merchandise.

Some corporate discounts are based on location: A fancy jeweler on Madison Avenue gives a discount to businesspeople who work in the neighborhood—he wants their business.

A certain camera shop offers a discount to photographers who work for Time, Inc., because he likes to tell his regular customers that all the *Life* magazine photographers buy from him. And so it goes.

If you are visiting your corporate headquarters, it pays to ask a local company representative which retailers offer corporate benefits. You just may be surprised by the choices.

INDEX

Pick your Big Apple getaway guide.

You can do it all—or do nothing at all—in and around New York City with Frommer's guides. From car-free escapes to dirt-cheap adventures, Frommer's makes the going easy, with the best hotels, restaurants and attractions, plus exact prices, detailed maps, and more.

Don't miss these other New York City guides:
Frommer's New York City Free and Dirt Cheap
Frommer's Memorable Walks in New York

The best trips start here. **Frommer's®**

Available wherever books are sold. A Branded Imprint of ⊕**WILEY**
Now you know.

Wiley and the Wiley logo are registered trademarks of John Wiley & Sons, Inc. and/or its affiliates.
Frommer's is a registered trademark of Arthur Frommer, used under exclusive license.

FROMMER'S® COMPLETE TRAVEL GUIDES

Alaska
Amalfi Coast
American Southwest
Amsterdam
Argentina & Chile
Arizona
Atlanta
Australia
Austria
Bahamas
Barcelona
Beijing
Belgium, Holland & Luxembourg
Belize
Bermuda
Boston
Brazil
British Columbia & the Canadian Rockies
Brussels & Bruges
Budapest & the Best of Hungary
Buenos Aires
Calgary
California
Canada
Cancún, Cozumel & the Yucatán
Cape Cod, Nantucket & Martha's Vineyard
Caribbean
Caribbean Ports of Call
Carolinas & Georgia
Chicago
China
Colorado
Costa Rica
Croatia
Cuba
Denmark
Denver, Boulder & Colorado Springs
Edinburgh & Glasgow
England
Europe
Europe by Rail

Florence, Tuscany & Umbria
Florida
France
Germany
Greece
Greek Islands
Hawaii
Hong Kong
Honolulu, Waikiki & Oahu
India
Ireland
Italy
Jamaica
Japan
Kauai
Las Vegas
London
Los Angeles
Los Cabos & Baja
Madrid
Maine Coast
Maryland & Delaware
Maui
Mexico
Montana & Wyoming
Montréal & Québec City
Moscow & St. Petersburg
Munich & the Bavarian Alps
Nashville & Memphis
New England
Newfoundland & Labrador
New Mexico
New Orleans
New York City
New York State
New Zealand
Northern Italy
Norway
Nova Scotia, New Brunswick & Prince Edward Island
Oregon
Paris
Peru

Philadelphia & the Amish Country
Portugal
Prague & the Best of the Czech Republic
Provence & the Riviera
Puerto Rico
Rome
San Antonio & Austin
San Diego
San Francisco
Santa Fe, Taos & Albuquerque
Scandinavia
Scotland
Seattle
Seville, Granada & the Best of Andalusia
Shanghai
Sicily
Singapore & Malaysia
South Africa
South America
South Florida
South Pacific
Southeast Asia
Spain
Sweden
Switzerland
Texas
Thailand
Tokyo
Toronto
Turkey
USA
Utah
Vancouver & Victoria
Vermont, New Hampshire & Maine
Vienna & the Danube Valley
Vietnam
Virgin Islands
Virginia
Walt Disney World® & Orlando
Washington, D.C.
Washington State

FROMMER'S® DOLLAR-A-DAY GUIDES

Australia from $60 a Day
California from $70 a Day
England from $75 a Day
Europe from $85 a Day
Florida from $70 a Day

Hawaii from $80 a Day
Ireland from $90 a Day
Italy from $90 a Day
London from $95 a Day

New York City from $90 a Day
Paris from $95 a Day
San Francisco from $70 a Day
Washington, D.C. from $80 a Day

FROMMER'S® PORTABLE GUIDES

Acapulco, Ixtapa & Zihuatanejo
Amsterdam
Aruba
Australia's Great Barrier Reef
Bahamas
Berlin
Big Island of Hawaii
Boston
California Wine Country
Cancún
Cayman Islands
Charleston
Chicago

Disneyland®
Dominican Republic
Dublin
Florence
Las Vegas
Las Vegas for Non-Gamblers
London
Los Angeles
Maui
Nantucket & Martha's Vineyard
New Orleans
New York City
Paris

Portland
Puerto Rico
Puerto Vallarta, Manzanillo & Guadalajara
Rio de Janeiro
San Diego
San Francisco
Savannah
Vancouver
Venice
Virgin Islands
Washington, D.C.
Whistler

FROMMER'S® CRUISE GUIDES

Alaska Cruises & Ports of Call

Cruises & Ports of Call

European Cruises & Ports of Call